Visit us at

www.syngress.com

SYNGRESS®

Check Point NGX R65 Security Administration

Ralph Bonnell Technical Editor
Simon Desmeules Assistant Technical Editor

Eli Faskha
Rajeev Gupta
Brendan T. Kearney
Patryk Krolikowski
Craig Wright

KEY	SERIAL NUMBER
001	HJIRTCV764
002	PO9873D5FG
003	829KM8NJH2
004	BPOQ48722D
005	CVPLQ6WQ23
006	VBP965T5T5
007	HJJJ863WD3E
008	2987GVTWMK
009	629MP5SDJT
010	IMWQ295T6T

PUBLISHED BY
Syngress Publishing, Inc.
Elsevier, Inc.
30 Corporate Drive
Burlington, MA 01803

Check Point NGX R65 Security Administration

Printed and bound in the United Kingdom

Transferred to Digital Printing, 2010

ISBN 13: 978-1-59749-245-4

Publisher: Amorette Pedersen
Acquisitions Editor: Andrew Williams
Technical Editor: Ralph Bonnell
Project Manager: Gary Byrne
Page Layout and Art: SPI
Copy Editors: Audrey Doyle and Adrienne Rebello
Indexer: SPI
Cover Designer: Michael Kavish

For information on rights, translations, and bulk sales, contact Matt Pedersen, Commercial Sales Director and Rights, at Syngress Publishing; email m.pedersen@elsevier.com.

Technical Editor

Ralph Bonnell (CISSP, Linux LPIC-2, Secure Computing Sidewinder Instructor, Crossbeam X-Series Instructor, Check Point Instructor, Check Point CCSE+, Nokia Instructor, Cisco CCNA, Microsoft MCSE: Security, RSA Security RSA/CSE, StoneSoft CSFE, Aladdin eSCE, CipherTrust PCIA, ArcSight ACIA, SurfControl STAR, McAfee MIPS-I, McAfee MIPS-E, Network Associates SCP, Blue Coat BSPE, Sygate SSEI, Sygate SSEP, Aventail ACP, Radware CRIE, PGP) is a senior information security consultant currently employed at FishNet Security in San Francisco, CA. Ralph has been working with Check Point products professionally since 1999. His primary responsibilities include the deployment of various network security products, network security product support, and product training. His specialties include Check Point and Juniper deployments, Linux client and server deployments, security product training, hardware hacking, firewall clustering, advanced scripting, Web programming, and lots of Nintendo. Ralph contributed to *Configuring Juniper Networks NetScreen & SSG Firewalls* (Syngress, ISBN: 1597491187). Ralph runs a Linux consulting business called Linux Friendly. He also manages his Web site, www.ralph.cx.

Assistant Technical Editor

Simon Desmeules (CCSI, NCSP, ISS/IDS, RSA/CSE, CNA) is the senior security analyst and technical trainer for GoSecure, located in Montreal, Canada. GoSecure's mission is to provide customers in industry and government with high-quality information security services and solutions to meet their specific challenges. Simon's main responsibilities include architectural design, technical consulting, managed security services, and tactical emergency support for perimeter security technologies for several Fortune 500 companies in Canada, France, and the United States. He has been delivering Check Point training for the past five years throughout Canada and the United States. His background includes positions as a firewall/intrusion security specialist for pioneer firms of Security, Maxon Services, and SINC. He has also developed a close relationship with Vigilar's Intense School based in Atlanta, GA, where he delivers Check Point training throughout the United States. He is an active member of the FW-1, ISS, and Snort mailing lists, consulting with fellow security specialists around the world. Simon has worked with Syngress while contributing to *Check Point Next Generation Security Administration* (Syngress, ISBN: 1-928994-74-1) and Check Point Next Generation *with Application Intelligence Security Administration* (Syngress, ISBN: 1-932266-89-5). He also was the technical editor of *Configuring Check Point NGX VPN-1/FireWall-1* (ISBN: 1-597490-31-8).

He would like to thank all of the students throughout North America who have passed through his classrooms and who have always brought new ideas and challenges. Des remerciements particuliers aux étudiants du Québec.

Contributing Authors

Eli Faskha (Security+, Check Point Certified Master Architect, CCSI, CCSE, CCSE+, MCP). Based in Panama City, Panama, Eli is founder and president of Soluciones Seguras, a company that specializes in network security and is a Check Point Gold Partner and Nokia Authorized Partner. He was assistant technical editor for Syngress's *Configuring Check Point NGX VPN-1/Firewall-1* (ISBN: 1597490318) book and contributing author for Syngress's *Building DMZs for the Enterprise* (ISBN: 1597491004). Eli is the most experienced Check Point Certified Security Instructor and Nokia Instructor in the region, and he has taught participants from over 20 different countries, in both English and Spanish. A 1993 graduate of the University of Pennsylvania's Wharton School and Moore School of Engineering, he also received an MBA from Georgetown University in 1995. He has more than eight years of Internet development and networking experience, starting with Web development of the largest Internet portal in Panama in 1999 and 2000, managing a Verisign affiliate in 2001, and running his own company since then. Eli has written several articles for the local media and has been recognized for his contributions to Internet development in Panama.

Rajeev Gupta (CCMA—Check Point Certified Master Architect, #13, CCMSE NGX Plus VSX, CCSI with CompTIA's CTT+, ITIL, CISSP) is a Check Point subject matter expert, currently working as the principal engineer in the Managed Security Services division of a leading provider of advanced communications and security services across the globe. With eight years of intense experience working with Check Point products, he is a highly respected resource at his company for strategizing clients' security solutions. He also is a key contributor toward product engineering, product marketing, and product management. During his more than four years of working at Check Point's worldwide support center, he became known as a Provider-1 expert extraordinaire, having impressed customers with his deep understanding of the product's underlying architecture.

Today, one of his major responsibilities includes managing day-to-day maintenance and operations of one of the world's largest fully redundant Provider-1 deployments. He is a keen contributor to Check Point usability testing, development and RnD support teams.

Brendan T Kearney (CCSA/CCSE, JNCIA-FWV, JNCIA-IDP, JNCIA-SSL, MCIA, ISS-TSS) is a senior help desk engineer for Surety Help Desk Inc., a 1-Step Check Point specialist IT security help desk provider with commercial and government clients throughout North America. Brendan served in the U.S. Marine Corps., where he worked in information technology. He has a 10-year background in security and IT infrastructure. He is an avid telemark skier in his spare time and lives with his better half, Tammy, in Bolton, CT.

Patryk Krolikowski (CCNA, CCNE, CNA, CNE, JNCIA, GIAC GCFW, SCSP) is a security consultant with CompFort Meridian Poland. His expertise includes Check Point, Juniper, Nokia, Symantec, and RSA design and implementations. Holding an MA in law and finishing a forensics PhD thesis on digital evidence seizure and handling, he is focused on computer forensics and incident response. Patryk is also a security publications author for *NetWorld* magazine and an active member of ISSA (Information Systems Security Association).

Craig Wright has personally conducted in excess of 1,200 IT security-related engagements for more than 120 Australian and international organizations in the private and government sectors and now works for BDO Kendall's in Australia.

In addition to his consulting engagements, Craig has also authored numerous IT security-related articles. He also has been involved with designing the architecture for the world's first online casino (Lasseter's Online) in the Northern Territory. He has designed and managed the implementation of many of the systems that protected the Australian Stock Exchange. He also developed and implemented the security policies and procedural practices within Mahindra and Mahindra, India's largest vehicle manufacturer.

He holds (among others) the following industry certifications: CISSP (ISSAP and ISSMP), CISA, CISM, CCE, GNSA, G7799, GWAS, GCFA, GLEG, GSEC, GREM, GPCI, MCSE, and GSPA. He has completed numerous degrees in a variety of fields and is currently completing both a master's degree in statistics (at Newcastle) and a master's degree in law (LLM) specializing in international commercial law (e-commerce law). Craig is planning to start his second doctorate, a PhD in economics and law in the digital age, in early 2008.

Contents

Chapter 1

NGX R65
Operational Changes

Solutions in this chapter:

- New SmartPortal Features
- New FireWall-1/VPN-1 Features
- Edge Support for CLM
- Integrity Advanced Server
- New VPN Features
- ClusterXL

☑ Summary

☑ Solutions Fast Track

☑ Frequently Asked Questions

Introduction

Check Point has come a long way since it was formed more than a decade ago. Check Point's latest major release is the NGX R65. This latest version incorporates features such as built-in antivirus, antispam, URL scanning, attack prevention, and route-based virtual private network (VPN) technology. This book will cover the new features introduced in this latest version.

The NGX R65 adds a significant number of features to the Management platform. In addition, a plug-in system was developed, making it easier to add new products to the SmartConsole suite of Management interfaces. This chapter summarizes the new features introduced since NGX R60.

Tools & Traps...

Service Contracts

Always ensure that you download and install an up-to-date Service Contract File for your SmartCenter Server (SCS). Validation of the systems licensing using the User Center helps you to maintain compliance with the Check Point licensing requirements and thus to stay within the law. Installing the Service Contract File on the SCS will allow it to be transmitted to the other gateways as a part of the upgrade procedure. Contract verification is a fundamental component of the Check Point licensing scheme.

See www.checkpoint.com/ngx/upgrade/contract for additional information on Service Contract Files.

New SmartPortal Features

The Check Point SmartConsole GUI clients have long been a significant competitive advantage for Check Point in the firewall space. Using secure internal communication (SIC), these clients provide a common user interface and communicate with the SCS over an encrypted, authenticated, private channel over any Internet Protocol (IP) network, including the Internet.

Before NGX, anyone who wanted access to the SCS needed to install the GUI clients, a possible problem for organizations with strict configuration management policies or for administrators who couldn't always use their own laptops. SmartPortal was introduced in NGX and allowed the firewall administrator to extend read-only browser-based access to the SCS to people outside the security team and to those on PCs without the GUI clients. It's essentially a secure Web interface into your SCS. NGX R65 added the ability to modify the internal user database so that SmartPortal users can create users and add them to existing user groups. The SmartPortal license is included in the SmartCenter Pro license and the UTM-1 appliances; otherwise, you have to purchase it separately.

Eventia Correlation Unit and Eventia Analyzer Server

SmartView Monitor is able to provide status updates from the Correlation Unit and Eventia Analyzer Server. Correlation Unit status checks include:

- Checking whether the Eventia Correlation Unit is active
- Checking whether the Eventia Correlation Unit is connected to the Eventia Analyzer Server
- Checking whether the Eventia Correlation Unit is connected to the log server
- Reporting on Eventia Correlation Unit and log server connection details and availability
- Monitoring offline job status reports
- Monitoring and reporting on low disk space

You can use Eventia Analyzer Server status to:

- Report the last handle event time that was recorded
- Report whether the Eventia Analyzer Server is active
- Report an inventory of correlation units the Eventia Analyzer Server is connected with
- Display the volume of events received in a selected period

The Eventia Correlation Unit's relation to other components will report trouble with the Eventia Correlation Unit's status. The Eventia Analyzer Server maintains system status to present information about connections to all Eventia Correlation Unit(s) that are currently associated.

SmartView Tracker

SmartView Tracker offers the ability to contact the SmartDefense Advisory information related to an explicit SmartDefense log. This can help an administrator to appraise configuration options to understand why the specific SmartView Tracker log occurred. SmartDefense's Advisory feature does not exhibit log entries that do not have an attack name and/or attack information.

IPv6 Reporting

IPv6 source or destination information will now display in the report. An administrator can define an Eventia Reporter filter using an IPv6 address, source, and destination.

DNS Implementation

Domain name system (DNS) implementation requires fewer resources. Furthermore, it is possible to control the requests for Time Out.

Remote License Management

The Eventia Reporter Server can search for the Eventia Reporter license on the Eventia Reporter machine if the license is not found on the Management Server.

Eventia Reporter on Multiple Versions of SmartCenter Management

Eventia Reporter in a distributed installation is able to integrate with multiple versions of SmartCenter Management from NGX R54 and later.

You can install Eventia Reporter as a stand-alone deployment or a distributed deployment. Eventia Reporter recognizes all the network objects in the SmartCenter Management database via an internal process referred to as *dbsync* when it is installed as a distributed deployment. Eventia Reporter can recognize objects from multiple versions (from NGX R54 and later) using dbsync.

Eventia Reporter and Analyzer Integration

Eventia Reporter, Eventia Analyzer Server, and Eventia Correlation Units are situated in the same package, and you can install them on the same server. You can use the high-level *evstop* and *evstart* commands to stop and start the Eventia Reporter and Analyzer.

Three new content inspection express reports are included with the new version of Eventia Reporter. They are the Anti Virus, Web (URL) Filtering, and Anti Spam reports.

New FireWall-1/VPN-1 Features

VPN technology has been an integral part of firewalls since the late 1990s. With the rise of the Internet in the early 1990s, most firms' first concerns were for a firewall that allowed them safe connectivity between their internal networks and the Internet. Once organizations began to use the Internet to connect separate offices, it became obvious that providing VPN functionality was a natural fit for firewall manufacturers. The fact that network address translator (NAT), IPSec, and antispoof checking have complex interactions has further driven the consolidation of these functionalities into a single perimeter device.

Although VPN technology was initially a separate add-on to FireWall-1, it soon became part of the standard package, and now, with version NGX, the firewall product itself has been renamed *VPN-1 Pro*, for reasons that aren't entirely obvious, given the large mindshare and recognition of the name *FireWall-1*.

NGX offers several new updates and upgrades in VPN functionality.

SmartDefense Profiles

SmartDefense/Web Intelligence is Check Point's way of providing an intelligent defense against attacks directed at open ports as well as a defense against other, more sophisticated types of attacks. Though previous versions of FireWall-1/VPN-1 included early versions of SmartDefense/Web Intelligence, these defenses have been upgraded and improved in NGX.

Because your site may have separate networks that each need a special level of protection, SmartDefense Protection Profiles have been updated and you now can tailor the SmartDefense protection configuration using the precise defenses required for each gateway. You can view the SmartDefense Protection Profiles using SmartPortal.

AMT Support

The NGX R65 now supports Intel Active Management Technology (AMT) for Linux and SecurePlatform to isolate endpoint computers that violate the network security policy. In addition, AMT Quarantine installs a special security policy that restricts inbound and outbound traffic on suspect endpoint hosts that protects the larger network from malicious activity.

Aggressive Aging

Aggressive Aging helps to manage the connections table capacity and memory consumption of the firewall to increase durability and stability. This feature introduces a set of short timeouts called *aggressive timeouts*. When a connection is idle for more than its aggressive timeout it is marked as *eligible for deletion*. When the connections table or memory consumption reaches the set user-defined threshold (or high-water mark), Aggressive Aging begins to delete *eligible for deletion* connections, until memory consumption or connections capacity decreases back to the desired level.

Aggressive Aging allows the gateway machine to handle large amounts of unanticipated traffic such as during a denial of service (DoS) attack.

Cooperative Enforcement

Administrators can ensure that users traversing the firewall are protected by the Integrity endpoint shield. When configuring a Check Point gateway, the administrator identifies whether hosts accessing the network from the internal interface have to be authorized by the Integrity Server. A user not authorized by the Integrity Server receives notification (through the Hypertext Transfer Protocol [HTTP] or e-mail) to this effect.

An administrator can define several additional parameters, such as:

- Check authorization of all clients
- A white list of machines that do not have the Integrity Server installed but can still traverse the firewall
- Tracking options for authorized or unauthorized clients
- Activating cooperative enforcement in monitor-only mode

Monitor-Only Deployment Mode

In the monitor-only deployment mode, the firewall requests authorization statuses from the Integrity Server but, regardless of the received statuses, connections are not dropped. In addition (if configured by the administrator), the Cooperative Enforcement feature generates logs regardless of deployment mode.

Handling an Unauthorized Host

Unauthorized hosts can be added to the host's exception list, or the administrator can take appropriate action to make these hosts compliant.

Internal URL Web Filtering

In the NGX R65, VPN-1 gateways with content inspection capabilities are able to inspect and control HTTP traffic. The Web Filtering function screens incoming URL requests against a database to determine whether the URL request should be blocked or allowed. Web filtering takes place according to predefined categories made up of URLs. The Web filter checks the URL of a Web page against a list of approved sites. In this way, complete sites or pages within sites that contain objectionable material (e.g., pornography, illegal software, or spyware) can be blocked.

Web (URL) filtering is based on the SurfControl engine which is now built into Check Point software. This provides for filtering rules based on the organization's needs, predefined categories made up of URLs and patterns of URLs, and a Web filtering database provided by Check Point.

Internal Antivirus Scanning

Since R61, antivirus scanning has been included in the NGX. Enabling antivirus scanning using the CA eSafe engine will allow you to scan an assortment of network protocols, trap them in the kernel, and forward them to the security server, which then transmits the captured files or data to the antivirus engine. The antivirus engine will allow or block data, depending on the reply from the antivirus engine. Antivirus scanning will apply to all traffic that has been permitted using the Security Policy.

SmartView Monitor can now provide statuses and counters for gateways with antivirus and Web filtering. The statuses are divided into the following two categories:

- Current status

- Update status (such as when the signature update was last verified)

Antivirus statuses are associated with signature checks and Web filtering statuses are associated with URLs and categories. SmartView Monitor can also run antivirus and Web filtering counters. For instance, the following reports are available:

- Top five attacks in the past hour

- Top 10 attacks since the last reset

- Top 10 HTTP attacks in the past hour

- General information regarding HTTP attacks

Signature Updates

You can schedule virus signatures to automatically update at any preferred period, or you can start manual updates of virus signatures at any time. Check Point provides antivirus and Web filtering updates. Check Point User Center credentials are necessary for the updates.

Continuous Download

The antivirus engine acts as a proxy, and will cache the scanned file prior to sending it to the client. Continuous Download will trickle data while the antivirus scan is taking place. If a virus is found during the scan, the file transfer is concluded. File types for which Continuous Download will not be used are configurable.

Scanning Files

You can scan files "by direction" or by IP address. In either instance, antivirus scanning will be performed only against traffic that has been permitted through the security rulebase.

Layer 2 Firewalling

Layer 2 firewall deployment enables a VPN-1 gateway to be inserted into an internal network without affecting the existing IP address routing scheme. Traffic authorized by the firewall is passed between bridged interfaces, which forward the traffic over Layer 2. This feature is supported only on stand-alone gateways.

VoIP Features

New Session Initiation Protocol (SIP) features to enhance Voice over IP (VoIP) include:

- Media Gateway Control Protocol (MGCP) NAT support
- MGCP on dynamic ports
- SIP NAT support in a Back-to-Back User Agent (B2BUA) configuration
- Static NAT for SIP proxies in the internal network
- Extended SIP state machines
- Blocked/allowed SIP commands
- Interoperability with Nortel, Broadsoft, Cisco, NEC, Polycom, Sylantro, Avaya, and others

SYN Cookies

A SYN-cookies mode has been added to SYNDefender to prevent a DoS SYN flood attack. In a SYN flood, external hosts overwhelm a server machine by sending a constant stream of Transmission Control Protocol (TCP) connection requests. The server machine continues to allocate resources until all its resources are exhausted. With SYN cookies, the server machine does not allocate resources until the server's SYN/ACK packets receive an ACK in return, meaning that the original request for a connection was legitimate. Using SYN cookies, the TCP three-way handshake is performed without saving state information. The connection is not registered in the connection table until the connection proves itself legitimate.

For a host, not saving any state information on an incoming SYN means the server is no longer vulnerable to backlog DoS SYN flood attacks. For a gateway, this means that processing time spent on spoofed SYN packets is reduced, and memory consumption is eliminated.

SYNDefender now has two active modes: relay mode and SYN cookie mode. In relay mode, when a SYN arrives, the connection table registers the connection in the usual way. In cookie mode, the firewall is not informed of the handshake with the external host or client until the client has shown itself to be legitimate. The SYN packet from the client is dropped and a SYN-ACK with a cookie set is sent directly to the client interface.

After receiving the ACK from the client, which completes the client handshake, SYNDefender transforms the ACK into a SYN and registers it in the connection table. Processing the connection then proceeds in the same way as relay mode.

Edge Support for CLM

The NGX R65 provides Edge support for the customer log module (CLM). This support will allow the administrator to choose the destination for the logs. The target can be the SCS; syslog is also supported.

Management Plug-In System

The NGX R65 introduces an additional infrastructure that enables the use of management plug-ins. The new plug-in architecture introduces the ability to dynamically add new features and support new products. Management plug-ins offer central management of gateways and features not supported by your current NGX R65 SmartCenter or Provider-1/SiteManager-1. Management plug-ins supply new and separate packages that consist only of those components that are necessary for managing new gateway products or specific features, thus avoiding a full upgrade to the next release.

Connectra Management

The NGX R65 is the first version to manage Connectra gateways centrally. This exposes Connectra to many more configuration possibilities than were available in previous versions.

Connectra Tab

SmartDashboard has a new tab for Connectra. All Connectra-related configurations are performed using the objects in this tab. The new Connectra tab in SmartDashboard contains a section for SmartDefense and Web Intelligence updates. SmartDefense and Web Intelligence configurations for Connectra are performed as part of "SmartDefense profiles." A Connectra-specific SmartDefense profile is used for all Connectra-related SmartDefense and Web Intelligence configurations.

Provider-1 Support

Provider-1/SiteManager-1 now supports Connectra objects (Connectra gateways, Connectra clusters, and Connectra cluster members). Provider-1 collects Connectra objects and their statuses, licenses, and packages from the CMAs to the MDS. Provider-1 then displays these collected objects in the MDG.

SmartView Monitor

SmartView Monitor can monitor Connectra gateways, and produce reports concerning statuses and activities.

Integrity Advanced Server

For Integrity 6.6 on the R65 installation CD, the embedded datastore now supports up to 2,000 concurrent users, removing the need for an external database. Logs, which are now stored on the embedded Check Point Log Server, integrate with Check Point and third-party reporting tools. (The Check Point Log Server is a high-performance log server that scales to the needs of the most intensive customers. Archiving, backup, and restore are much simpler now with the embedded datastore.) Customers with more than 2,000 concurrent users should continue to use Integrity 6.5 until Integrity 7.0 is released.

New VPN Features

NGX offers several new updates and upgrades in VPN functionality. We will discuss some of the new features for VPN support with NGX R65 in the following sections.

Understanding the New VPN Options

Rather than creating individual encryption rules to handle the traffic between VPN terminator gateways, the user need only create a VPN community and then specify the gateways and properties. With NGX R65, Check Point has preserved this useful and simple mental model and has added some additional functionality.

Allowing Directional VPN Rules

Enforcement of VPN rules by direction of connection is now possible. By going to the **Policy | Global Properties | VPN | Advanced** dialog box, you can check the box allowing directional specificity in the VPN element in the rulebase. Whereas in NG AI, directionality in VPN communities was an all-or-nothing proposition, the ability to now specify directionality is useful.

Allowing Backup Links and On-Demand Links

A pair of VPN gateways can now have multiple links between them (say, through multiple Internet service providers [ISPs]), allowing more than one communication path between them. This allows the configuration of back-up links and on-demand links.

Allowing Wire Mode VPN Connectivity

You can now enable VPN connections in NGX as wire mode, reflecting the fact that communications over the VPN are inherently trusted. When you label a connection as wire mode, packets traversing this connection are not inspected by stateful inspection, enabling these connections to successfully fail over. In wire mode, dynamic routing protocols are available for VPN traffic.

Allowing Route-Based VPNs

NGX now supports the Open Shortest Path First/Border Gateway Protocol (OSPF/BGP) for VPN traffic routing. Every tunnel is represented as a virtual adapter, allowing OSPF and BGP traffic to be encapsulated.

Allowing Permanent Tunnels

Permanent tunnels are "nailed-up" connections. This permits more advanced monitoring of VPN traffic through these tunnels, and prevents latency problems for applications that are sensitive to link setup delays.

Same Local IP and Cluster IP Address for VTIs

The NGX R65 provides the capability to arrange the same local IP and cluster IP address for virtual tunnel interfaces (VTIs) on the equivalent cluster member, reducing the total number of IP addresses required in a cluster configuration.

Antispoofing for Unnumbered Interfaces on IPSO

The NGX R65 now provides support for antispoofing on unnumbered interfaces on the Nokia IPSO.

Dynamic Routing and VTIs

The R65 provides support for networks that use dynamic routing to deploy a remote IP address of VTIs in clusters.

Configurable Metrics for Dial-up Routes

The R65 provides the capability to separately configure the metric of dial-up routes.

Interoperability between SecurePlatform and IPSO

SecurePlatform gateways using VTIs can use OSPF as of R65. This provides enhanced interoperability between SecurePlatform using numbered VTIs, and the Nokia/IPSO platform using unnumbered VTIs.

Route-Based VPN Improvements

NGX R65 management gateways may be located in the encryption domain without having to filter out its IP address from the dynamic routing protocol distribution for route-based VPN configurations.

Customer-Defined Scripts for VPN Peers

Customer scripts are capable of running on the R65 in cases where a VPN peer has stopped partaking in a community that has RIM enabled.

Route-Based VPN and IP Clustering Support

The R65 supports IP address clustering with route-based VPN on IPSO.

RIM Performance Improvements on IPSO

The R65 features a performance improvement with RIM for the process of injecting routes on Nokia IPSO.

SSL Extender

The SSL Network Extender (SNX) is now fully supported on the Microsoft Windows Vista operating system. With NGX R65 it provides the capability to add:

- An ICS policy per user group with the facility to characterize an integrity Clientless Security (ICS) policy for each individual user group

- An encryption domain per user group allowing the capacity to describe an encryption domain for each individual user group

The NGX R65 also has a considerably improved connection speed associated with the Secure Sockets Layer (SSL) extender.

SecureClient Mobile

SecureClient Mobile is a client for mobile devices to add VPN and firewall capabilities. It substitutes for SecureClient for PocketPCs, works on a variety of platforms, facilitates simple deployments, and features an easy upgrade path. SecureClient Mobile's VPN is based on SSL (HTTPS) tunneling and permits handheld systems to connect to resources protected by Check Point gateways in a secure manner. The client can be controlled by third-party applications via a programmable and extensible interface.
SecureClient Mobile operates in the following modes:

- **Centrally managed mode** The client bonds with a gateway configured for SecureClient Mobile, and downloads a set of policies that were sent to the gateway from SCS. The client can then enforce the policies it received.

- **SNX mode** This mode lets a client connect to a gateway configured only for an SNX. The client does not download policies in this mode, but will implement a set of policies that were loaded upon client installation. It can integrate with any gateway configured to provide SNX network mode. This mode is supported by Check Point VPN-1 Pro R55 HF10 versions and later, and on Connectra 2.0 and later.

TIP

SecureClient Mobile is supported on the Windows Mobile 2003/SE/5.0 operating system.

ClusterXL

In this section, we'll discuss interface bonding and multicast routing failover support.

Interface Bonding

Interface bonding facilitates the construction of a redundant, fully meshed topology in High Availability mode configurations. A fully meshed topology requires two interfaces on a gateway that attach to two switches (one active and one passive). This bonds the interfaces, letting them operate as a unit, sharing an IP and Media Access Control (MAC) address. If a failure occurs on the active switch connection, the active interface senses the failure and will fail over to the supplementary bonded interface that is connected to the second switch.

Multicast Routing Failover Support

The Multicast group, source address, and incoming and outgoing interface indexes of Multicast traffic are synchronized among all cluster members for cluster deployments in the NGX R65. This synchronization provides the capacity to continue Multicast sessions if a failover condition occurs. The NGX R65 supports PIM-DM and PIM-SM Multicast routing protocols.

Summary

Check Point releases a major upgrade to its core VPN-1 product every two or three years, and version NGX R65 is the latest in this line.

SmartDefense and Web Intelligence have received moderate upgrades in the NGX R65. This is still a fascinating set of tools for the network security administrator to understand and configure against all sorts of higher-level attacks.

Eventia Reporter provides a way to tackle those large and growing log files and provide detailed, informative reports and traffic analysis.

VPN functionality has seen significant improvements and now delivers on the full promise of the enhanced community-based VPNs we saw in the previous version.

SecurePlatform continues to evolve and improve. The product line is now split, with the addition of SecurePlatform Pro, which offers dynamic routing and support for Remote Authentication Dial-in User Service (RADIUS) authentication for firewall administrators. Dynamic routing adds some risk and some complexity, and is now available to those larger organizations that wish to more fully integrate the underlying router in their Check Point firewalls into their existing dynamic routing configuration.

Solutions Fast Track

New SmartPortal Features

☑ SmartPortal allows the firewall administrator to extend browser-based access to the SCS to persons outside the security team and to those on PCs without the GUI clients.

☑ SmartPortal is essentially a secure Web interface into your SCS for viewing policies and logs.

☑ You can install SmartPortal either on a dedicated server or on the SCS itself.

☑ With SmartPortal, you can limit access to specific IP addresses.

New FireWall-1/VPN-1 Features

☑ The "Hacker versus Firewall" arms race has moved up the stack to a higher level.

☑ SmartDefense and Web Intelligence have capabilities in three broad categories: defense against attacks, implicit defenses, and abnormal-behavior analysis.

☑ The SmartDefense Service is an annual subscription service that provides ongoing and real-time updates and configuration advisories.

Edge Support for CLM

☑ The NGX R65 provides Edge support for the customer log module (CLM). This support will allow the administrator to choose the destination for the logs.

☑ The NGX R65 introduces an additional infrastructure that enables the use of management plug-ins.

☑ The NGX R65 is the first version to manage Connectra gateways centrally.

Integrity Advanced Server

☑ For Integrity 6.6 on the R65 installation CD, the embedded datastore now supports up to 2,000 concurrent users, removing the need for an external database.

☑ Logs, which are now stored on the embedded Check Point Log Server, integrate with Check Point and third-party reporting tools.

☑ Customers with more than 2,000 concurrent users should continue to use Integrity 6.5 until Integrity 7.0 is released.

New VPN Features

☑ Rather than creating individual encryption rules to handle the traffic between VPN terminator gateways, the user need only create a VPN community and then specify the gateways and properties. With NGX R65, Check Point has preserved this useful and simple mental model and has added some additional functionality.

☑ Enforcement of VPN rules by direction of connection is now possible.

☑ You can now enable VPN connections in NGX as wire mode, reflecting the fact that communications over the VPN are inherently trusted.

ClusterXL

☑ Interface bonding facilitates the construction of a redundant, fully meshed topology in High Availability mode configurations.

☑ If a failure occurs on the active switch connection, the active interface senses the failure and will fail over to the supplementary bonded interface that is connected to the second switch.

☑ The Multicast group, source address, and incoming and outgoing interface indexes of Multicast traffic are synchronized among all cluster members for cluster deployments in the NGX R65.

Frequently Asked Questions

Q: Limiting access to specific IP addresses was always an important part of two-factor security with SmartConsole clients. Can I do that with SmartPortal?

A: Yes, limiting access to specific IP addresses is retained in the new interface. You can configure this by creating or editing the hosts.allowed file on the SmartPortal Server.

Q: Where do I install the SmartPortal Server?

A: You can install SmartPortal either on a dedicated server or on the SCS itself.

Q: Which Web browsers are compatible with SmartPortal?

A: SmartPortal is compatible with these browsers:

- Internet Explorer
- Mozilla
- Firefox
- Netscape

The only other requirements are that you enable JavaScript and disable pop-up blockers.

Q: Is a SmartDefense Services subscription required to use SmartDefense or Web Intelligence?

A: No. SmartDefense and Web Intelligence are built in. You need the subscription only to get real-time updates and configuration advisories.

Q: I don't see where in my rulebase I can select SmartDefense. Where is it?

A: SmartDefense and Web Intelligence are configured on their own tabs within SmartDashboard.

Q: What types of defenses does SmartDefense/Web Intelligence provide?

A: SmartDefense/Web Intelligence provides defenses against attacks, implicit defenses, and abnormal-behavior analysis.

Q: What type of objects can be cloned?

A: Only network and host objects can be cloned, but that's a good start.

Q: Do I need a separate license for SecurePlatform?

A: No. SecurePlatform (the regular version) is free. SecurePlatform Pro requires a separate, additional license.

Chapter 2

SmartClients and SmartManagement

Solutions in this chapter:

- SmartDashboard
- SmartView Tracker
- SmartView Monitor
- SmartUpdate
- SmartLSM
- The SecureClient Packaging Tool
- Management Plug-ins
- The Check Point Configuration Tool/cpconfig

☑ Summary

☑ Solutions Fast Track

☑ Frequently Asked Questions

Introduction

The Check Point security suite is managed by the SmartCenter Server software. This chapter covers the set of graphical client software used to manage the SmartCenter server. Many people say this set of SmartClient management interfaces is among the best in the industry. One example of such an impressive interface is SmartView Tracker, a tool that lets you have a detailed view of all log files collected from different Check Point components. Moreover this is all in real time, with tons of flexible filters and views (see the "SmartView Tracker" section for more details).

SmartDashboard

SmartDashboard is a powerful GUI, yet it is intuitive and user-friendly, and has been the hallmark of the Check Point FireWall-1/VPN-1 framework. For anyone interested in learning FireWall-1/VPN-1, it is critical to understand and become fully familiar with this all-encompassing user interface, which is fully integrated with myriad offerings from Check Point. Understanding its components will help users to translate the security policy vision of any organization into reality.

This section covers the main elements of SmartDashboard, emphasizing changes introduced in the NGX R65.

The SmartDashboard Log-in Dialog Box

Check Point introduced its new plug-in technology in the NGX R65, and you can see the first signs of its introduction at the log-in interface to SmartDashboard, as shown in Figure 2.1.

Figure 2.1 The SmartDashboard Log-in Dialog Box

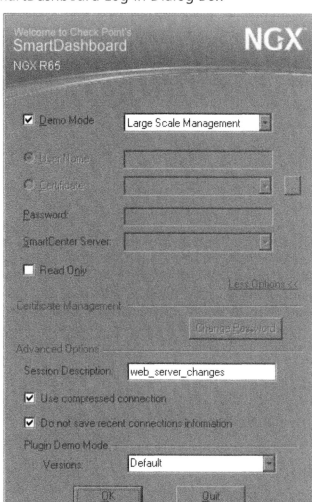

Note that **Plugin Demo Mode** becomes active only while you're logging in with **Demo Mode** selected. Also notice the **Session Description** section under **Advanced Options**. Check Point enhanced this feature in the NGX, allowing administrators to make it *mandatory* to provide an appropriate name to a session, which can be tracked in audit logs to monitor what was or was not done by a specific user while logged into SmartDashboard. Also note that only one user can log in with read/write permissions, but in the NGX, Check Point gives users the ability to disconnect any other user logged in as read/write if desired. This can come in handy in configurations with more than one administrator. Administrators commonly do not disconnect from the console after they have finished their work; instead, they just minimize the window and do other things (or even leave the office), leaving your hands tied if, for example, your boss wants you to configure virtual private network (VPN) access for one of the directors right away. Now, instead of waiting for your colleague to come to the office, you can just disconnect his session and take over.

NOTE

cpconfig allows you to define only one administrator, and is done during SmartCenter Server installation. You can add other users through SmartDashboard. You can convert all cpconfig administrators to administrators in SmartDashboard by using the $FWDIR/bin/cp_admin_convert.exe utility if you want to make access to SmartDashboard more secure.

Key Components

SmartDashboard is composed of four main sections, officially referred to as "panes." They are:

- The Object Tree pane
- The Rule Base pane
- The Object List pane
- The SmartMap pane

You will mostly be working through these panes to build a complete policy package encompassing various security policy elements as "tabbed" in the rulebase section of SmartDashboard. Figure 2.2 shows the NGX R65 SmartDashboard.

Figure 2.2 The Default View of SmartDashboard Showing All Four Panes

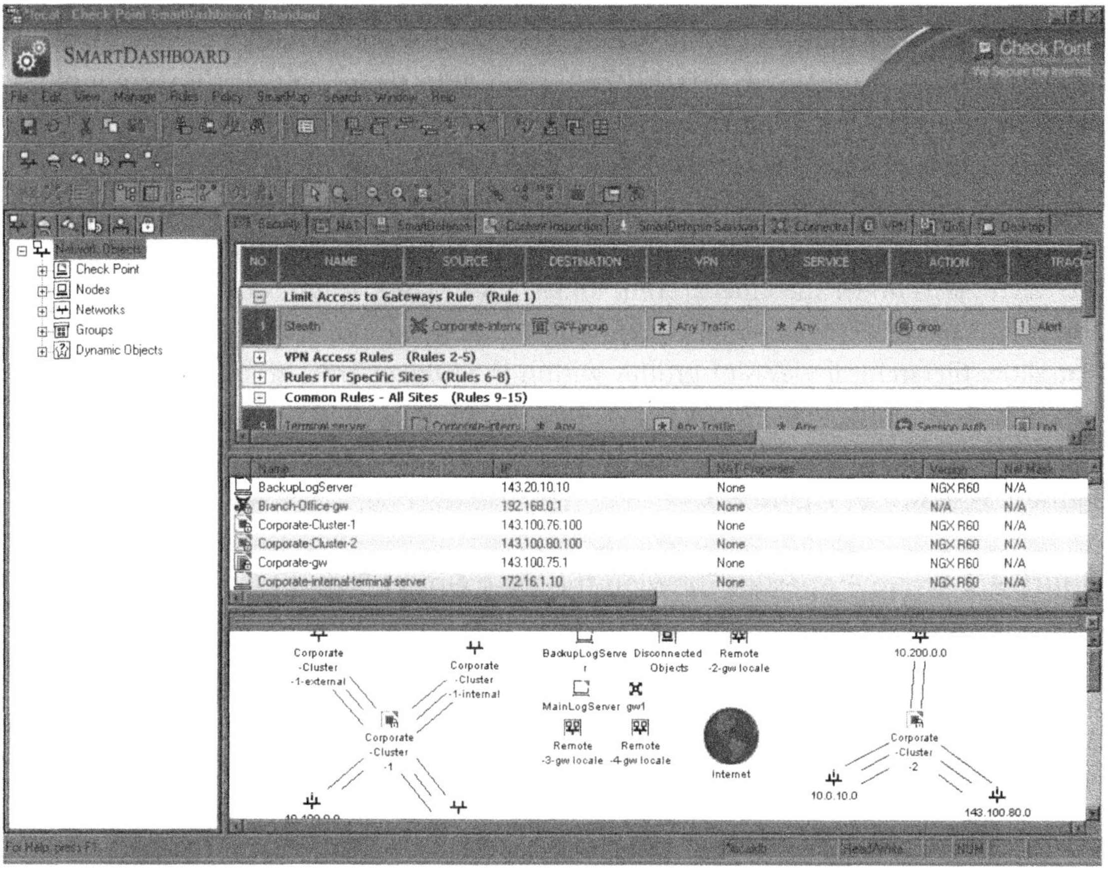

> **TIP**
>
> You can display these panes or remove them from the View menu. You may want to remove a pane from the View menu to avoid clutter and focus on certain panes, or perhaps you do not want some of your users to view information that they do not need to see. For example, you may not want an administrator to be allowed to perform object operations and see the rulebase, in which case it may be a good idea to remove the Rule Base pane from the View menu.

We will discuss each pane in SmartDashboard in the following sections.

The Object Tree Pane

The Object Tree pane provides a first-glance peek at various entities, including network objects, services, resources, servers, OPSEC applications, users, and VPN communities that have been either predefined or user-defined. All of them are organized under separate distinct tabs, each topped with a meaningful icon. The objects under each tab are systematically organized into meaningful folders—for example, network objects under the Networks folder, host objects under the Nodes folder, and SmartCenter or gateway objects under the Check Point folder. Several new features have made network object management much easier, chiefly the "cloning" of node objects, SmartGroups that allow hierarchical views of groups within the Object Tree, group conventions, tool tips, and a unique rule identifier. Another interesting feature available in the NGX R65 is the ability to view object details in Group Properties while creating a group, as shown in Figure 2.3.

Figure 2.3 Group Properties Showing the View Object Feature

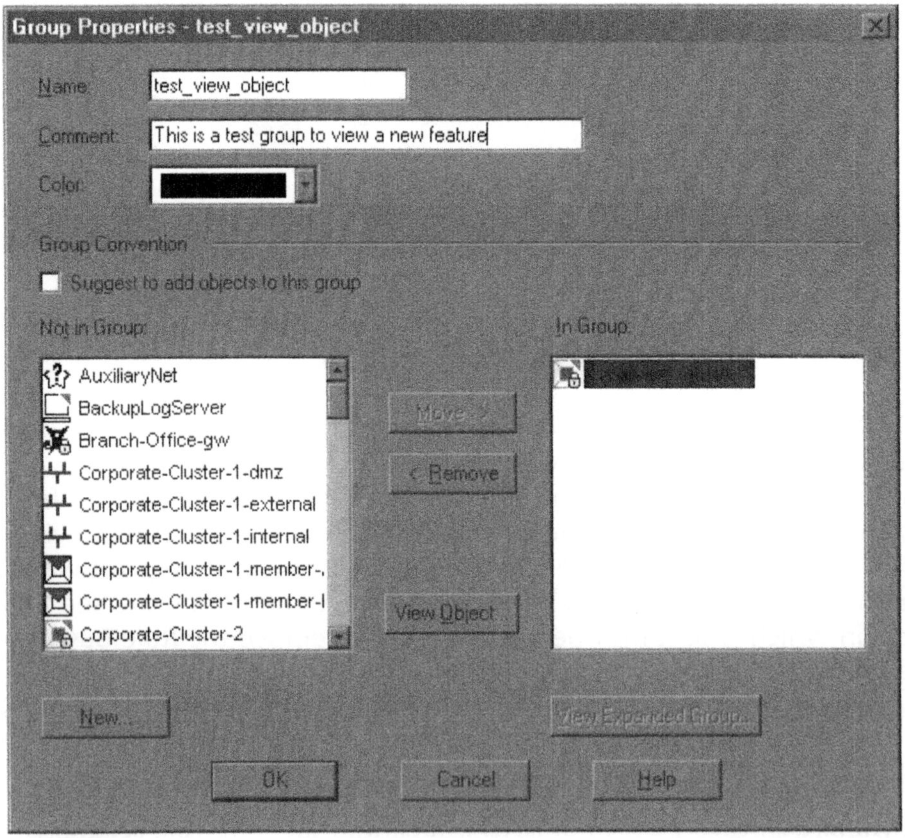

Although the Object Tree is the main work area for creating, editing, deleting, and configuring objects, you can also perform these operations through the Manage menu by choosing Network Objects, or any other suitable category.

The Rule Base Pane

The Rule Base pane is one of the most important sections of SmartDashboard and is where you define the rules that comprise various security policy elements. It also includes a Connectra tab, which is new to the NGX R65 and allows central management of Connectra VPN gateways. This is part of the new management plug-ins feature in the NGX R65, which are intended to enhance the management capabilities of a SmartCenter Server without requiring a complete upgrade. As of this writing, Check Point has released only one such management plug-in, which enables central management of a Connectra gateway. The Connectra tab in the Rule Base pane appears because a Connectra plug-in was installed on the SmartCenter Server to which SmartDashboard is connected, as shown in Figure 2.2 in the SmartDashboard Key Components section.

We will briefly examine the features of some of the important tabs in this pane to highlight their major characteristics and enhancements.

The Security Tab

This is the most used and most important tab within SmartDashboard, as it is where you create rules using objects to define an organization's main security policy element to control inbound and outbound access to different types of networks, hosts, services, and other resources, such as Web servers and e-mail servers. Each rule is a collection of basic elements categorized into fields—Rule Number, Name, Source, Destination, Service, Action, Track, Install On, Time, and Comment—and organized into columns. Another column, the VPN column, appears only if a policy has been created with the VPN configuration method set to **Apply** in **Simplified mode to all new Security Policies**, which is configurable from within the **Policy | Global Properties | VPN tab**. Each rule has a unique rule ID that does not change during the life of the rule, even if that rule number keeps changing in the rule base as more rules are added or deleted. You can view that unique ID from the context menu, which you can reach by right-clicking the **Rule Number** column of the rule and choosing **Copy Rule UID**. Then you simply paste it into the SmartView Tracker Query Properties pane to filter log data based on this rule UID. Another important enhancement in SmartDashboard allows administrators to view all of the logs for a specific rule in the rule base, which you can obtain by right-clicking the rule's **NO** column.

The NAT Tab

You define NAT rules in the NAT tab. Check Point defines Automatic NAT rules if the user selects **Automatic NAT**, but you have to manually define any rules to allow Manual NAT. Manual NAT is needed if translation is required to or from a network other than the external network, for port address translation, or when translation needs to be disabled between certain networks. The important enhancement in the NGX relates to the ability to provide a section title to NAT rules, similar to the same feature available in the Security rule base.

The SmartDefense and SmartDefense Services Tabs

SmartDefense Services is a new tab in the NGX. The SmartDefense tab is the main console for configuring SmartDefense protections at the network, transport, and application levels, including the Web Intelligence level. The Services tab is a licensed subscription feature to keep these protections constantly updated to ensure mitigation of evolving threats. The NGX R65 enables administrators to define multiple SmartDefense profiles that can be centrally managed from within SmartDashboard. Each gateway can be assigned a different profile containing different protections and defense configurations.

The Connectra Tab

The Connectra tab is new in the NGX R65, and it is based on the management plug-in installed on the SmartCenter Server to centrally manage Conncetra gateways.

Depending on the products that have been licensed, installed, and configured for policy, there are other tabs in the Rule Base pane, including the VPN, QoS, and Desktop Security tabs, but they offer similar views and configurations as were available in previous NGX versions.

The Objects List Pane

The Objects List pane depicts the objects as selected in the Object Tree. It provides a useful and quick view of not only the objects, but also some high-level details about them. Furthermore, you can sort them in the order you want. For example, if you want to know what port a specific Transmission Control Protocol (TCP) or User Datagram Protocol (UDP) service is using or what the session timeout setup is for that service, you can select **TCP** or **UDP** as required in the **Service** tab of the Object Tree, move over to the Objects List pane, sort out the order by clicking on the **Port** or the **Session Timeout** column to quickly find the needed service, and view the details right away. In the NGX R62 and R65, another new feature allows you to choose fields that you want to be visible within the Objects List pane. You can do this by going to the **View** menu and selecting **Customize network Objects List** or by right-clicking any of the columns in the Object List pane and selecting/deselecting the columns that are required/not required.

The SmartMap Pane

The SmartMap pane continues to reflect Check Point's underlying belief that a picture is worth more than a thousand words. The SmartMap pane lays bare the complexity of topology hidden beneath numerous gateways, networks, and hosts used in large sets of rules in the rulebase. It is Check Point's attempt at facilitating your work as an administrator to quickly understand the layout of objects and their relationships as reflected in their use in the rulebase to help resolve any inadvertent misconfigurations and deployments. SmartMap's graphical display of the topological layout can be exported as a bitmap (*.bmp) or JPEG (*.jpg) image file, or as a Visio file if Microsoft's Visio is installed on your client machine.

Configuring SmartMap Display and Characteristics

SamrtMap provides extensive options for configuring a desired visual representation of your topology as well as for performing operations related to objects and rules. The following list describes some of the main options available, as shown in Figure 2.4:

Figure 2.4 Menu Options for SmartMap

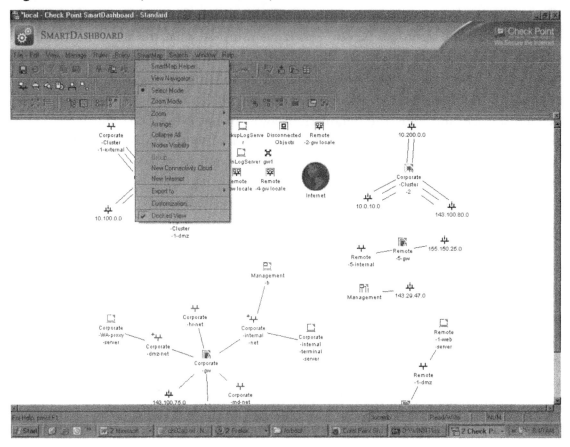

- To enable/disable SmartMap, go to **Policy | Global Properties |
  SmartMap**.

- To enable/disable the SmartMap pane display in SmartDashboard, go to
  View | SmartMap.

- To view the SmartMap display outside SmartDashboard, disable **SmartMap |
  Docked View**.

- To magnify a specific area of SmartMap, go to **SmartMap | Zoom Mode**
  and select the area you want to zoom.

- To customize the level of magnification, choose **SmartMap | Select
  Mode** and, while in the SmartMap area, choose **SmartMap | Zoom |
  desired option** from the submenu.

- To navigate through different parts of SmartMap, launch the secondary window from **SmartMap | View Navigator**.

- To rearrange the SmartMap layout, go to **SmartMap | Customization | Arranging Styles**.

- To optimize the entire SmartMap layout, go to **SmartMap | Arrange** and choose **Global Arrange**.

- To optimize the layout of a selected area, go to **SmartMap | Arrange | Incremental Arrange**.

SmartView Tracker

SmartView Tracker is one of the most useful tools for administrators to gather complete, wide-ranging information regarding network activity. Besides being a highly critical asset in your forensic and auditing arsenal, this application can help you to make sure your products are operating correctly, that the access controls configured in your security policy are being enforced properly, and that you are alerted instantly in case of an attempted attack on your firewall. Further, it will help in troubleshooting any number of day-to-day network and security-related issues. Depending on its configuration in the rules and other related elements, the SmartCenter Server/Customer Log Module collects information regarding each network event in the form of logs, and SmartView Tracker uses these logs to visually present that information. SmartView Tracker provides you with a complete solution to:

- Observe, identify, and scrutinize security-related events

- Gather data related to any troubleshooting issues

- Observe traffic patterns to help in statistical analysis

Log View Types

You can launch SmartView Tracker from within SmartDashboard or directly from the Check Point SmartConsole R65 application and you will see the main window shown in Figure 2.5. Here you will see three tabs: Log, Active and Audit.

Figure 2.5 SmartView Tracker Showing the Log, Active, and Audit Tabs

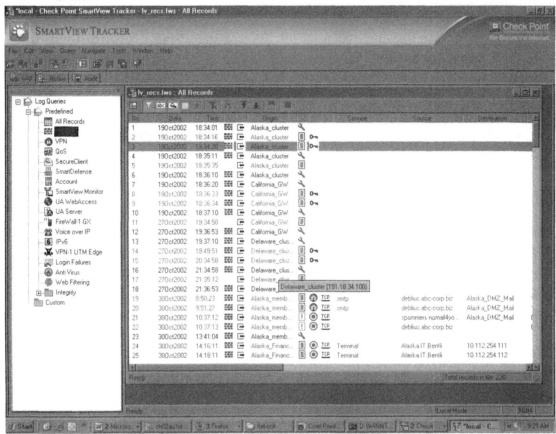

We will discuss each tab in the following sections.

The Log Tab

The Log tab is the default mode of SmartView Tracker and it provides a visual representation of logs in the current fw.log file. These logs are received from various Check Point and OPSEC partner products. This view also presents the most exhaustive set of predefined queries in the Query Tree to help administrators control the number of records they need to display based on one or more matching conditions. Older log files can be opened using the *File > Open* menu item. Log files can be opened only if they reside on the firewall or management server in the *$FWDIR/log* directory.

The Active Tab

The Active tab has serious performance implications, but in rare cases you can use it to view the live connections currently active on the firewall. One of the most useful features of the Active tab is the ability to immediately block selected active sessions based on different criteria. This functionality is part of the Suspicious Activity Monitoring (SAM) concept, which is also extended to the SmartView Monitor (discussed shortly). You invoke SAM by first selecting an active connection from the list and then selecting **Tools | Block Intruder**. Here you'll get detailed information regarding the source, destination, and service involved in the connection. You're also given some options regarding how the connection should be blocked. You can block all connections with the same source, destination, and service, or block a connection coming from a particular source or going to a particular destination. You can also set a time limit (in minutes) for which the connection will be blocked and decide whether this policy is enforced on only one or all gateways.

You can clear a connection you previously blocked indefinitely by clearing the SAM database, which you can do by selecting **Tools | Clear Blocking**.

The Audit Tab

Available via the Audit tab, audit logs display information related to administrator login, SmartDashboard usage, and operations performed on various objects. This information is particularly helpful in an environment with many administrators want to pin down responsibilities for their actions in SmartDashboard. If the current set of log files are rotated or deleted, first audit log records the time and date of the log rotation or deletion.

Filters and Queries

SmartView Tracker's versatility lies in its ability to provide some clever and elegant criteria to build conditions such that only relevant information is displayed from the huge amount that is being constantly collected. The two features of SmartView Tracker which combine to empower the harried administrator to narrow down just the information he needs to see are filters and queries.

Configuring a Filter

Check Point continues to enhance granularity in its filtering capabilities, which you can find interesting and exceedingly useful for quickly analyzing and auditing user-level or even rule-specific data.

To examine the desired data, choose **View | Query Properties** and right-click the needed log field in the **Filter** column. Alternatively, you can right-click the desired column in the **Records** pane and select **Edit Filter**. The Filter window will display the fields that are specific to the column type you've chosen. Then, you can configure the Filter window to see the desired log data, and click **OK**.

To view logs related to a specific rule number, make sure the **Current Rule Number** field is selected in the **Query Properties** pane. Right-click the **Curr. Rule No**. column in the **Records** pane and choose a suitable policy from the drop-down list box. Select the **Current Rule Number** from the filter options to view logs that are specific to the rule number(s).

TIP

Another interesting filtering feature allows you to search for logs based on source, destination, user, rule number, or rule name. Right-click on the desired log record in the **Records** pane and choose either **Follow Source, Destination, User, Rule Number** or choose the rule.

Query

Each of the Log, Active, and Audit modes in SmartView Monitor has its own query tree grouped into two folders, named Predefined and Custom. Predefined queries can neither be modified nor saved, but you can use them to customize queries to display only the log data that you are interested in by applying filters on the log records within the Record pane or by choosing only certain columns in the Query Properties. You can choose to save these customized queries, which automatically show up, in the Custom folder.

Follow these steps to create a customized query:

1. Double-click a predefined query under the Query Tree or choose **Query | Open** after highlighting the desired predefined query.

2. Make changes to the number of columns in the Query Properties pane and/or apply any number of different filter options to the desired fields in the Record pane.

3. Select **Query | Save as** and give the query a new name, which will be saved under the Custom folder in the Query Tree.

> ## Tools & Traps…
>
> ### Change in Location of Customized Queries
>
> You may be surprised why you are no longer seeing your customized query files on the local GUI client machine under the <>\SmartConsole directory. In the NGX R65, customized queries are stored in the SmartCenter database so that they are available to multiple administrators using different GUI client machines.

SmartView Monitor

SmartView Monitor is one of the most useful tools for not only monitoring the vital functions of your Check Point firewall but also detecting performance issues and spying on users to some extent. Thanks to its intuitive GUI, it takes an administrator only seconds to do what would normally require an entire day of digging through various CLI commands. SmartView Monitor parses and filters data coming from SmartCenter Servers. This allows you to check hardware and application status (including resource usage), monitor network traffic based on different patterns, and get a clear overview of your VPN tunnels. Furthermore, new in the R65 release is a feature called Cooperative Enforcement, which lets you monitor hosts that are out of compliance. In addition, SmartView Monitor incorporates the SAM incident response system, letting you alter access privileges when potential intrusion is being detected.

The SmartView Monitor Interface

You can launch SmartView Monitor from within any other GUI console by navigating to the **Window | SmartView Monitor** menu or by simply pressing **Ctrl+Alt+M**. In the left pane (the Tree View) are expandable menus from which you can choose a desired view. All of the results of the choices you've made in that pane are visible on the right-hand side of the pane (in the Results View). If you need a detailed view of a particular result from the Results View pane, a third window comes into play, as shown in Figure 2.6. Its contents differ slightly depending on the view. For instance, when you select **System** from the **System Counters** menu, the bottom–right pane displays an alphanumeric representation of data shown in the Results View.

Figure 2.6 SmartView Monitor Showing the Status of All Gateways

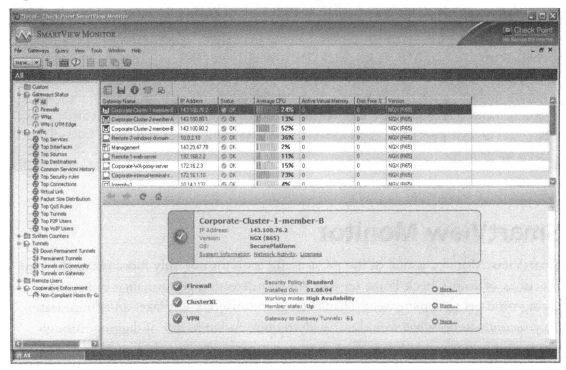

As noted earlier, SmartView Monitor's main purpose is to give you insight into how your security system is performing. This is done via both predefined and custom views. You can choose from the following views:

- Gateway status

- Traffic

- System counters

- Tunnels

- Remote users

- Cooperative enforcement (available only in a predefined view)

The R65 also brings some enhancements to SmartView Monitor. For instance, it is now possible to monitor Check Point's Eventia Analyzer. You also can access antivirus and Web filtering-related counters, such as the top 10 attacks, Hypertext Transfer Protocol (HTTP) attacks, and so on.

TIP

Another mini window/utility bar is available at the bottom of the console. Here's how it works. Opening a new view actually does two things. First, it opens a view in the Tree View pane. Second, a new tab appears in the utility bar. When you open a new view/query, by clicking on it the Tree View, the new tab appears in that utility bar. It is a kind of a history tab, but with one big difference: It is not static. Once the query starts, it remains active in the tab. Now, instead of trying to remember which queries were really important, you can take a quick look at the tabs and easily switch among active queries.

Gateway Status

The query view gives you information pertaining to the performance status and resource usage of all the servers (not just the gateways) on which you have supported software installed. That software can be either Check Point products (such as VPN-1, ClusterXL, and SmartCenter Server) or OPSEC-certified applications. In addition to general information regarding average CPU utilization, active virtual memory, disk usage, and product version installed, you also can poll for additional data. You can achieve this by clicking on the particular device for which you want more information, as shown in Figure 2.6. This fills the Gateway Details pane (on the lower right) with even more informative content. This is the right place to look for such data as application versions, current status, and components. Three other tabs are available in the Gateway Details pane: the System Information tab, Network Activity tab, and Licenses tab. We will discuss them next.

The System Information Tab

The System Information tab, which is divided into CPU, Disk, and Memory sections, gives you much more in-depth information regarding hardware status. This enables you to quickly identify the need for hardware upgrades.

The Network Activity Tab

By clicking on the Network Activity tab, you can see detailed statistics regarding the packets that have been received and sent from each interface. This information is further divided into Accepted, Dropped, Rejected, and Logged packets. You can also list the routing table by clicking on the link at the bottom of the window.

The Licenses Tab

The Licenses tab will list the license that is associated with a specific device, including its expiration date, Internet Protocol (IP) address, and features provided.

Traffic View

When you click on the Traffic link in the Tree View pane, 13 different queries show up. You can now use those queries to monitor network traffic patterns, network and bandwidth usage, and other traffic-related data. Many useful queries can be made from this pane, but perhaps the most important concerns the top P2P users. This will allow you to quickly identify workstations that are eating up resources and bandwidth by running peer-to-peer software.

When you start a query you are presented with a simple filtering tool that lets you narrow your query results to a particular connection/interface direction (inbound and outbound), interfaces, and gateways or clusters. When you click on **Traffic Views**, the bottom-right window displays a text-based legend regarding what is being shown in the Results View pane. You can change the way the information is presented via the toolbar above the Results View pane. For instance, you can see statistics represented by bar/line/pie or table diagrams. If you need to take a closer look at what is happening in the Results View pane and you don't want to worry that with the next refresh interval everything will be lost, you can freeze the view (select **Traffic | Freeze View**) and take as much time as you want for analysis. And speaking of analysis, the Recording feature, which is available from the **Traffic | Recording** menu, enables you to record everything that is happening in a particular query and then use it for further analysis. You also can export data being shown in. html, .csv, or plain text format by using the **File | Export View** menu.

TIP

If you want to display an important view as soon as you open SmartView Monitor, right-click on the view and choose the **Run at startup** option. Be careful, though, because SmartView Monitor doesn't let you choose more than one view.

NOTE

You need a separate license for SmartView Monitor to use all of its features. Without this license, you can view only static information; all real-time dynamic views are not available. We have seen many unhappy users who have realized that their brand-new license doesn't cover SmartView Monitor.

System Counters View

System Counters allow you to gather detailed information regarding resource utilization. You can use this to visualize both current and historical data. With System Counters, not only can you monitor hardware, but you can also get detailed statistics regarding such things as encryption throughput in VPN tunnels, SmartDefense or Web Intelligence rule hits, packet fragmentation, and Simple Mail Transfer Protocol (SMTP) security server usage.

Tunnels View

SmartView Monitor lets you monitor and detect issues with VPN tunnels based on different filtering conditions—for instance, gateways involved, communities for which the tunnel has been established, peer IPs, types of tunnels (regular or permanent), and so on. There are four out-of-the-box views that you can start with. One that is considered the most useful is Down Permanent Tunnels. Check Point makes a distinction between permanent and regular tunnels. Permanent tunnels are those that are kept from disconnecting, even though no traffic is being sent through them. They are created to make administrators' lives easier in terms of monitoring and trouble-shooting. Having 30 permanent tunnels can be cumbersome to monitor constantly. You are mostly interested in those that are malfunctioning for any reason and are down. That's when you can use this view. By right-clicking on the tunnel, you can get more detailed information about it. When the tunnel is down, sometimes all that it takes to fix the issue is simply resetting the tunnel. You can do that from that view; just right-click on the tunnel and select **Reset Tunnel**, as shown in Figure 2.7. If you don't like GUI tools, you can achieve the same result using the CLI on the VPN node. The command that lets you list and delete tunnels and associations is # *vpn tu* (see Figure 2.7a).

Figure 2.7 Resetting the VPN Tunnel with SmartView Monitor

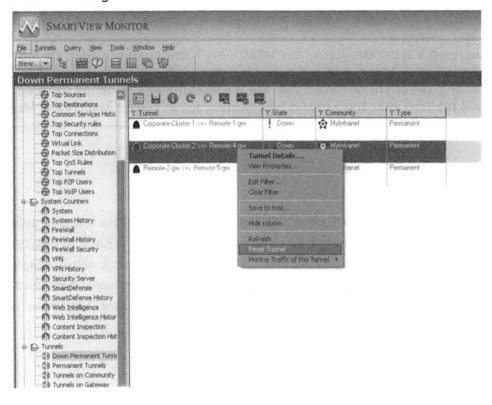

Figure 2.7a Resetting the VPN Tunnel with # vpn tu

```
[cpfw]# vpn tu

* * * * * * * * *      Select Option       * * * * * * * * *

(1)              List all IKE SAs
(2)              List all IPsec SAs
(3)              List all IKE SAs for a given peer (GW) or user (Client)
(4)              List all IPsec SAs for a given peer (GW) or user (Client)
(5)              Delete all IPsec SAs for a given peer (GW)
(6)              Delete all IPsec SAs for a given User (Client)
(7)              Delete all IPsec+IKE SAs for a given peer (GW)
(8)              Delete all IPsec+IKE SAs for a given User (Client)
(9)              Delete all IPsec SAs for ALL peers and users
(0)              Delete all IPsec+IKE SAs for ALL peers and users


(Q)              Quit

* * * * * * * * * * * * * * * * * * * * * * * * * * * * * * * * * * *
```

Remote Users View

The Remote Users View is somewhat connected with the Tunnel View—they both relate to VPN tunnels. With the Remote Users View, you can track SecuRemote VPN users who are currently logged on. Custom filters let you choose the information that will be displayed and narrow search queries to specific criteria, such as Distinguished Names (DNs), VPN gateways, SCV state, authentication method, and so on.

Cooperative Enforcement

Cooperative Enforcement is new in this version of the NGX. Thanks to compatibility with the Integrity Server (which provides endpoint protection and compliance checks), now you can easily query for workstations that are out of compliance status. So, when you have the Cooperative Enforcement feature enabled on the gateway (in either Monitor mode or Enforcing mode), you can check which workstations have been blocked or would be blocked (Monitor mode). This view is unique—you cannot make any modifications to it and you cannot create custom views.

Custom Views

As an administrator, you may come to the conclusion that out-of-the-box filters are not enough and do not suit your needs. That is when you should reach for the "creative" part of SmartView Monitor: custom filters. Two options are available for you. You can either alter existing views or create new ones from scratch. The first option is recommended when you generally like the view but some aspects of it need to be changed, such as narrowing to particular services (in the Top Services view) and shortening the refresh cycle. Elements that you can modify differ greatly and depend on the view type. The choices available with the Traffic View, for instance, will not be the same as those in the Gateways Status View. Generally, you should play a bit with all the accessible filter types to determine what you can modify.

On the other hand, you might not want to alter anything, but rather create totally new views. You may even want to place custom views in a separate folder so that they don't mix with preexisting ones. You can achieve this by first right-clicking on the **Custom** tab at the top of the **Tree View** pane and then choosing **New Folder** from the menu. You then can create custom queries in that particular folder by first clicking on the new folder and clicking the **New** button (the first button on the left in the upper toolbar).

Alerts

One of the most common questions administrators ask when implementing the NGX is where the alerts go once they've chosen the Alert action in the rulebase. The answer is that they go to SmartView Monitor. Accessing Alerts from SmartView Monitor is simple. Just click on the exclamation mark next to firewall icon in the upper toolbar, or select the **Tools | Alerts** menu. You can choose between playing a beeping sound or displaying the Alerts window when signifying an alert.

TIP

Don't choose alerts in too many rules in the SmartDashboard. Doing so will result in numerous alerts being displayed when you open the SmartView Monitor console. After some time, you will stop paying attention to them, and that's a bad sign. As soon as you start ignoring alerts, you'll miss a critical one.

Suspicious Activity Rules

You might think that when you buy the NGX R65 you get just one firewall. Actually, you get two. The other is built into SmartView Monitor. It's not a full-blown firewall, but rather a human-decision-based add-on to SmartDefense. For example, say you noticed some weird or even hostile communication coming from a particular source that wasn't blocked by your rulebase. How would you normally block it? You would have to create another rule, and then install the policy, and that takes time. With the Suspicious Activity Rules feature, you can act much faster, and simply click on the firewall icon in the upper toolbar, which will bring up a window with a rulebase. By filling it in accordingly to detect communication (Gateway, Source, Destination, Service, and Action), you can quickly block a workstation or even an entire subnet; see Figure 2.8. And you don't have to install the policy. It works right after you click the **Enforce** button in your rule.

Such actions are not meant to be permanent, however. You usually investigate a problem and then either adjust your regular rulebase or forget about it. But if you forget, you might end up with an innocent user complaining about connectivity issues, and you have no clue what the problem might be. That's why you can make Suspicious Activity Rules time-restricted and enforce them for a particular amount of time. When you create the rule, you can fill in the **Expiration** field. The expiration time you provide can be relative (meaning enforce for 10 minutes from now on, for instance) or absolute (enforce until a specified date).

The SAM table is stored in a kernel table in memory on the firewall. If the firewall is rebooted all of the SAM firewall entries are lost. The SAM table can be viewed by typing fw tab -t sam_blocked_connections and a summary can be viewed by adding a -s to the end of that command.

Figure 2.8 Creating Suspicious Activity Rules via SmartView Monitor

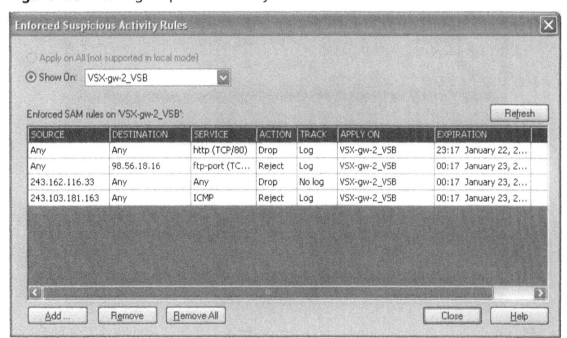

SmartUpdate

Check Point gives users a tool called SmartUpdate, which is one of the SmartConsole GUIs available with the NGX R65. Like all other SmartConsole GUIs, this one is created to make your life as an administrator easier—this time in terms of licensing and package management. This tool lets you keep your Check Point products licensed and up-to-date. Before we jump into some more details, let's look at the tool's interface (see Figure 2.9).

Figure 2.9 SmartUpdate Showing the Packages Tab
and the Packages Repository Contents

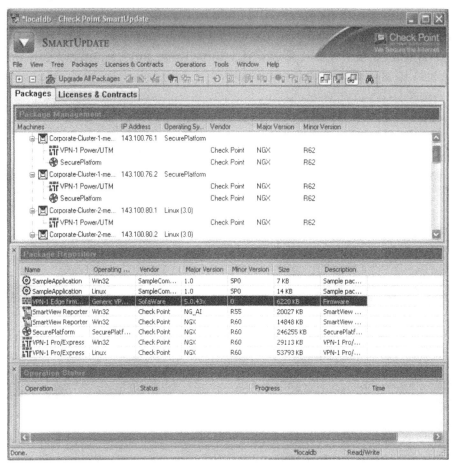

As you can see, there are four main parts of the GUI: the Licenses & Contracts tab, the Products tab, the Operation Status (the bottom pane), and, depending on the tab chosen, the License or Package Repository pane.

License Management

Let's start with the Licenses & Contracts tab. But first, you need to be aware of a licensing nuance introduced with the NG series of Check Point products. You can have two different types of licenses: Central and Local. The main reason for that move was to simplify a complicated licensing problem. With Central licenses, all you need to remember is the IP address of your SmartCenter Server where these types of licenses are uploaded. So, it doesn't matter if you have Connectra or VPN-1 products that need to be licensed. You generate Central licenses with SmartCenter's IP address. Having them on the SmartCenter Server, you can further assign them to particular modules. That differs greatly from Local licensing, which some administrators might find difficult to cope with. The Local licensing model is based on the IP address of each module for which you have a license. You must apply the license on that specific module. This doesn't matter that much when you have a simple infrastructure, but the Local licensing method can drive you mad if you're trying to manage several gateways. Imagine how frustrating it would be to readdress 10 gateways. You would have to generate 10 new licenses if you changed the IP addresses of your modules.

The process of applying licenses is divided into two steps. First, you need to add a license to the license repository, and then attach it to a specific module. To add a license, you select **Licenses & Contracts | Add License**. From here, you have three choices. You can add a license from a file, you can connect directly to the UserCenter, or you can manually fill in the license form. The last option is rarely used. Most often, all needed licenses are first downloaded from the UserCenter and then uploaded to SmartCenter with the **From File** option.

Once you have the license uploaded, you can attach it to the module. You can do this from the menu by selecting **Licenses & Contracts | Attach Licenses**. This launches a short wizard that lets you choose the module to which you want to attach licenses, and then choose the licenses you have in the repository that can be assigned to the module you've chosen. If you suspect that some licenses are not visible under the module but should be, you can manually force the module to present you with the current list by right-clicking on the module and then choosing **Get Licenses**. You can also see the progress of this operation in the **Operation Status** pane.

As you can imagine, if something can be attached, it should also be possible to detach it. And that is also true with SmartUpdate. To detach a license, select the license below the module, right-click on it, and select **Detach License**. You can also detach all licenses assigned to a module. This time, right-click on the module itself and choose **Detach All Licenses**.

NOTE

Be careful when detaching Local licenses. Unlike Central licenses, when a Local license is detached it is also removed from the repository. You'll get a warning about that fact, but sometimes it is easy to miss it.

The last thing you can do with a license is completely remove it from the repository. If the license expired, it does not make sense to keep it. It would just make your repository messy. You can delete a license by opening the **Licenses Repository** pane (select **Licenses & Contracts | View Repository**).

The R65 introduced one more element to licensing: contracts. Contracts are different from licenses. They show your support contract validity, list covered gateways, and show expiration dates. The validity of a contract needs to be confirmed before performing software upgrades. If any of the modules need to be upgraded, the contract information is downloaded to them during that process. You can add a contract to SmartCenter from the SmartUpdate menu by selecting **Licenses & Contracts | Update Contracts**. Then you have two options. You can use a contract file or connect to the UserCenter.

Package Management

The second part of SmartUpdate is package management. Unlike license management, package management requires additional licensing. If you decide to buy a license, you need to take the number of the devices you want to manage into account (also known as *device-based licensing*). In return, you will receive a GUI tool for upgrading not only the software packages but also the operating system of the managed devices.

Tools & Traps...

Package Management

Although package management seems to be a great feature, you should be extremely careful with it. Based on experience, it is better to perform major upgrades using the traditional, command-line method. Even if you upgrade from the CLI and it fails, it is easier to debug and troubleshoot. In case of a failed upgrade, SmartUpdate should revert to the last good version after rebooting.

Before you start playing with packages, it is good to see a module's list of already installed packages. Right-click on the module and choose **Get Gateway Data**.

As with licenses, two basic steps are involved. First, you upload the package to the SmartCenter Server Package Repository and then distribute it to the module. To upload a package, select **Packages | Add Package**. Again, as with licenses, you have three ways of placing packages into the repository:

- **Directly from Check Point** This is shown in Figure 2.10. Note that you need to have a valid UserCenter user account to do this. After verifying your credentials, you will be presented with a list of available packages. Notice that all of these are packages; choose only those that apply to your modules.

Figure 2.10 Selecting Packages for Download from the Check Point Download Center

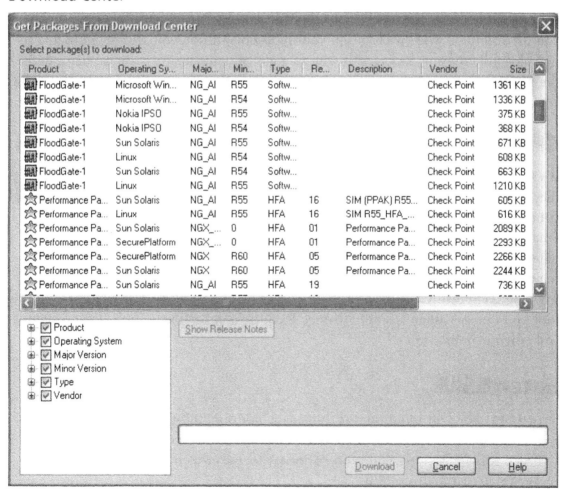

- **From the CD**

- **From a file** This is the most commonly used method.

After you've downloaded the package you require, you need to install it. This process is divided into several steps. First, it is good to verify whether there are enough system resources to perform the install, and you can do this by selecting **Packages | Pre-Install Verifier**. If verification was successful, you can move on to the distribution/installation phase, which involves either transferring the package to the selected module or both transferring and installing it. You can follow this process by observing the **Operation Status** pane.

SmartUpdate gives you another option, and that is to conduct a global upgrade on all available modules. To accomplish that task you select **Packages | Upgrade All Packages**. According to Check Point, this is a recommended method of keeping your products up to date. With Upgrade All Packages, SmartUpdate verifies whether you have all the needed packages in your repository. If not, you will be prompted to download the missing packages. If you do a global upgrade, it is wise to first transfer the packages to the appropriate modules and then start the installation. This will help you to save some resources.

CPInfo

If something goes wrong and you need to ask tech support for help, the first thing they will ask you to do is generate a CPInfo file containing detail information regarding your modules. You can create a CPInfo file in two ways: using the CLI or using SmartUpdate. The latter is recommended, as you do not have to switch between different CLIs. You can invoke this capability from the **Tools | Generate CPInfo** menu with the specific module selected, or by right-clicking on the module and selecting **Generate CPInfo** from the expanded menu. With the SmartUpdate CPInfo tool, you can also assign a proper Service Request number that Check Point support will assign to your case.

SmartLSM

SmartLSM allows an administrator to manage not only full-featured Check Point gateways but also hundreds of small ones, called ROBOs (Remote Offices/Branch Offices), as Edge devices. As this book doesn't focus on such devices, we will not cover SmartLSM in great detail.

How It Works

For SmartLSM to work, you first need to have the SmartLSM feature enabled on the SmartCenter Server. You can achieve this from the CLI with the command *LSMenabler on.*

Then you need to define SmartLSM profiles from within the SmartDashboard. You can do this by right-clicking on the **Network Objects** menu in the Object Tree and selecting **New Check Point | SmartLSM Profile**. From there, you can assign SmartDefense profiles, select VPN communities, enable or disable authentication schemes, or assign the SmartCenter Server and set the policy fetch interval. After defining a profile, you can start to use the SmartLSM SmartConsole.

TIP

SmartLSM is especially useful when it comes to policy installation. Thanks to the "fetch interval" option you can offload the SmartCenter Server by assigning a policy to a profile instead of separate ROBO gateways. Using randomly chosen timeslots, these profiles poll the policy from the server at specified intervals.

GUI and Basic Functionality

The SmartLSM console is divided into two main sections:

- **Gateways List pane** This shows various information regarding all gateways defined in the SmartLSM console and the SmartDashboard.

- **Status View pane** This is divided into two sections: Critical Notifications and Action Status. The Critical Notifications window displays all the gateways that might require a closer look. The Action Status window shows the results of the actions you took on the gateway, such as Restart, Reboot, and Stop.

As you can with other SmartConsoles, you can access SmartLSM functions directly from the menu, the toolbar (the most common place), or the object's context menu. Using SmartLSM, you can create gateways and assign profiles to them. You can also invoke some commands on them. For example, you can launch the Edge server's management portal, push policies and dynamic objects, and create clusters. You can also modify a gateway's properties (see Figure 2.11). In addition, you can convert regular gateways. For example, if you have several different gateways installed at remote locations and you want to use SmartLSM as your primary management tool, you can convert them into ROBO gateways with the CLI command *Convert*. This process works both ways: You can convert a regular gateway to a ROBO and vice versa.

Figure 2.11 Modifying the VPN-1 Edge ROBO Gateway from within SmartLSM

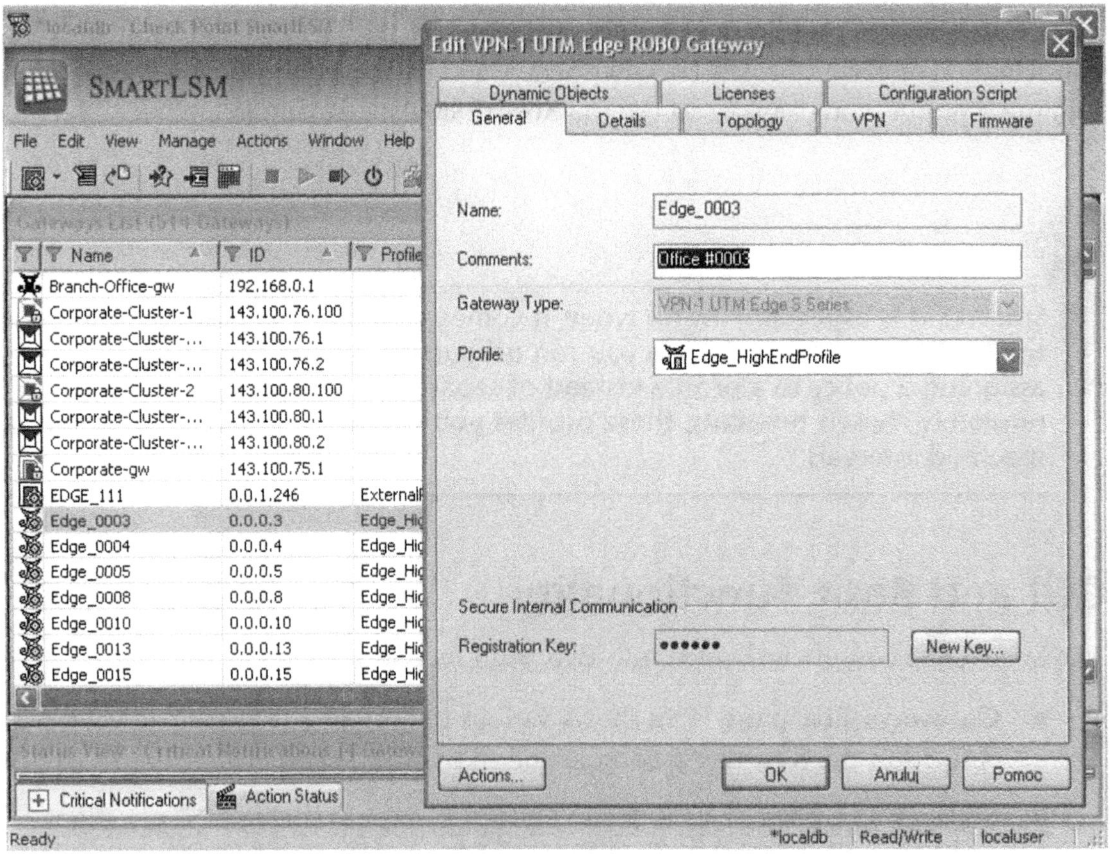

The SecureClient Packaging Tool

One of the most typical situations administrators face is calls from inexperienced users asking for help when they install and configure SecuRemote or Secure Client. That might be a real nightmare if you have 200 users who *must* be "VPNized" within the next 24 hours. But you're not on your own. In such situations, the SecureClient Packaging Tool will serve you well.

With this tool, you can preconfigure the VPN client and set all needed parameters before sending it to users. After preparing the package, you can put it on the Web or on a file server for distribution. Users then can download the package and install it locally. You can also use third-party deployment tools if you like. In addition, you can define the client's installation process—for instance, as silent or fully interactive, resulting in an automatic reboot or requiring the user's "touch".

Using the SecurClient Packaging Tool

So, you have that magic tool. How do you use it then? There are several steps that need to be accomplished before pushing ready-to-roll packages to your users.

Creating an Installation Profile

To create an installation profile, you need to invoke **Profile | New** from the menu, at which point a wizard pops up, asking you to define several parameters. Here are the steps to follow:

1. First provide the profile name.

2. Now choose the mode in which the client initializes its connection to the VPN server. This can be either Connect mode or Transparent mode. You can also give your users the freedom of switching between the two. It is good to know how choosing the mode will influence users. The main difference is in connection initialization. From the user's perspective, Connect mode looks like a standard VPN client. You need to open the client and connect to the site if you want to establish the tunnel, and then disconnect after you are done. In Transparent mode, however, if you send a packet directed to a host in the site's encryption domain, you get a pop up asking whether you want to establish a VPN tunnel. You should also remember that *Transparent mode* is the term used only for client versions prior to NG FP1. In the NGX R65, the function is called Auto Connect mode. It's a different name but it works in the same way.

3. Provide some information regarding the policy that should be enforced on the client. For example, you can disable the user's ability to turn the policy off (by selecting the **Restrict Secure Client user intervention** box). You can also force SecureClient to automatically log on to a specified Policy server containing security policies for your clients.

4. At this point, you can set some encryption-related parameters, prevent users from stopping the client, or even add a custom dynamic link library (DLL) file that should be used if you have a third-party authentication scheme such as smartcards or tokens.

5. Change some topology-related settings. One interesting feature you can use is called Partial Topology. This is useful when you have to publish installation packages in unprotected locations, such as freely accessible Web sites or public File Transfer Protocol (FTP) servers. With Partial Topology, you can hide some of the topology information from a nosy parker.

6. Add certificate-related information.

7. Choose the installation process behavior—for instance, silent; or maybe provide some information to the user. You can also allow users to alter some settings during installation, such as the destination path.

8. Choose whether this setting should be SecuRemote or Secure Client, and enable Secure Domain Logon and third-party Windows GINA integration, if needed.

9. Finish creating the profile or create the profile and start generating the installation package.

Generating the Package

Creating only an installation profile is not enough. To build a complete client package you need to wrap your newly created profile with some real client software. To do this you have to download a special version of the installation package from the Check Point Web site. It's called the Administrative package and it comes in the form of an MSI file. Here's what you need to do:

1. Extract the contents of the MSI administrative package with the cpmsi_tool. exe utility, which you can find on a workstation with SmartConsoles installed. It should be in the [Drive]\Program Files\CheckPoint\ SmartConsole\R65\Program\Util\directory if you used the default path (see Figure 2.12).

Figure 2.12 Extracting the Secure Client Package with cpmsi_tool.exe

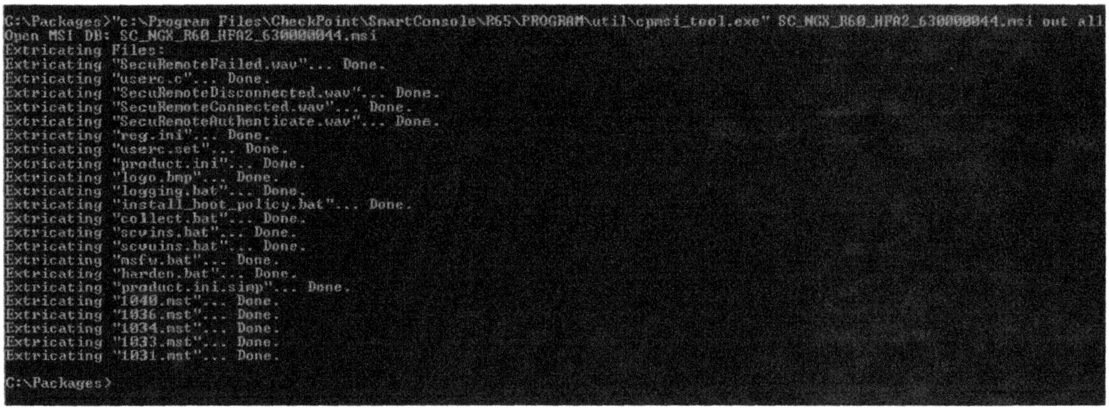

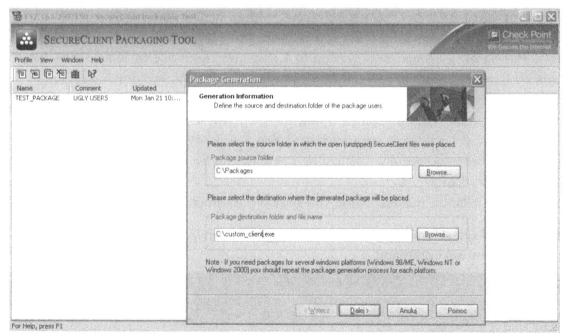

2. When you have all the contents extracted, you can go back to the SecureClient Packaging console, click on the newly created profile, and select the Christmas-gift-looking icon on the toolbar. This will display the Package Generator Wizard.

3. Select the source folder (the one that was used to extract the MSI file) and the destination folder with the package name. This is where the new package (.exe or .msi) will be created (see Figure 2.13).

Figure 2.13 Invoking the Package Generation Wizard

Now all you have to do is deploy the package.

NOTE

When you have the SecureClient Packaging Tool started, you will not be able to log in to the SmartDashboard with read/write privileges; only read-only privileges. And vice versa; when you have the SmartDashboard started, you will not be able to get to the SecureClient Packaging Tool.

Management Plug-ins

Management plug-ins, as we mentioned earlier, are new with the NGX R65. The plug-in concept is to bring all Check Point product management capabilities together into one console and have everything centrally managed. Moreover, you don't need to reinstall or upgrade the entire SmartCenter Server to manage additional products. Management plug-ins are simply separate packages that can be installed as soon as new features become available. As we also mentioned, the only plug-ins that are available as of this writing is the Connectra plug-in.

Installing the Connectra Management Plug-in

Not long ago, Connectra was a stand-alone product with its own management system. The only integration with SmartCenter that was possible was sending logs to it. Now, there's a brand-new version of Connectra: the R62CM (CM stands for *centrally managed*). With it, you can fully integrate Connectra into the SmartCenter Server in terms of management.

You can install this management plug-in when you install the R65 or upgrade to it. Either way, the process is straightforward. You can verify whether the Connectra plug-in has been successfully installed by invoking the *fwm ver* command from SmartCenter's CLI.

If the installation was successful, you should see something similar to Figure 2.14.

Figure 2.14 Checking Whether the Connectra Plug-in Was Installed with the fwm ver Command

```
[cpmgmt]# fwm ver
This is Check Point SmartCenter Server NGX (R65) HFA_02, Hotfix 602 - Build 004
Installed Plug-ins:  Connectra NGX R62CM
[cpmgmt]#
```

After installation, you can start your SmartDashboard. You'll notice a new tab, Connectra, as shown in Figure 2.15.

Figure 2.15 SmartDashboard Showing the Connectra Tab after Connectra Management Plug-in Installation

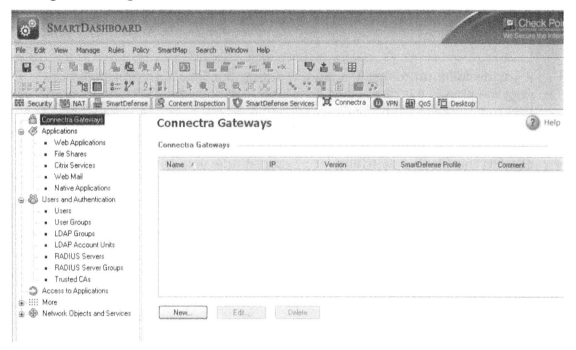

Now, you can take advantage of using one console for managing not only your Check Point firewall but also your Connectra Secure Sockets Layer (SSL) VPN application.

Uninstalling the Connectra Management Plug-in

If you don't need the plug-in anymore or you installed it by mistake, you can uninstall it from the CLI on the SmartCenter Server:

1. Log in to the CLI in Expert mode.
2. Run the plug-in cleanup utility:

   ```
   /opt/CPPIconnectra- *R65/bin/plugin_preuninstall_verifier
   ```

3. Uninstall the package. As it is a regular RPM package, you can do this using a typical Linux RPM tool:

```
rpm -e CPPIconnectra-R65-00
```

4. Reboot the server.

TIP

If you decided not to install a plug-in during the SmartCenter installation/upgrade phase, you can always do it later. Just copy the CPPIconnectra-R65-00.i386.rpm package from the /linux/CPconplg directory on the installation CD. You can do this using such tools as pscp or winscp, provided you created an /etc/scpusers file on the server and put the "admin" user there. After copying the file and switching into Expert mode, you can install it using this command:

  rpm –ivh /[path_to_the package]/ CPPIconnectra-R65-00.i386.rpm
  Then reboot the server, and you're done!

The Check Point Configuration Tool/cpconfig

cpconfig is one of the most frequently used and versatile CLI management tools. It does not have its GUI representation, and it is available on SmartPlatform. The only place you will definitely not find cpconfig is in a GUI client workstation. You can use cpconfig either to finish the system installation process or to configure/reconfigure your favorite firewall or management server.

cpconfig Configuration Options

Although you might think that cpconfig is a constant tool that doesn't change at all, that's not quite right. Depending on the products installed on the host machine, options available from within cpconfig differ.

Let's look at most of the common configuration options for which you can use this utility (see Figure 2.16).

Figure 2.16 cpconfig Invoked on a Stand-alone UTM-1 R65 Platform

```
[r65]# cpconfig
This program will let you re-configure
your Check Point products configuration.


Configuration Options:
_____

(1)   Licenses
(2)   Administrator
(3)   GUI Clients
(4)   SNMP Extension
(5)   PKCS#11 Token
(6)   Random Pool
(7)   Certificate Authority
(8)   Certificate's Fingerprint
(9)   Disable Check Point SecureXL
(10)  Automatic start of Check Point Products

(11) Exit

Enter your choice (1-11) :_
```

Licenses

With cpconfig, you can add and remove licenses for your products. You can add licenses both manually and from a file. We don't know too many administrators using the former method. It's just too cumbersome.

Administrator

With cpconfig, you can add an administrative account.

GUI Clients

With the GUI Clients option you can specify workstations, networks, subnets, or IP address ranges from which administrators can connect to the SmartCenter Server using the SmartConsole. This is a simple yet effective way to keep "curious" people away from your configuration.

SNMP Extension

Using the SNMP Extension option you can configure Simple Network Management Protocol (SNMP) daemons, thus allowing your server to share its status information with other management tools.

Secure Internal Communication (SIC)

SIC is by far the most critical element of successful communication between different Check Point components—gateways and, especially, SmartCenter. It is used to set up trust between them. You will not find that option on the SmartCenter server—only on modules that need to be connected to SmartCenter.

Automatic Start of Check Point Modules

This option lets you choose which Check Point modules will be starting automatically when the machine boots. These can be for Eventia Reporter, QoS service etc.

Summary

With the introduction of the SmartConsole management console, Check Point gave the term *central management* a new meaning. Furthermore, SmartDashboard combined with management plug-ins gives you a powerful yet easy-to-understand management interface. However, it would be impractical to bring all administrative tasks together. That is why Check Point created other, dedicated tools that make your life much simpler.

For instance, with SmartView Tracker, you can painlessly debug communication, track intrusion attempts, and observe concurrent connections. SmartView Monitor, meanwhile, offers you a more in-depth landscape of your systems in terms of performance and resource utilization, allowing you to detect possible bottlenecks before it is too late. With SmartUpdate, you can manage both licenses and packages (although package management needs another license). And when you have 100 gateways spread all over the country, you can use SmartLSM for management purposes. It is also important that the R65 allows you to prepare a diagnostics package (with CPInfo) that you and your support team can use to resolve issues quickly.

Solutions Fast Track

SmartDashboard

☑ SmartDashboard is composed of four main sections, officially referred to as "panes."

☑ **Plugin Demo Mode** becomes active only while you're logging in with **Demo Mode** selected.

☑ The Object Tree pane provides a first-glance peek at various entities, including network objects, services, resources, servers, OPSEC applications, users, and VPN communities that have been either predefined or user-defined.

SmartView Tracker

☑ SmartView Tracker enables you to view logs and query for log-based information (e.g., SmartDefense, Antivirus, VPN).

☑ With SmartView Tracker, you can view current active connections on your firewall.

☑ SmartView Tracker can track modifications of your configuration.

SmartView Monitor

☑ SmartView Monitor parses and filters data coming from SmartCenter Servers.

☑ SmartView Monitor allows you to check hardware and application status (including resource usage), monitor network traffic based on different patterns, and get a clear overview of your VPN tunnels.

☑ With SmartView Monitor's Suspicious Activity Rules feature, you can respond rapidly to unwanted communications with SAM rules.

SmartUpdate

☑ SmartUpdate is one of the SmartConsole GUIs available with the NGX R65.

☑ SmartUpdate lets you keep your Check Point products licensed and up-to-date.

☑ There are four main parts of the SmartUpdate GUI: the Licenses & Contracts tab, the Products tab, the Operation Status (the bottom pane), and, depending on the tab chosen, the License or Package Repository pane.

SmartLSM

☑ SmartLSM allows an administrator to manage not only full-featured Check Point gateways but also hundreds of small ones, called ROBOs (Remote Offices/Branch Offices), as Edge devices.

☑ For SmartLSM to work, you first need to have the SmartLSM feature enabled on the SmartCenter Server.

☑ The SmartLSM console is divided into two main sections: Gateway List pane and Status View pane.

The SecureClient Packaging Tool

☑ The SecureClient Packaging tool enables you to prepare pre-configured SecureClient packages with built-in configuration profiles for automated installs.

☑ With the SecureClient Packaging tool you can create different installation profiles based on users' expertise levels.

☑ The SecureClient Packaging tool helps you to safeguard your topology data.

Management Plug-ins

☑ Management plug-ins are simply separate packages that can be installed as soon as new features become available.

☑ Connectra is the only plug-in available so far.

☑ You can install and uninstall management plug-ins at any time.

The Check Point Configuration Tool/cpconfig

☑ You can use cpconfig either to finish the system installation process or to configure/reconfigure your favorite firewall or management server.

☑ You can use cpconfig to define the first Administrator.

☑ You can use cpconfig to restrict GUI clients from accessing your SmartCenter.

Frequently Asked Questions

Q: Where can I configure port forwarding in SmartDashboard?

A: All network address and port translation is done in the NAT tab.

Q: How can you set the global VPN configuration method to Simplified mode?

A: You need to open SmartDashboard and go to **Policy | Global Properties | VPN tab.** Once this is done, all new security policies will be created as Simplified.

Q: Is there any way I can customize fields visible within the Objects list?

A: Yes, that is a new feature available starting with the R62. You can do this by selecting View | **Customize Network Objects List.**

Q: Can I export a SmartMap layout to some graphical format?

A: Yes, SmartMap allows you to export its contents to three different formats: .bmp, .jpg, and Visio (the latter only if you have Microsoft Visio installed on the local workstation).

Q: How can I optimize the layout of a selected area in SmartMap?

A: You can achieve this by going to **SmartMap | Arrange | Incremental Arrange menu.**

Q: It is possible to track all active connections with the Audit log in SmartView Tracker?

A: No. You do this from the Active tab.

Q: How can I track a workstation that tried to establish a Secure Shell (SSH) session to my mail server?

A: You can do this from within the Log tab. Right-click on the **Service column header**, select **Edit filter**, find the **ssh** and **ssh_version_2** services, and move them to the right-hand pane with the **Add** button. Then right-click on the **Destination column header**, select **Edit filter**, and either find your mail server object on the list or type its IP address, and move it to the right.

Q: What is the purpose of the Custom folder in SmartView Tracker?

A: The Custom folder is used when you decide to create your own custom query. The query is placed in that folder right after creation.

Q: How can I install a SAM policy?

A: You do not need to install a SAM policy. When you configure Suspicious Activity Rules, they are enforced automatically.

Q: I don't see the Traffic View in SmartView Monitor. Why?

A: You might need an additional license to have all real-time views available. You can only see static ones without it.

Q: What is the easiest way to reset a VPN tunnel?

A: You can use SmartView Monitor and its Tunnel View from the Tree View pane—for instance, Permanent Tunnels View. Then right-click on the tunnel you wish to reset and select **Reset Tunnel**.

Q: What is the difference between a Central and a Local licensing model?

A: Central licenses are generated with the SmartCenter Server IP address regardless of which module needs to be licensed. Then, from within the SmartCenter Server, you can attach that license to the specific module. A Local license is different. You need to generate a Local license with the IP address of the specific module and apply it directly on that module. If for some reason you have to change the IP address of the module, the license must be regenerated.

Q: Can I use all SmartUpdate features with a standard license?

A: No, if you want to use the package management feature you must have a separate license.

Q: How can I create a diagnostics file for Check Point support?

A: You can do it with the CPInfo tool. The easiest way to do this is with the SmartUpdate console. Select the module and then select **Tools | Generate CPInfo**.

Q: What is the easiest way to manage 200 Edge devices in different locations?

A: The best way is to use SmartLSM. Remember, you need to create SmartLSM profiles (from within SmartDashboard) before using full SmartLSM management capabilities.

Q: What is a ROBO gateway?

A: ROBO stands for Remote Office Branch Office and it describes remote gateways such as Edge devices that can be managed via SmartLSM.

Q: Can I make a regular gateway a ROBO gateway?

A: Yes, you can do it using the "convert" tool accessible from the CLI.

Q: What do I have to do to create a preconfigured SecureClient install package?

A: Three steps are required: two from within the SecureClient Packaging Tool console and one from the CLI on the workstation where the SmartConsoles are installed. With the SecureClient Packaging Tool you need to create an installation profile. Then extract the SecureClient MSI package with the cpmsi_tool.exe utility. Lastly, build the package with the SecureClient Packaging Tool.

Q: What SecureClient package do I need to create a custom SecureClient installation file?

A: You need an administrative version, which you can download from the Check Point Web site.

Q: What management plug-ins can I use in the R65?

A: At the time of this writing, only one plug-in is available: Connectra.

Q: How do I uninstall a management plug-in?

A: Plug-in are standard RPM packages. You can uninstall them using the *rpm −e* command from the CLI. You must be in Expert mode to do this.

Q: I forgot to install the Connectra management plug-in during the system installation phase. Do I have to reinstall the system?

A: No, you can easily install the package at any time. The Connectra plug-in comes in a form of RPM file and can be uploaded to the SmartCenter Server from your installation CD (from the /linux/cpconplg directory). You can install it with the *rpm –ivh* command in Expert mode.

Q: I used SmartUpdate and uploaded a package from a file to the Package Repository. Where does it reside physically?

A: The Package Repository is in the directory represented by the *$SUROOT* environment variable on the SmartCenter Server.

Q: How many administrators can be defined with cpconfig?

A: Only one. The rest of them must be created using SmartDashboard.

Q: I want to configure a network interface on my gateway. I opened cpconfig but I don't see such an option.

A: This is common. There are two similar configuration tools in the CLI: cpconfig and sysconfig. Options that you're looking for are available from the latter.

Chapter 3

Management Portal

Solutions in this chapter:

- SmartCenter Installation

- Dedicated Server Installation

- A Tour of the Dashboard

- New in SmartDashboard NGX

- Your First Security Policy

- Other Useful Controls on the Dashboard

- Managing Connectra and
  Interspect Gateways

- SmartPortal

☑ Summary

☑ Solutions Fast Track

☑ Frequently Asked Questions

Introduction

SmartPortal is one of Check Point's newest additions to the SmartCenter server product family. This feature allows a user to browse the security policies and logs of a SmartCenter server using the Internet Explorer Web browser, without needing a full-blown SmartClient software installation. This chapter covers the installation and usage of the SmartPortal interface, which is the interface used to configure your NGX installation: the SmartDashboard.

Once we are done with the tour, new users of Check Point should know where to return in order to configure more advanced features of NGX; those familiar with Check Point NG will see where things have changed and what new features they can use to make management of their systems easier. We will then run through setting up a simple security policy and applying it to your NGX firewall gateway. The new SmartPortal management interface will be visited; we will look at how to install it and how it will help administrate your organization's Check Point systems.

SmartCenter Installation

Check Point provides for three Integrity-NGX configurations through SmartCenter and two Integrity-NGX configurations by means of Provider-1.

Basic Configurations

1. **Integrity Only** This configuration is intended for users who do not want to connect Integrity to SmartCenter and wish to deploy the Integrity product alone.

2. **Integrity and Smart Center on one host** This configuration is designed to provide the advantage of allowing both SmartCenter and Integrity to run on the same host. This configuration is aimed at:

   a. Sites with concerns regarding the cost of hardware, limited clients, and a low volume of SmartCenter traffic.

   b. Sites that wish to evaluate the product lines.

3. **Integrity connected to a remote SmartCenter** This configuration is designed to allow both SmartCenter and Integrity to be deployed on separate machines. This provides the benefits of greater system control and performance, but at a higher cost. This configuration can be more robust as the load is

divided between two hosts. Since SmartCenter must not be open to the public network as is required with the Integrity module, the system may be more tightly secured.

4. **Integrity on the MDS host (Provider-1)** This configuration is designed for sites that are attached to a single Check Point Management Agent (CMA).

5. **Integrity associated to a remote CMA on Provider-1** This configuration is designed to provide the ability to connect to both systems using separate hosts.

Installation Paths

Each of the aforementioned basic configurations and a variety of combinations that are derived from them are valid. Further, it is feasible to install additional Check Point products with the Integrity module. The following list presents a few of the many methods of installing and configuring this product.

Common Installation Scenarios

In the subsequent configuration methods, Integrity characterizes a non-clustered Integrity as well as any Integrity cluster node.

- Integrity on a primary SmartCenter machine.
- Integrity on a primary SmartCenter machine and gateway.
- Integrity on a secondary SmartCenter machine and gateway.
- Integrity on a Log Server machine. In this case the user may want to send the Integrity logs to this Log Server, thereby having the Integrity logs on the Integrity machine itself.
- Integrity on a Log Server machine and gateway.
- Integrity on a dedicated machine.
- Integrity on a dedicated machine and gateway.
- Integrity along with other Check Point products (such as Eventia Reporter).

Install

The Integrity server consists of the following packages: Integrity, SmartPortal, and SmartCenter. The Integrity wrapper installs the right packages automatically. If you prefer to manually install the packages, verify the following:

- When you are installing Integrity on the same machine as the SmartCenter, the SmartCenter should be installed as the primary management.

- When you are installing Integrity as a distributed configuration, SmartCenter should be configured as a Log Server.

- Every additional Integrity node should be treated as Integrity in a distributed mode (that is, SmartCenter should be configured as a Log Server).

- The UTC time for Integrity and SmartCenter machines should be the same in a distributed configuration.

- The installation should not be interrupted and the packages should be installed in the order listed above.

- A reboot is required only after all the packages are successfully installed.

For additional information about installation refer to the Advanced Server Installation Guide.

Uninstall

To completely uninstall Integrity and the packages associated with it, manually uninstall the following three packages in the order they appear: Integrity, then SmartPortal, and finally SmartCenter.

When Integrity is installed on the same or different machine as SmartCenter, it is possible to uninstall Integrity while leaving SmartCenter installed. But, you cannot uninstall SmartCenter without uninstalling Integrity, since Integrity is dependent on SmartCenter services.

Integrity Advanced Server

The Embedded Data store in Integrity 6.6 (as is distributed on the R65 installation CD) currently supports up to 2,000 concurrent users. This is designed to remove the requirement for an external database. Logs are now stored on the embedded Check Point Log server. This will still integrate with both Check Point and third party reporting tools. It is recommended that sites requiring greater than 2,000 concurrent users continue using Integrity 6.5 until Integrity 7.0 is released.

Dedicated Server Installation

When deploying SmartPortal on a dedicated server, the following actions should be taken to successfully integrate the SmartPortal Server with the SmartCenter server.

1. During the SmartPortal installation you will be asked to choose a SIC (Secure Internal Communication) password that will be used to establish trust with the SmartCenter server.

2. On the SmartCenter server create a network object to represent the SmartPortal server.

   ■ Fill in the network objects properties.

   ■ Select SmartPortal from the Check Point Product list.

3. Add access rules to allow administrative access to the SmartPortal Server.

4. Create administrator users with SmartPortal permissions if you want to restrict access to SmartPortal.

   ■ Administrator users can be limited to SmartPortal access only using a Permission profile. Create a Permission profile by selecting the **Allow access SmartPortal only** permission for the specific administrator.

A Tour of the Dashboard

Those unfamiliar with the Check Point NG interface may find the SmartDashboard interface a little daunting at first sight, what with so many different panes, views, and toolbars on one screen! Indeed, a large screen is a good place to start Check Point—say, at least 800 × 600—but 1280 × 1024 over 19" is much more workable, and an excuse for the larger monitor you'd wanted for months.

The key to working with the interface is understanding what each area is for and sticking to those you need. We will take a quick tour to help with this.

Logging In

First, we need to log in. Usually, you'd be connecting SmartDashboard to your SmartCenter, but there is also the option of Demo mode. This allows you to get familiar with the interface and take a look at some advanced configurations without risking any damage, because the only configuration you are changing is the local Demo databases. You can choose a number of different Demo databases, varying in complexity from a firewall only to advanced VPN scenarios. When you use Demo mode, SmartDashboard shows that it is connected to a SmartCenter named *local—that's really just some static files. You can run SmartDashboard in Demo mode without any SmartCenter installed—choose a Demo Installation from your NGX CD.

For our tour, we will log in using Demo mode with the Basic Firewall+VPN database, as shown in Figure 3.1.

Figure 3.1 Logging in Using Demo Mode

The SmartDashboard window includes a number of different panes. Our tour begins with the rulebases—those Check Point administrators who remember FireWall-1 v4 will recall when there was nothing more than the Security and Address Translation rulebases!

Tools & Traps...

Stuck on Solaris?

The vast majority of Check Point installations run SmartDashboard on Windows. However, SmartDashboard is also available for Solaris as a Motif application. If you really are not able or willing to run SmartDashboard on Windows, it is an option. However, be warned that the Motif version requires an additional license. In this chapter we will be looking at the Windows version only, but most here will apply to the Solaris version, too.

The Rulebase Pane

The tabs in Figure 3.2 are the default tabs we see in the Demo mode. Each tab configures a different product feature, the Security tab being the most commonly used—the firewall rulebase. Some of the tabs reflect a particular policy, where different policies can be loaded and applied to different gateways, whereas others apply globally across all the gateways managed by your SmartCenter. The combination of policies that you view at one time is called a *policy package*. Other tabs will appear if other product features are enabled.

Figure 3.2 Rulebase Pane Tabs

To get your first firewall policy up and running, you probably will use only the Security and perhaps Address Translation tabs, but here is the full list.

Security Tab

This tab is the policy-based definition of the firewall security policy. Rules here define what traffic is permitted through a firewall, whether to log the traffic, and whether the traffic requires encryption or authentication. The Security rulebase is part of the Security and Address Translation policy.

Address Translation Tab

These policy-based rules define what Network Address Translation (NAT) should be performed on traffic through a firewall. They are part of the Security and Address Translation policy.

SmartDefense Tab

This tab is the global configuration of the firewall's attack detection and prevention features. This includes everything from low-level IP packet sanity checks up to application layer controls for Instant Messengers and Voice-over IP (VoIP). The functionality here has expanded greatly since the introduction of SmartDefense back in NG FP2.

Web Intelligence Tab

This tab is the global configuration of Web (HTTP)-related SmartDefense features, including new features that were introduced in the R55W (Web Intelligence) version of NG.

VPN Manager Tab

This is the global configuration of VPN gateways when using VPN Communities. This method of VPN configuration applies only when a *Simplified Mode* Security and Address Translation policy is enforced on the gateways, so this tab is not present if a *Traditional Mode* Security and Address Translation policy is part of the current policy package. The difference between Simplified and Traditional Mode will be explained in Chapter 10.

QoS Tab

This policy controls the behavior of the Quality of Service (QoS) (Floodgate-1) gateway module where it has been enabled. It allows granular control of bandwidth usage per protocol and source and destination IP. This tab is not available in the Basic demo database.

Desktop Security Tab

This tab is the policy defining the desktop firewall rulebase that will be downloaded to SecureClient remote users when they connect. Check Point's SecureClient secure remote access solution consists of client software (SecureClient) installed on each remote user machine; the VPN-1 gateway, which acts as the endpoint for the VPN tunnel to the client; and the SecureClient Policy Server, which runs on the gateway. The Policy Server will supply the latest Desktop Security policy to clients when they connect.

Web Access Tab

This tab is the global configuration of UserAuthority WebAccess modules. UA WebAccess software can be installed on Web servers to provide URL level access control and single sign-on integration with gateways. This tab is disabled by default—if you are installing a WebAccess module, enable it in the **Global Properties, UserAuthority** page (see Figure 3.3).

Figure 3.3 Enabling the Web Access Tab

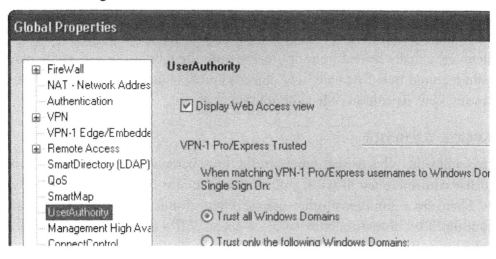

Consolidation Rules Tab

This policy controls the behavior of the Eventia Reporter Log Consolidator, if installed. To display this tab, use **View | Products | Reporter Log Consolidator**. Note that this removes all other tabs—to return to the previous view of tabs, use **View | Products | Standard**.

The Objects Tree Pane

To the left of the rulebases, you should see the Objects Tree, as shown in Figure 3.4.

Figure 3.4 The Objects Tree Pane

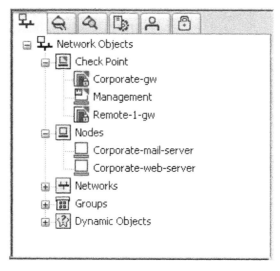

The tree is a convenient way to browse, edit, and create the objects that you need to define for your rulebases. Objects are needed to represent the SmartCenter, gateways, networks, and hosts you reference in policies, user accounts, and so on.

There are actually several trees of objects—use the tabs at the top of the pane to select the required tree. To create new objects, simply right-click the top of the tree and choose New. To edit an object, double-click it.

Network Objects

This tree holds the objects that represent the hosts, gateways, networks, and address ranges that you reference in your policies. You can also create groups of network objects. There are a number of other special types of objects that can be defined here, representing DNS domains, external VPN peers, VoIP configuration, server load balancing controls, and routers managed by the Check Point OSE product.

By default, the Network Objects tree branches reflect each type of Network Object or can be sorted by color or name. Alternatively, a Group View will show each Network Object group as a branch, and its members within that branch—right-click the top of the tree to switch between **Arrange by Group** or **Classic View**.

Services

A wealth of objects reside here that define protocols that can be used in policies. The tree divides the objects by protocol type. The objects range from the obvious—like the telnet object that represents TCP port 23—to the obscure—such as SSL_v3, which represents an SSL connection, but enforces version 3 of the protocol.

Resources

Resource objects control the behavior of the firewall security servers—these are transparent proxy servers integrated into the firewall gateway. Security servers can be used for http, ftp, and smtp traffic. There is also a generic TCP proxy. A typical use of security servers is enabling redirection of Web and mail traffic to third-party CVP or UFP servers that perform antivirus scanning or URL cataloging. An additional type of resource object is the CIFS resource that can be used to control and audit use of Microsoft networking—allowing the restriction of what server shares can be accessed. This CIFS enforcement is performed without the use of a security server.

Servers and OPSEC Applications

Check Point can integrate with a wide range of other servers and applications. Objects are defined here to represent applications that will be integrated. These include certificate authorities, authentication servers, LDAP servers, and content checking servers. There is one predefined object: the *internal_ca* Certificate Authority (CA) object. This represents the internal CA that is integrated into the SmartCenter Server.

Users and Administrators

To connect to the SmartCenter for the first time, an administrator account is used that was created as part of the installation process using the *cpconfig* utility. This account is visible in SmartDashboard in the object *cpconfig_administrators*. Once connected using this account, additional administrator accounts should be created here in SmartDashboard for each user that will require access to the SmartCenter. Each account can then have different access permissions as required.

In addition, nonadministrative user accounts can be created to make use of the firewall and VPN authentication features. These accounts can be defined with a fixed password, certificate, or authentication backed off to an external authentication server.

To avoid the overhead of user account management in SmartDashboard, the provision of the user database can be passed to an external server in two ways: first, External User Profiles can be created that back off all authentication requests that do not match a locally defined user. Second, it is possible to fully integrate with a LDAP directory server. This includes using the server for authentication plus the ability to manage user accounts on the LDAP server directly through SmartDashboard—once configured, the directory will become accessible in this object tree. Integration with LDAP for user authentication is a licensed feature—Check Point calls it SmartDirectory. If you have a SmartCenter Pro license, SmartDirectory should be included.

VPN Communities

This provides a tree view of community objects—the same as those displayed in the VPN Manager rulebase tab.

The Objects List Pane

This pane shows objects in a list format. The contents of the list are controlled by what is currently selected in the Objects Tree. For example, select the **Network Objects—Nodes** branch to see a list of all nodes.

The SmartMap Pane

SmartMap provides a visual representation of the network topology that can be gleaned from the network objects that have been defined. SmartMap can be disabled in **Global Properties, SmartMap** page. If you are not using SmartMap, disable it—this avoids the overhead of SmartDashboard calculating the visual topology.

Menus and Toolbars

Although most of the policy and object management can be performed via the panes we've looked at, there is plenty more that can be achieved via the drop-down menus or, for some of the most common actions, the toolbars.

Working with Policy Packages

To save changes to objects and the current policy package, create new policy packages, or open a different policy package, use the File menu. Remember that a policy package is all the policies you can see on the rulebase pane. If you wish to take a copy of just one of the policies—say the Desktop Policy—and save it in a new package, use the **Copy Policy to Package** option and specify a name for your new policy package.

Installing the Policy

Saving the Policy Package does not actually change the policy running on your gateways—it's just updating the SmartCenter database. To update your gateways, use the **Policy** menu, **Install Policy** option—or find the toolbar icon for Install Policies.

There are plenty more menu options to explore in your own time. The final option we will look at is the big daddy of all: **Global Properties**, from the **Policy** menu.

Tools & Traps…

One Policy for All?

If you have a number of different gateways, you should consider whether to keep a single policy package for all gateways, or instead, create new packages for each new gateway. The latter is usually the best option if there is very little overlap between the security policies of each gateway.

Continued

> If you have a single policy for all, use the **Install On** column of your security rules to define which rules apply to which gateways.
>
> If you go for different packages for each gateway, use the menu option **Policy | Policy Installation Targets** in order to define which gateway(s) a policy applies to.

Global Properties

The Global Properties window, as the name suggests, defines settings and fine-tuning of your Check Point systems that apply globally (rather than per policy or per gateway). To open the window from the menus, choose **Policy | Global Properties**, or from the toolbar, choose the icon that looks like a bulleted list (see Figure 3.5).

Figure 3.5 The Global Properties Window

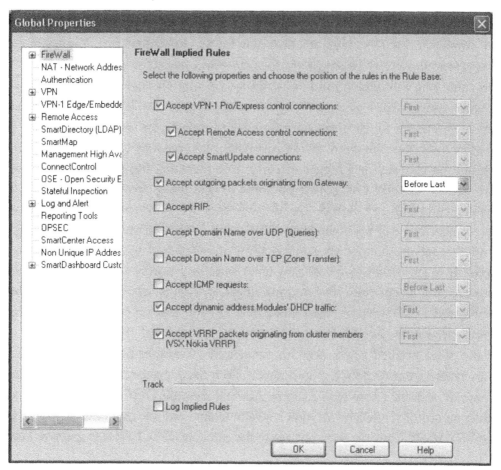

A detailed look at everything here easily could fill a whole book! We'll take a look at the more useful settings as well as new additions to NGX. Looking at new additions is fun since it's an NGX book. NG users will find this useful.

FireWall Page

The FireWall page shows Implied Rules settings. These "rules" are imposed over every security policy installed to your gateways. The idea is that they allow traffic that your gateways might need to function correctly—so you avoid pushing a policy that sends your gateway AWOL. There are obvious security implications here—to a degree, you are opening up "holes" in your security policy. Actually, as long as you are aware of what shape and size holes are involved, there is no need to panic. Fortunately, exactly this facility exists in SmartDashboard: with the **Security** rulebase displayed, use the **View** menu to choose **View | Implied Rules**. This will show the Implied Rules that are currently enabled by adding them to the view of your Security rulebase.

The tickbox for **VPN-1 Pro/Express Control Connections** enables a vast array of implied rules: the initial reaction may be to untick that box. However, on closer inspection, these rules are pretty specific—and in fact, if you disable these implied rules you will likely spend an awful lot of time recreating them as manual rules before you get back to a correctly functioning gateway. The decision is yours: the author's preference is to leave the option checked unless you are very confident you know what rules you will need to add manually. Are you sure you can avoid either a malfunctioning gateway or a bigger security hole than the implied rules may have left?

The option **Accept Outgoing packets originating from Gateway** is often left enabled, although we should consider whether we want to implicitly trust any and all connections from the gateway. Should the firewall gateway itself become in some way compromised, do we want to allow it unfettered access to the internal networks? It is preferable to investigate what outgoing traffic will be required from the gateway and accept only that in your rulebase. This is often just DNS queries to the configured DNS servers—remember that VPN-1 control connections (required to permit gateway to SmartCenter connections) are allowed elsewhere.

Of the other implied rules, most are undesirable. Consider the options for RIP and DNS: a sensible security policy would never allow these protocols without considering the source IP address. Those for Dynamic Address module DHCP traffic and Nokia VSX may be useful if relevant to your configurations, and are harmless enough. Note that the VSX VRRP setting does not apply for standard IPSO VRRP gateway clusters.

Finally, it is a good idea to enable **Log Implied Rules**. That way you can reassure yourself that you know exactly what connections are being allowed by the settings here, thanks to logging in SmartView Tracker. By default, Log Implied Rules is not enabled.

NAT—Network Address Translation Page

The default settings here are good for most configurations: be aware of the new option of **Merge manual proxy ARP configuration**. This allows the use of Automatic ARP when the old local.arp publishing method also is required on a Windows gateway. In gateway versions prior to NGX, if Automatic ARP configuration was enabled, the local. arp mechanism was disabled.

VPN Page

There are some global options here affecting site-to-site VPN gateways; however, most VPN configuration is performed in VPN community objects and VPN gateway objects.

VPN-1 Edge/Embedded Page

Where the SmartCenter is managing remote *VPN-1 Edge* or other similar software-based devices (e.g., *Nokia IP40*), this page controls some global behavior. This includes, new in NGX, the ability to inspect Web and mail content passing through these devices using central checking servers. Web traffic can be verified against a central UFP (URL filtering) server; SMTP and POP3 mail can be redirected via a central antivirus scanning CVP server.

Remote Access Page

On the Remote Access page and its subpages, there is a wide range of configuration settings—usually best left at their defaults unless a specific configuration requires otherwise. New in NGX is the ability to configure SSL Network Extender, SecureClient Hotspot, Office Mode IP reuse across gateways, and SCV connection exceptions.

SmartDirectory (LDAP) Page

If you wish to use LDAP integration, don't forget to enable it here first!

Stateful Inspection Page

Fundamental to the operation of the firewall gateway is stateful inspection: that is, tracking the progress of a TCP connection (or other protocol sessions) to ensure that all traffic that arrives is consistent with the connection state. This page allows this behavior to be fine-tuned, or to a degree, disabled.

Dropping out-of-state TCP packets is sometimes disabled in scenarios where TCP connections remain idle for long periods, so the gateway will timeout the connection and then drop packets in the future. If at all possible, avoid this; first try extending the *TCP Timeout* on the object for the service affected. Extending the timeout globally may significantly increase the amount of stale data in the gateway state tables.

New in SmartDashboard NGX

For readers familiar with previous versions of SmartDashboard, this chapter may have yet to uncover much that is new for them. For those readers in particular, we will now have a look at the improvements in NGX.

Security Policy Rule Names and Unique IDs

In previous versions, every rule had a number. At a stretch, the administrator may have bothered to scroll over to the far left column of the rule to add a comment. Neither helped clearly identify the purpose of each rule when browsing through the rulebase.

NGX introduces *rule names*, now the first column in every rule. Describing each rule in one or two words should make the rulebase far more readable. Figure 3.6 shows an example of annotating a rulebase in this way.

Figure 3.6 Naming Rules

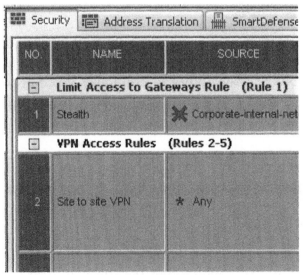

Also new are *Unique Rule IDs*. Every rule now has a hidden, unique ID that does not change throughout the rule's life span—unlike the visible rule number, which will change when rules above are added or removed. This feature comes into its own when viewing log entries in SmartView Tracker. Now it is possible to identify which rule triggered the log entry—whether or not the rule number has since changed. For good measure, the rule name is included in the log entry, too. An example of the logging you'll see is shown in Figure 3.7.

Figure 3.7 Logging with Rule IDs and Names

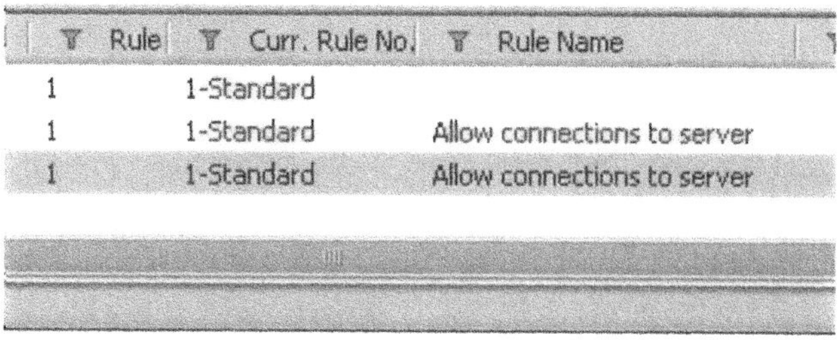

Rule
Curr. Rule No.
Rule Name
1
1-Standard
1
1-Standard
Allow connections to server
1
1-Standard
Allow connections to server

There is also an option in SmartDashboard to launch SmartView Tracker and view all logs relating to a rule. Right-click the rule to try this, as shown in Figure 3.8.

Figure 3.8 Launching SmartView Tracker for a Specific Rule

NO.
NAME
SOURCE
1
Allow connections to
Any
Any
Add Rule
Delete
Copy
Cut
Paste
Copy rule UID
View rule logs in SmartView Tracker
Add Section Title
Hide
Disable Rule(s)
Select All
Ctrl+A
Show
Query Column...
Clear Query

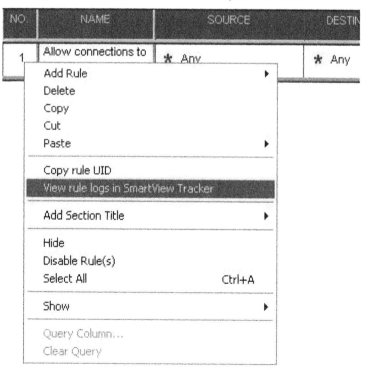

Group Object Convention

It is possible to specify a *convention* when defining a group. This consists of conditions based on object name, color, and IP, as shown in Figure 3.9.

Figure 3.9 Groups with Conventions

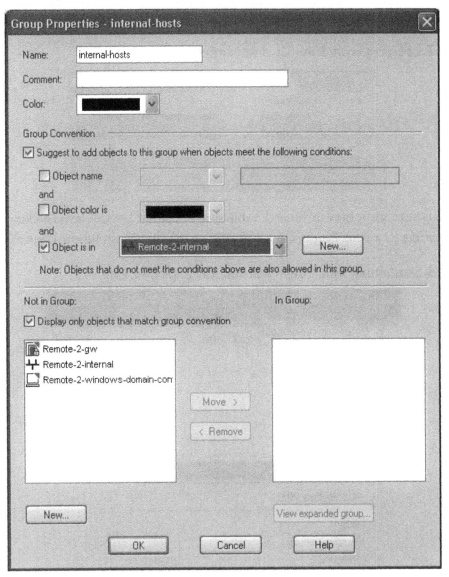

This can be used to assist when adding members to a group: a list of existing objects that meet the convention is provided. In addition, in the future when a new object is defined, SmartDashboard will check whether it meets a group convention. If so, you will be prompted to add the object to the relevant group.

Group Hierarchy

The Network Objects view in the Object Tree pane has been enhanced for Group objects to allow "drilling down" into groups. Right-click the **Groups** branch and choose **Show Groups Hierarchy**, as shown in Figure 3.10.

Figure 3.10 Enabling Group Hierarchy View

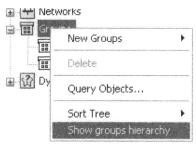

The tree will now show the members of groups, including subgroups. An example is shown in Figure 3.11.

Figure 3.11 Drilling into Groups

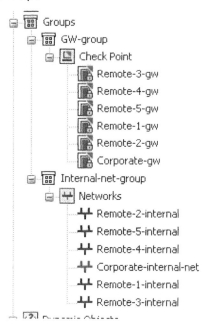

Clone Object

For those times when you need to create a large number of similar objects, **Clone Object** is here to help. Right-click any Node or Network object and you have the option to **Clone**. This creates a new object with the same properties. Just change the name and IP and you are done.

Session Description

In previous versions, it was possible to supply a Session Description when logging in to SmartDashboard, and this would be written to the Audit Log. This provided a rudimentary way of tracking the reason for which administrators had logged into SmartDashboard, should they choose to supply one.

SmartDashboard NGX provides the ability to require a Session Description in order to log in: enable this in **Global Properties, SmartCenter Access**. However, as yet there is no way of forcing the administrator to enter something helpful.

Tooltips

In the rulebase, tooltips are provided for host and network objects—hover your mouse pointer over an object for a summary: for example, for a network, its IP, subnet mask, and object comment (see Figure 3.12). This is particularly useful when analyzing a rulebase, allowing you to understand what the objects used in rules are representing. Of course, to make the tooltip really useful, you do need to have provided a helpful Comment in the object definition. This should be considered standard practice in order to make the effect of your rulebase clear. Losing track of what objects represent can easily lead to your defined security policy not providing the protection that you expected, or perhaps (in practice, more often) blocking legitimate traffic.

Figure 3.12 Tooltips Are Your Friend

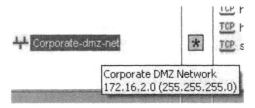

We've now completed our SmartDashboard tour and highlighted the new features in NGX. With some luck you are now familiar enough with the interface to create a simple security policy.

Your First Security Policy

We will now run through the steps of configuring and installing your first security policy. In our example, SmartCenter Express has been installed on a Windows 2003 Server named "sleigh." You have a dedicated firewall gateway host running Nokia IPSO that has VPN-1 Express gateway installed, named "vixen."

Having installed the SmartCenter software successfully, you should be able to connect your SmartDashboard for the first time. If you have installed SmartCenter on a Windows platform, you will be able to run the SmartDashboard locally. Otherwise, you will need to install the SmartConsole package on a Windows host and connect to the SmartCenter over the network—make sure your *cpconfig* GUI clients settings allow the host to connect. Log in by specifying the administrator credentials that you configured in *cpconfig* and the hostname (or IP) of the SmartCenter, as shown in Figure 3.13.

Tools & Traps...

More Options?

You may have noticed the More Options link at the bottom of the Smart-Dashboard Log In dialog. Clicking this will allow you to tune how the SmartDashboard attempts its connection to the SmartCenter. The options are:

- Change Certificate Password If you are using a certificate to authenticate your connection, SmartDashboard allows you to change the password that protects the certificate.

- Session Description Specify a description that will be supplied to SmartCenter when connecting. As discussed earlier, this can now be enforced.

- Use Compressed Connection By default, the connection to the SmartCenter is compressed. If you wish, you can disable this—for a very large configuration database, doing this may help reduce load on the SmartCenter when a client connects.

- Do not save recent connections information By default, SmartDashboard will remember the last user ID and SmartCenter(s) to which connections were made. For more security and less convenience, check this option—no information will be remembered and prefilled.

Figure 3.13 Connecting to Your SmartCenter

NOTE

The first time you connect the SmartDashboard to the SmartCenter, you will be prompted to confirm the identity of the host to which you are connecting. This is achieved by verifying the fingerprint of the Internal CA. If you are at all concerned that the host you've connected to might not actually be your SmartCenter, you can compare the fingerprint with the one for your SmartCenter Internal CA; you can get that from the *cpconfig* utility on the SmartCenter. Once you have done this once, the host running SmartDashboard will trust that SmartCenter. Note that you will be warned again if the Internal CA on the SmartCenter is reset.

Once connected, you will notice in the Objects Tree that an object for the SmartCenter has been created automatically. Double-click the object to review the object settings: verify that the hostname, IP address, and OS are correct. If there are discrepancies, it might indicate a problem with the installation; double-check that the SmartCenter's host OS is configured correctly. The object for our SmartCenter *sleigh* is shown in Figure 3.14.

Figure 3.14 SmartCenter Object for Sleigh

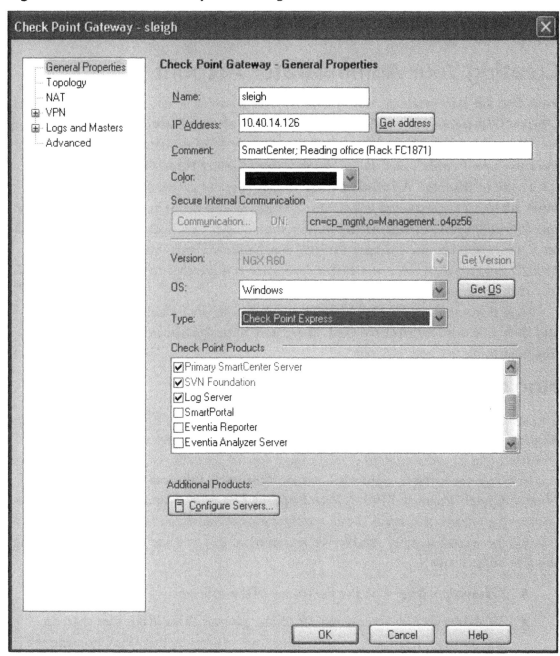

The Products Installed list indicates that *sleigh* is running a Primary SmartCenter, Log Server, and SVN Foundation (SVN is the base Check Point software module).

In our example, no gateway is installed on *sleigh*, so Firewall, VPN, and QoS are all unchecked. We have provided a useful comment—here it identifies the location of the SmartCenter.

Creating Your Administrator Account

Your first job is to create an administrator's user account. Select the **Users** tab of the Objects Tree, right-click on **Administrators**, and choose **New Administrator**. Your user ID will be *clauss*. In order to configure your level of privileges, create a new **Permissions Profile** called *fulladmin*. You should select **Read/Write Access**, and the ability to **Manage Administrators** so that you can create further accounts for other admins, operators, and so on. Don't forget to choose an authentication method, too—in the object **Admin Auth** tab, you should select a Check Point password and set it. Note you can use stronger external mechanisms if you wish, such as *RSA SecurID*. Additionally, you can create a certificate and use that to authenticate instead of a regular password.

Now that you have an administrator account, save your changes (**File | Save**) and then exit from SmartDashboard. Then, start SmartDashboard and log in again, this time using the new account.

Hooking Up to the Gateway

You are now ready to hook up the SmartCenter to your new VPN-1 gateway, *vixen*. As part of the installation of NGX on *vixen*, you were supplied a *SIC activation key*: you need that in order to define your object for the gateway.

To create your object, right-click on the **Network Objects** tree and choose **New | Check Point | VPN-1 Pro/Express Gateway**. You are prompted for the choice of a wizard or manual classic configuration. Unless you have a real aversion to wizards, the wizard is pretty reliable. We recommend that you use the wizard, supplying the following details:

- **Gateway name** Use the hostname of the gateway.
- **IP Address** Use the *external* IP of the gateway (also make sure that, on the gateway host itself, its own hostname resolves to this IP). Choosing the external IP is important for VPN configurations as clients or peers may use this IP for building the VPN tunnel, and the internal, private IPs are unlikely to be reachable. It is critical for the gateway's hostname to resolve correctly locally because the Check Point services on the gateway will use the

resolved IP when locating the firewall object for that gateway. On UNIX platforms, verify the hosts file is correct on the gateway. On Windows, it is not so straightforward: ping the gateway's own hostname in order to determine which physical interface is considered the primary by Windows, then use that interface as the external interface.

- **Gateway Type** Express or Pro (we are using Express). This depends on what license you have.

- **Firewall or VPN** Will you be using the VPN features of VPN-1? If not, only enable FireWall—this simplifies configuration. You can always switch on VPN later if needed. We'll have VPN from the start.

- **SIC Activation Key** After you supply this key and click Next, the SmartCenter will attempt a connection to the gateway.

Hopefully the SIC connection is successful—if not, take a look at the sidebar, "Can't Communicate?"

Tools & Traps...

Can't Communicate?

What if SmartCenter can't connect to the remote gateway?

There are a number of reasons why the SmartCenter may fail to connect to the new gateway—you will get an error indicating that the SIC initialization process has failed. Common problems include:

- Routing from SmartCenter to the gateway external IP. Check routing tables—it may be that traffic is being routed to an existing Internet gateway. Configure routing so that traffic to the new external network range hits the new gateway.

- Routing from the gateway to the SmartCenter. Check gateway routing tables—ensure the gateway has the routing information required to reply to the SmartCenter.

Continued

- SIC initialization at the gateway. If there have been previous attempts to configure management of the new gateway, it may be that the gateway is no longer expecting a new SIC key. Use *cpconfig* on the gateway to reset SIC.

- Default policy on the gateway. If there have been previous policies loaded to the gateway, they may be blocking the connection from the SmartCenter. You can make sure that no policy is running by running the command **fw unloadlocal** on the gateway. Be warned that this will leave the gateway unprotected, so disconnect any live untrusted networks first!

The wizard will now ask you whether to automatically retrieve interfaces and topology from the gateway. This will fetch a list of interfaces and inspect the routing tables on the gateway in order to identify what subnets are connected to each interface of the gateway, creating any necessary objects for you—on complex networks this can save you a lot of time. It is also important that the interface list is defined accurately, so automatically fetching the list is highly recommended.

When the wizard completes, you can check the box to **Edit the Gateways Properties** to review the configuration of the new object. The hostname, IP address, OS, and Products Installed should all be as required.

Reviewing the Gateway Object

It's worth reviewing all the objects settings: first, to make sure the wizard got it right (they aren't perfect, you know), and second, so that you are aware of the available options to be configured if you need to later. The object for *vixen* is shown in Figure 3.15.

Figure 3.15 Gateway Object for Vixen

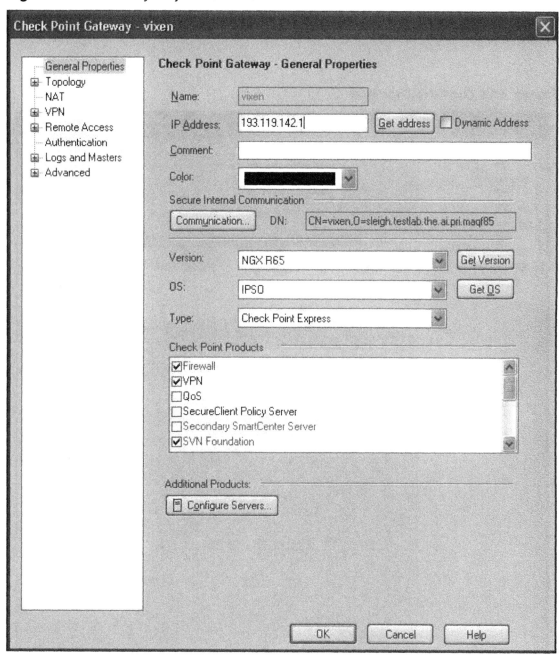

If you are satisfied that these general properties look good, move on to the Topology page for the object. Here you'll see a list of interfaces on the gateway and the IP addresses behind those interfaces, based on the routing tables. On your *vixen*

gateway, the eth4c0 interface has an additional routed subnet behind that interface and SmartDashboard has created objects to reflect that. The topology is shown in Figure 3.16.

Figure 3.16 Gateway Topology

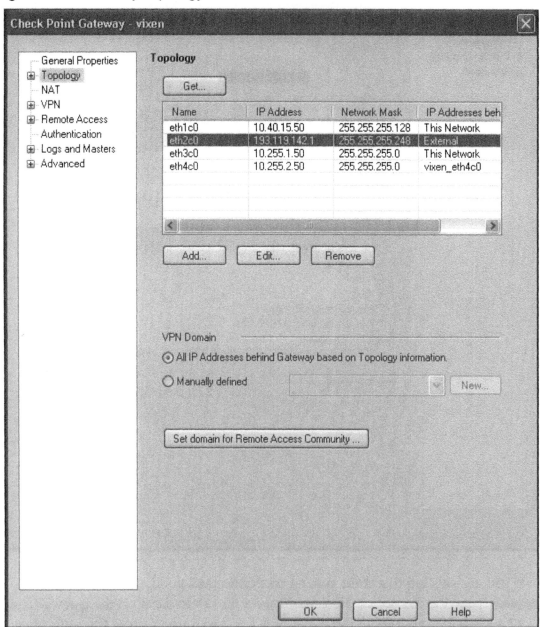

To edit the settings for each interface, just double-click the interface name. As well as the name and IP, the topology should be reviewed to ensure it correctly reflects what IP addresses lie behind that interface. Accurately configuring this allows anti-spoofing protection to be enabled on the interface—essential in securing your networks against spoofed packets arriving at untrusted interfaces.

You may want to browse through the raft of other pages and settings available in the gateway object, but these are best left at their defaults for now.

Tip

SmartDashboard provides a handy shortcut for launching the Web interface to your SecurePlatform or IPSO gateways: right-click on the Check Point object and choose **Manage Device**. However, note that SmartDashboard will attempt to connect to the device using https on port 443, so if this isn't what your gateway listens on, this won't work for you.

Defining Your Security Policy

Before defining rules in your policy, you will likely need to define a few objects to represent internal hosts and networks. SmartDashboard automatically created objects for two of your internal networks when it fetched the gateway topology, so you can just change those object names to something more meaningful rather than creating new objects.

You will also create a group, *sleigh_internal*, which will include all your internal networks. To add the networks to the group, just drag and drop them into the group using the Objects Tree.

Figure 3.17 shows the Objects Tree with all our objects defined. You have objects for your networks plus an object for the Internet mail relay server on our DMZ. There is also a group that was automatically defined for use in the gateway topology.

Figure 3.17 The Objects Tree

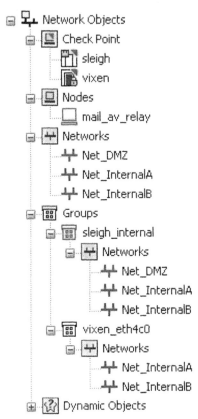

Policy Design

A firewall security policy should be designed with the principle of least privilege in mind: accept only the traffic that is required, drop anything else. When the firewall gateway implements the rulebase, each new connection is compared against the rulebase top down—when a rule is matched, that action is followed and no more rules are checked. Check Point helps you out with best practice by dropping any traffic that is not accepted by either implied rules or a rule you have added to the policy—in other words, there is an invisible rule at the bottom of rulebase: *drop anything*.

Two rules are usually explicitly added as part of every policy: the Stealth rule and the Clean Up rule.

A *Stealth rule* is placed near the top of the policy and explicitly blocks access to the firewall. It should be placed above other more general rules that would otherwise allow access (maybe a rule allowing internal users access to the Internet—i.e., any address—which would include the firewall itself). Don't forget to add a rule above the Stealth rule to allow access for administrators—for example, ssh to the gateway.

A *Clean Up rule* is placed at the bottom of the policy and explicitly drops and logs all traffic that has not matched other rules. This traffic would have been dropped by the gateway anyway because of the invisible drop-anything rule, but the Clean Up rule ensures it gets logged.

In addition to the aforementioned rules, your security policy should be developed in order to reflect the formal network usage policies of your organization.

Creating Rules

Before we begin creating rules, it is a good idea to save the Policy Package using a descriptive name. You will notice that the current policy name is "Standard." It is good practice to use policy names that identify the date/time of the policy, or some versioning reference. There are two reasons for this—first, it is easy to check what revision of the policy package is installed on a gateway—SmartView Monitor will show the current installed package name. Second, it makes it easy to roll back changes to the policy (although be aware that saving the policy does not provide version control over changes to objects—we'll discuss Change Management later in this chapter). To save the policy under a new name, use **File | Save As**.

To add a rule to the rulebase, use the **Rules Toolbar**. This provides buttons for adding rules at the top or bottom of the policy, and above or below the current selected rule. Clicking one of these buttons adds a rule that by default will drop all traffic. First you should give the rule a **Name**; then we can modify the rule **Source**, **Destination**, and **Service** by dragging objects into the fields or right-clicking and adding objects from a list. Then choose the **Action** you wish to take if a connection matches this rule (right-click and choose from the list); to start with, choose between **Accept** or **Drop**. Other options can be used to perform authentication or require encryption. The **Reject** option drops traffic but informs the client by means of either a TCP Reset or ICMP destination unreachable message.

The full security rulebase for our example is shown in Figure 3.18.

Figure 3.18 A Full Example Rulebase

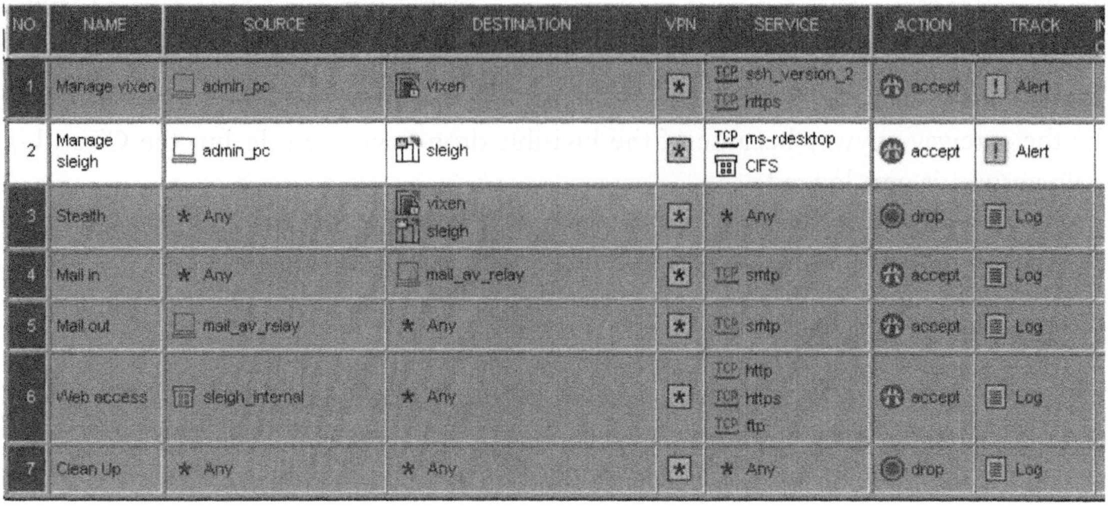

NO	NAME	SOURCE	DESTINATION	VPN	SERVICE	ACTION	TRACK	I
1	Manage vixen	admin_pc	vixen	✱	TCP ssh_version_2 TCP https	accept	Alert	
2	Manage sleigh	admin_pc	sleigh	✱	TCP ms-rdesktop CIFS	accept	Alert	
3	Stealth	✱ Any	vixen sleigh	✱	✱ Any	drop	Log	
4	Mail in	✱ Any	mail_av_relay	✱	TCP smtp	accept	Log	
5	Mail out	mail_av_relay	✱ Any	✱	TCP smtp	accept	Log	
6	Web access	sleigh_internal	✱ Any	✱	TCP http TCP https TCP ftp	accept	Log	
7	Clean Up	✱ Any	✱ Any	✱	✱ Any	drop	Log	

Reviewing the rules, you have allowed our administrators PC access to the gateway and SmartCenter for the required protocols. You had to define a new Service object (right-click in the **Services** tab of Objects Tree) to represent the Microsoft Remote Desktop protocol (TCP port 3389). You ensured that ssh access to the gateway is using the more secure ssh version 2, not version 1, by using the special service *ssh_version_2*.

Once you have your policy defined, remember to review the implied rules that are enabled in Global Properties. The defaults in NGX are sensible, but make sure that you are aware of what they are. In the example in this chapter, you have left Control Connections and Outgoing Packets from Gateway enabled. It is a good idea to enable Log Implied Rules so that it is clear what connections are being accepted and dropped.

Tools & Traps...

Time Management

On the far right of your Security rules, you will see the column *Time*. This allows you to specify time periods during which a rule will be applied—from times of the day to days and months of the year. You achieve this by creating

Continued

Time objects that represent a time period, and then add that to the rule. To define objects use the Manage menu, **Manage | Time**, and create a new **Time** type object. Note that Time objects are also used for scheduled events such as times at which a log server should start a new log file; these are **Scheduled Event** type Time objects.

Network Address Translation

To be allowed to access the Internet, and for your mail relay to receive incoming mail, you need to configure some address translation. Add **Hide NAT** to your internal networks (hiding behind the gateway itself) and **Static NAT** to your mail relay. The mail relay will be translated to an address supplied by our ISP, in the same range as our gateway external IP. This is simple to configure using Automatic NAT—edit the relevant objects and configure the NAT page. Figures 3.19 and 3.20 show the NAT configuration on an internal network object and the mail relay object.

Figure 3.19 Internal Network Hide NAT Configuration

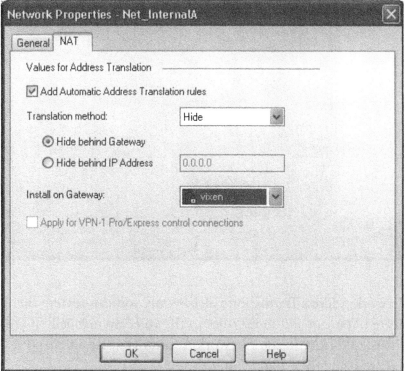

Figure 3.20 Host Object Static NAT Configuration

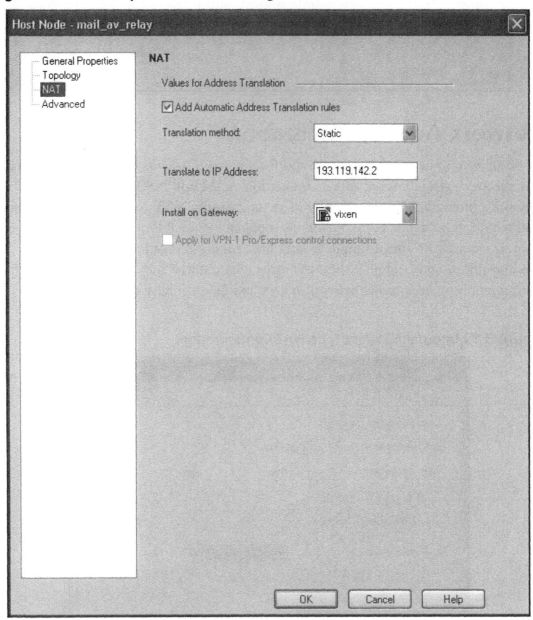

In the Network Address Translation rulebase tab, you can review the rules that have been created. You can add more rules to the rulebase manually if you need to—this is discussed further in the Network Address Translation chapter.

At last you are ready to test your policy!

Installing the Policy

To install the policy, use the Policy toolbar—the policy install button shows a rulebase with a downward arrow above it. SmartDashboard will prompt you to select which gateways the policy should be installed on—in this case, there is only one gateway to choose from, and it will be selected by default. If you later choose to enable the QoS or Policy Server modules on the gateway, you will also be able to select whether you wish to update the QoS and Desktop Security policies. Clicking OK to continue the process will show the Install Progress dialog box. This will indicate that the policy is first Verifying and then Installing. The Verify phase identifies any logical problems with your policy—for example, rules that "hide" later rules, making the later rule redundant. Installation is the process of connecting to the gateway, transferring the policy and database files to the gateway, instructing the gateway to update its policy, and waiting for a successful confirmation from the gateway. If all this succeeds, you will see a reassuring large green tick appear, as in Figure 3.21.

Figure 3.21 Success!

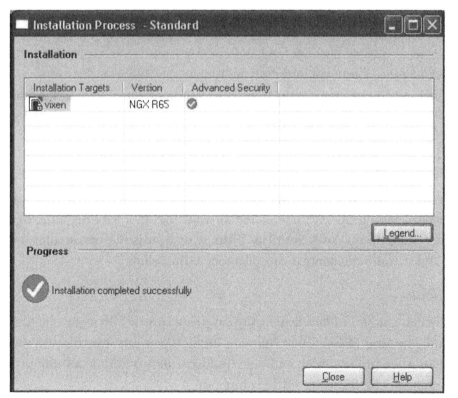

If you see anything else—red crosses, warnings, or the like—click the **Show Errors** button that will appear in order to view the reasons for this. This may not be critical in some cases—sometimes it is just a recommendation about your policy. Other times it will indicate the policy has not been installed, maybe due to connectivity to the gateway or some other serious error during the policy compilation process.

Before you make any further changes to the policy, you may want to save the current policy using a new name, indicating a new policy version.

Once you have your policy installed it is time to test whether connectivity is as expected: now is probably a good time to read the SmartView Tracker chapter so you can observe your connections being accepted, and the bad guys being dropped. Hopefully.

Other Useful Controls on the Dashboard

Once you are comfortable with the core features we've covered so far, you might want to explore some more SmartDashboard features. We'll quickly look at some of them now.

Working with Security Policy Rules

Rulebases tend to quickly become long and cumbersome—you might even end up with a few hundred rules. Keep in mind that the longer the rulebase, the more work the gateway needs to do per new connection. This can be reduced by making sure that the most common connections match rules early in the rulebase. The tools described in this section will help manage bigger rulebases.

Section Titles

As your rulebase gets larger you can use Section Titles to summarize the purpose of a group of rules, making the rulebase easier to read. To add a Section Title, right-click a rule number and choose **Add Section Title**. A section is the set of rules between two titles and it can be expanded or collapsed with a click.

Hiding Rules

Individual rules can be hidden (leaving a gray stripe instead) by right-clicking the rule number and choosing **Hide**. Once rules are hidden, you can store/restore the current list of hidden rules, unhide rules, and view hidden rules (without unhiding them!) using the menus—the **Rules | Hide** submenu.

Rule Queries

In order to locate rules that apply to a particular host or service, for example, use a *Rule Query*. These will hide all rules that don't match your query. To define queries, use the Search menu: **Search | Query Rules**.

Searching Rules

You can perform a simple text search through the Security Policy using the Search menu: **Search | Find in Rulebase**. This is useful as a quick way to locate an object in a rule, or, if you use the Comments field in a structured way, to locate some keyword or perhaps a change control reference.

Working with Objects

We'll take a look at a few useful tools we can use when we are working with Network Objects.

Object References

You can track all references to an object—right-click on any object and choose **Where Used?** This is very useful when you forgot why exactly you created that object all those months ago.

Who Broke That Object?

Curious about the last person to edit an object? Right-click the object and choose **Last Modified**. You'll see when it was changed, by whom, and from where.

Object Queries

Under the Search menu, the **Query Network Objects** tool allows simple searching and filtering of Network Objects. You can also define a *Network Object group* based on your query.

Working with Policies

The policy you see in SmartDashboard is not automatically applied to the gateway—you have to install the policy (push it down to the gateway) first! If you are managing multiple gateways, this becomes more of an issue—are you sure you've installed the latest policy to all the gateways? Do you have different policies on each gateway? Which rules in your policy are relevant to a gateway?

What Would Be Installed?

If you are working with multiple gateways but a single policy, it is not always easy to see which rules would be applied to a particular gateway. You can use the Policy menu, **Policy | View Policy Of** tool in order to view selected gateway(s) rules. To return to the normal view, use the same tool and click **Clear**.

What's Really Installed?

You can check what Security policy is actually running on a gateway—rather than the one that you see in SmartDashboard, or the one that you think should be running. From the menus, choose **File | Installed Policies**.

No Security Please

It is possible to request that the Security Policy be unloaded from remote gateways: from the menu, choose **Policy | Uninstall**. This is a bad idea, as it leaves your firewall gateway with no protection (although it will no longer forward traffic, so connections cannot be made through the firewall). Ironically, the only time you would want to remove a policy from a gateway is when you've accidentally pushed a policy that blocks the connections from the SmartCenter to the gateway—in which case, the SmartDashboard will not be able to request the policy unload anyway! For those times, you will need to run the command **fw unloadlocal** from the command line of the gateway itself—but disconnect untrusted network interfaces first to avoid leaving the gateway open to attack.

For the Anoraks

You can view the underlying script that is generated by your security policy, should that sort of thing interest you. In the menus, select **Policy | View**. The script displayed corresponds to the *<policyname>.pf* file on the SmartCenter. This tool is rarely required.

Tools & Traps...

Why and What Is "Install Database"?

Under the Policy menu there is an option **Policy | Install Database**. In early versions of NG, this option was used to update the *user database* on gateways, without reinstalling the actual security policy rulebase. It is now prohibited to

Continued

use **Install Database** to a gateway, because it can result in inconsistencies where the rulebase refers to objects that are no longer part of the user database. However, **Install Database** now has a different function: it is used to install the *configuration database* to hosts running nongateway Check Point software: for example, a dedicated Log Server. You can even install the database to the SmartCenter itself, although this happens anyway when you do a normal **Install Policy** to a remote gateway. Installing the database to the local SmartCenter might be used to modify the log management settings of the SmartCenter without having to perform a full Policy Install to a gateway.

Change Management

It is possible to take a snapshot of the whole configuration database: rulebases, users, and objects. To do so, use the **Database Revision Control** feature from the File menu. To take a snapshot, **Create** a new version. It is possible to review that snapshot at a later date and, if you need to, restore it. You can even choose to create a new version on every policy install—if you do this, make sure you manage the number of database versions you have created: each snapshot increases the size of the SmartCenter configuration directories, and you risk the stability of the SmartCenter if you have hundreds of versions. Note that each version is tied to the SmartCenter software revision, so if you upgrade your SmartCenter there is little point in maintaining the previous database revisions. Do not mistake Revision Control for a full system backup: if you badly corrupt your live database version, you may not be able to connect to SmartDashboard in order to restore an older database.

Tools & Traps…

Backing Up Your SmartCenter Configuration

A step further than Revision Control is a configuration database export. You can export the entire SmartCenter configuration database including rules, objects, and the internal CA using the *Upgrade Tools*. These utilities are designed primarily for exporting from one version of SmartCenter and importing into an upgraded installation, but can also be used to export and import on the same software revision.

Continued

> The tools are found in the SmartCenter directory *$FWDIR/bin/upgrade_tools* (Windows: *%FWDIR%\bin\upgrade_tools*).
> For example, to export your running configuration:
> *upgrade_export C:\temp\exported*
> To import this configuration archive:
> *upgrade_import C:\temp\exported*
> Warning: on Windows, before running the import, check that the file properties of *%CPDIR%\conf\dependencies.c* are not set to Read Only. If they are, set to Read/Write before running the import.

Managing Connectra and Interspect Gateways

Check Point SmartDashboard NGX allows the definition of Check Point objects for Connectra and Interspect gateways. Check Point Connectra is a SSL VPN gateway product; Check Point Interspect is an internal network security gateway. However, configuration management of these devices from SmartDashboard is limited to launching a dedicated management client for the device: Interspect SmartDashboard or a Web browser session to the management port of a Connectra gateway.

Configuring Interspect or Connectra Integration

Right-click on **Network Objects** in the Objects Tree and choose **New | Check Point | Connectra Gateway** or **Interspect Gateway**.

Define the object's name and IP, then use the **Communication** button to initialize SIC keys. Configured objects are shown in Figures 3.22 and 3.23.

Figure 3.22 Check Point Connectra Object

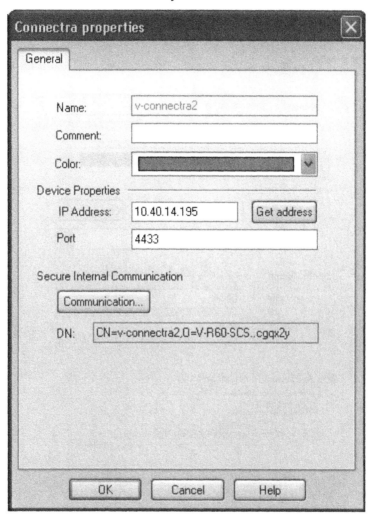

Figure 3.23 Check Point Interspect Object

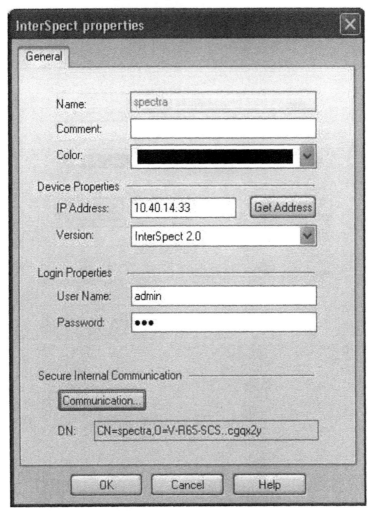

Once the object has been defined, you need to update the SmartCenter running configuration in order to allow connections from the device. To do this, use the SmartDashboard menu option **Policy | Install Database**. Then on the new object, you can right-click and choose **Manage Device** in order to launch the management client for the device.

In the Connectra or Interspect management interface, configure Central Management/Logging as per the device documentation. You will need to specify the SmartCenter name/IP and the object name that you have given to the new object.

After these changes have been made, the device logs should begin to appear in SmartView Tracker.

SmartDefense Updates

SmartDashboard also provides centralized SmartDefense Updates for Connectra and Interspect. If you have purchased a SmartDefense subscription for the device, you can update its SmartDefense features directly from the SmartDashboard rather than the management interface of the device: right-click on the object and choose **SmartDefense Service Update**. The latest SmartDefense database can then be downloaded to the SmartCenter and pushed out to internal Connectra and Interspect gateways, as shown in Figure 3.24.

Figure 3.24 Updating Connectra SmartDefense from SmartDashboard

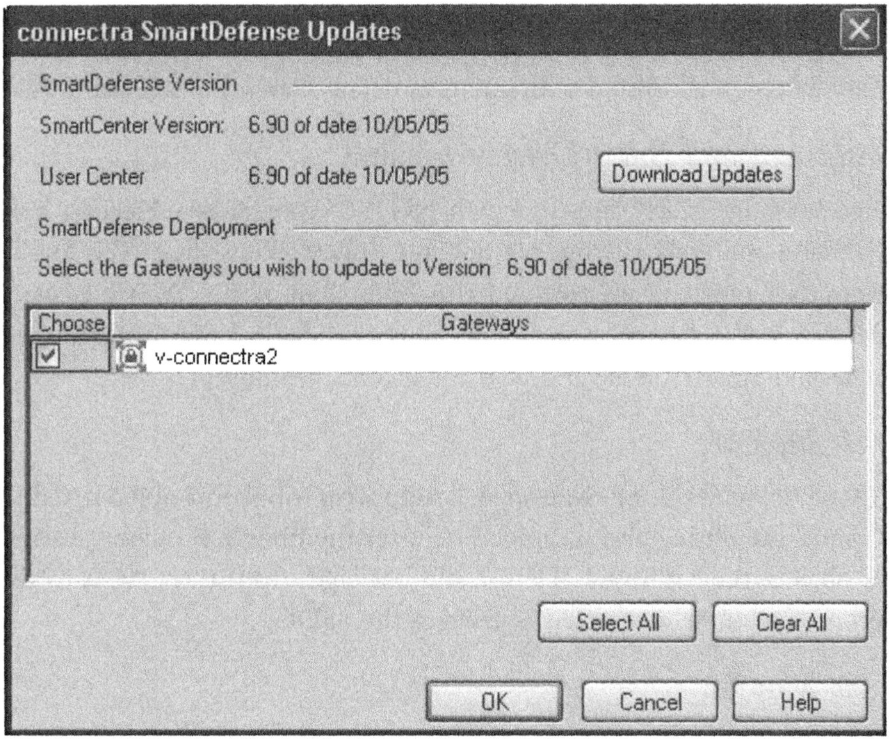

SmartUpdate Enhancements

In NGX 65, the license Repository window of SmartUpdate displays both contracts and regular licenses. Selecting a particular contract will show the contract's properties including the contract ID and expiration date. It will also provide information as to the gateways that are included within the contract.

The License management window can display if an individual license is linked to a contract. SmartUpdate will also verify if the contract file on the gateway is more up to date then the contract file on the SmartCenter Server, adding an additional menu item to enable the more up-to-date contract information to be loaded into the management server.

Connectra Central Management

NGX R65 is the first version of Check Point's products to centrally control Connectra gateways. This offers many more methods to configure Connectra than in preceding versions.

Connectra Tab

SmartDashboard has an additional tab for the configuration of Connectra that provides the capability to access all related configuration details using the objects in this tab.

SmartDashboard and SmartDefense Update

The Connectra tab in SmartDashboard with NGX 65 integrates a selection linking for SmartDefense and Web Intelligence updates. SmartDefense and Web Intelligence configurations for Connectra are executed as a component of the "SmartDefense profiles." A SmartDefense profile particular to Connectra is provided for the configuration of Connectra-related SmartDefense and Web Intelligence features.

Provider-1 Support

With NGX 65, Provider-1/SiteManager-1 supports Connectra objects (Connectra gateway, Connectra cluster, and Connectra cluster members). Provider-1 assembles Connectra objects, their statuses, licenses, and packages from the CMAs to the MDS. It will then present these assembled objects in the MDG.

SmartView Monitor

As of NGX65, SmartView monitor can monitor Connectra gateways and also produce reports concerning status and activities recorded on the system.

SmartPortal

The complexity and power of the Check Point management clients has a downside: the client software is a substantial suite of applications, not exactly lightweight. There are a number of situations when this is not ideal:

- There is often a requirement for operators to be able to view the logs or summary of status of the gateways, without any need for the full functionality of the SmartConsole suite.

- In a managed service environment, customers may want to view the logging from their sites' gateways, but not wish to install any software.

- Remote administrators may need to check on the status of the gateway, but are unable to install the software on the system they are using.

SmartPortal provides a browser-based alternative to the SmartConsole clients—ideal for these scenarios.

SmartPortal Functionality

The SmartPortal interface provides:

- **Status information** Similar information to the Gateway Status view of SmartView Monitor

- **Log viewer** Access to the traffic and audit logs, similar to SmartView Tracker

- **Policy and objects summary** A view of the Security Policy rulebase and object details

Installing SmartPortal

The SmartPortal server is available as an option when you first install NGX on the supported platforms: Windows, Solaris, Red Hat EL 3.0, and SecurePlatform.

Note that SmartPortal requires a license, although that license is included in most VPN-1 Pro and some extended VPN-1 Express licenses. To check yours, run *cplic check swp* on your SmartCenter.

If you didn't choose SmartPortal at install time, you can just run the wrapper again on Windows or Solaris—it should detect that NGX is already installed and give you the option to install additional products. Do this and choose SmartPortal. On SecurePlatform, you will need to install SmartPortal manually: enter Expert mode from a console session and run the command:

rpm −i /sysimg/CPwrapper/linux/CPportal/CPportal-R65-00.i386.rpm

Usually you would install SmartPortal on the SmartCenter; however, it is possible to install it on other Check Point hosts or its own dedicated server. The SmartPortal server then makes an onward connection to the SmartCenter. A dedicated server would be advisable if there are likely to be many concurrent SmartPortal users.

Once the product is installed, ensure that the relevant object has **SmartPortal** checked in the **Check Point Products** list. Having done so, perform a database install to the SmartCenter (**Policy | Install Database**).

To access the portal, point your browser to https://smartcenter-host:4433.

TIP

Smart Portal officially supports a range of browsers: Internet Explorer, Mozilla Suite, Firefox, and Netscape. The latest versions of these browsers are recommended. However, with the NGX initial release code, Firefox 1.0.4 failed to connect, throwing a script error (Firefox 1.0.3 works just fine!). A change to the SmartPortal code to support Firefox 1.0.4 is expected in the first NGX hotfix release.

Tour of SmartPortal

At the welcome page (see Figure 3.25), supply your administrator credentials (this should be an account created in SmartDashboard) and the name (or IP) of the SmartCenter server.

Figure 3.25 Welcome to SmartPortal

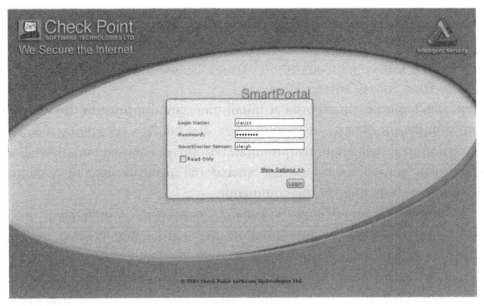

After a few seconds you should be connected to the SmartPortal front page, as shown in Figure 3.26. If the SmartPortal connection fails, check that you have correctly followed the installation steps and are using the correct SmartDashboard administrator credentials. Check that the SmartCenter Server name you supplied resolves successfully on the server running SmartPortal.

Figure 3.26 Logged In: SmartPortal Front Page

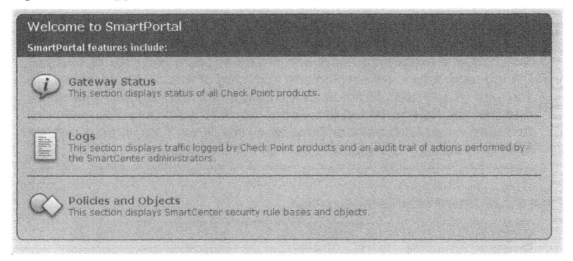

A sidebar allows selection of the different features.

The **Gateway Status** page will show a summary of status for each gateway and the SmartCenter itself (see Figure 3.27). To see more detailed status information, click the name of the gateway.

Figure 3.27 SmartPortal Gateway Status Page

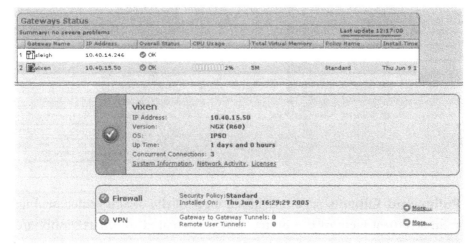

The **Logs** page can show either the **Traffic Log** or the **Audit Log**. The view is similar to SmartView Tracker but with a restricted set of columns shown. The Traffic Log is shown in Figure 3.28. Note the toolbar allowing navigation of the log, automatic scrolling, searching, filtering, and access to older log files. If the administrator has write access to the logs, it is possible to switch and purge logs. Clicking the record number will open a new window showing that log entry.

WARNING

SmartPortal is entirely read-only with regard to policy and objects; however, the log page *does* allow purging and switching of logs. In a scenario where you wish to give users access to view configuration and logging only, make sure that you have restricted the user accounts to Read Only. You may need to define a new Administrator Permissions Profile with SmartPortal only and Read Only access and associate that with the user account.

Figure 3.28 SmartPortal Traffic Log Page

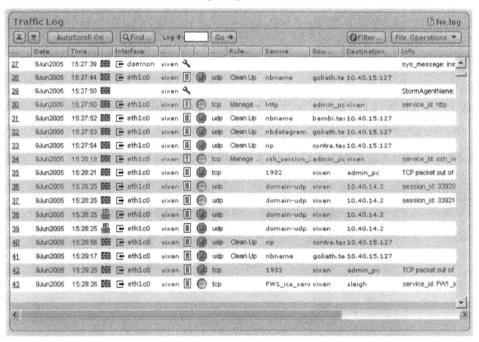

The **Policy and Objects** page provides a view of the *Security* rulebase. Figure 3.29 shows the SmartPortal view of the policy that was created in SmartDashboard.

Figure 3.29 SmartPortal Policy View

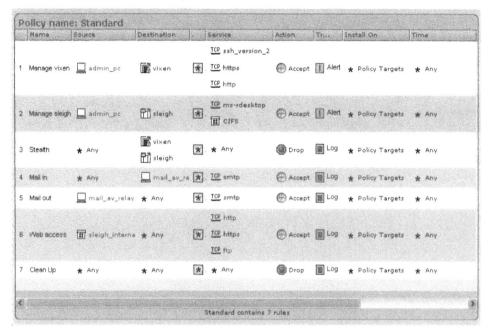

If you have multiple policy packages, you can view the security rulebase from these packages, too.

There are a number of pages for viewing objects: Network Objects, Services, Users, and Time objects. The views are equivalent to the Objects List view in SmartDashboard. A simple Filter on object name can be used to narrow down the list.

Tools & Traps...

Securing Access to the SmartPortal Server

Access to the SmartPortal server is not restricted by the GUI clients settings that apply to full SmartConsole access. By default, any client can connect to the SmartPortal. To restrict by client IP, create the file *hosts.allowed* in the SmartPortal *conf* directory:

Windows   *C:\Program Files\CheckPoint\SmartPortal\R65\SmartPortal\ conf\hosts.allowed*

Continued

Linux/SecurePlatform/Solaris */opt/CPportal-R65/portal/conf/hosts.allowed*
Add lines in the format
ALL: <IP host address 1>
ALL: <IP host address 2>
For each trusted host, or, for trusted networks:
ALL: <IP network address 1>/<subnet mask>
An example:
ALL: 10.40.6.0/255.255.254.0
ALL: 192.168.12.1

Summary

SmartDashboard provides an extremely powerful interface for configuring your Check Point installation—from the traditional firewall gateways, through VPN gateways, to the new Connectra and Interspect devices. It effectively provides a single management interface for your entire Check Point security infrastructure.

The interface, though complex, can be broken down into separate panes. Each provides different functionality and views of your configuration, and you can choose which panes are visible. This allows you to tailor the interface to suit the areas you need to work with and your preferred methods of accessing the settings.

The rulebase pane can be tailored to show just the policies and products you manage, again allowing simplification of the interface by hiding the functionality that you don't need to see. Conversely, when you have several different gateway products installed and therefore a number of different policies defined, these can be combined into a single policy package for the gateway.

The objects panes provide many different views onto your object database—with some experimentation you should be able to find a view ideal for your working style and requirements. Despite the ever-increasing range of object types available, these are broken down into different categories, and within each category, can be sorted and displayed so you see just the types that you are using.

The degree of fine-tuning allowed via the Global Properties windows increases in every software release, but the tree structure of the windows helps with navigation to the setting you need to adjust. The majority of the settings here can be left unchanged for most scenarios, so these pages can remain hidden away. We have outlined those that we do need to be aware of.

The NGX release introduces a range of new features to the interface that should be very helpful to administrators, making management and clear understanding of your configuration easier.

Your first security policy should be straightforward to define once you are familiar with the interface. Configuring a simple security rulebase and automatic NAT should have a typical Internet gateway up and running within minutes, or maybe an hour at the longest.

NGX begins to integrate management of Check Point Connectra and Interspect devices, continuing toward the goal of the SmartCenter being the single point of management for the whole network security infrastructure.

The new NGX SmartPortal Web interface provides a clientless management solution, enabling operator and managed customer access to view the status, logging, and configuration of a management server.

Solutions Fast Track

A Tour of the Dashboard

☑ Get familiar with SmartDashboard in Demo mode.

☑ Use the Objects Tree and Objects List to configure objects representing the network infrastructure.

☑ Use the rulebase pane to manage SmartDefense, Web Intelligence, and VPN communities.

☑ Define policy packages including security, NAT, QoS, and Desktop policies.

New in SmartDashboard NGX

☑ Use rule names and UIDs to clearly identify which rule triggered a log entry.

☑ Group object convention can assist in defining groups and managing group membership.

☑ Drill down into defined groups by viewing the group hierarchy.

☑ Easily create similar objects with cloning technology.

☑ Requiring a Session Description might help with change tracking.

☑ Tooltips make it easier to see details of objects used in rules.

Your First Security Policy

☑ Define yourself an administrator account.

☑ Verify and configure the Check Point objects we need.

☑ Define objects we need to describe the network infrastructure.

☑ Define a simple rulebase.

☑ Configure NAT if needed.

☑ Install and test your new policy.

Other Useful Controls on the Dashboard

- ☑ Work better with rules using titles, hiding, searching, and query filters.

- ☑ Work better with objects by tracking references, making changes, and using queries.

- ☑ Work better with complex policies on multiple gateways.

- ☑ Full database change management using Revision Control.

Managing Connectra and Interspect Gateways

- ☑ Setting up connections to the devices to receive logging.

- ☑ Central SmartDefense management.

SmartPortal

- ☑ Installing or enabling SmartPortal.

- ☑ Status page shows state of Check Point hosts.

- ☑ Log page shows traffic and audit logs.

- ☑ Policy page shows Security policies.

- ☑ Objects pages show object lists.

Frequently Asked Questions

Q: What software do I need to install in order to use the SmartDashboard in Demo Mode?

A: You only need the SmartDashboard software. The CD installer on Windows will present Demo as an install option. No SmartCenter is needed because the Demo database files are stored locally in the SmartConsole *PROGRAM\cpml_dir* directory.

Q: When I try to log into the SmartCenter, I get told that someone else is already logged in. I need to log in to make changes—Read Only access is no good for me. It gives me the option to disconnect them—should I do this?

A: Only one administrator can log into SmartDashboard in Read/Write mode at once. It is much better to get hold of the other administrator and ask him or her to cleanly log out of SmartDashboard, to avoid problems that could occur if they are in the process of making changes to the SmartCenter configuration. However, if his SmartDashboard or whole PC has crashed, or he can't be reached, you will need to force a disconnect.

Q: If I log into SmartDashboard in Read Only mode, do I see any changes made by a SmartDashboard user in Read/Write mode?

A: Your SmartDashboard will be notified if another user has Saved changes, and when this happens the Toolbar Refresh icon is enabled: left-hand end of the toolbar, a circular arrow icon. Click the icon to load up the updated database. Note that this may take some time, so be patient!

Q: Why don't I see the VPN Manager tab?

A: You are using a Traditional Mode VPN policy—VPN Manager configures Communities, and these are used only with Simplified Mode VPN policies. The traditional policy will not include a VPN column; instead, Encrypt is available as an Action. To convert the policy to a Simplified Mode policy you can use the **Policy | Convert To** menu option. Be aware that conversion can not always preserve the exact functionality of the policy, so be prepared to review and troubleshoot the new policy. When creating new policies, the selection of Traditional or Simplified policy is implied by the setting in the **Global Properties—VPN** page.

Q: I don't see a QoS rulebase tab; how can I add a QoS policy for my QoS (Floodgate-1) gateway?

A: Use the menu option **File | Add Policy to Package** and choose **QoS**.

Q: When I try to install a policy, it fails because one rule conflicts with another. What does that mean?

A: The rulebase works on a first-match basis—this means that the gateway compares connections to the rules from top down until it finds a match and follows that action. When you request a policy install, the SmartCenter verifies that the rulebase does not include rules that would never be matched—that is, there is a rule somewhere above it that will always catch the connection first. If this is the case, the error about conflicting rules is shown.

Q: Do I need to create network objects to represent every network and server protected by the firewall?

A: No, you only need objects for those hosts and networks you need to reference specifically in your configuration. This will include rules in your policies, objects used for NAT, and networks used in your gateway anti-spoofing settings. If you want to minimize the objects you require, you can create network objects that represent a large network range, rather than an object for an individual subnet. If you wish to represent a range of addresses that is not an exact subnet, use an Address Range object. Use large network objects and address ranges in rules (Security & NAT) where possible to make the rulebase clearer and more efficient.

Q: Is it possible to change a gateway's SmartDefense settings without installing the Security policy?

A: No, the SmartDefense and Web Intelligence settings are pushed to the gateway as part of the Security policy, so a policy install is required after a SmartDefense change or update.

Q: Tech Support has asked me to edit some settings using **dbedit** or **Database Tool**. What is this and why do I need to use it?

A: SmartDashboard allows you to manage the majority of possible settings in the configuration database; however, there are a number of settings that are not available in the main interface. Some are tucked away within **Global Properties | SmartDashboard Customization | Advanced Configuration | Configure**. However, some other settings are not available there either. Some are hidden because they are very rarely used, to keep the SmartDashboard interface tidier. Some are hidden and undocumented as they are not intended to be changed—perhaps they will be utilized in a future software release. The utility **dbedit** allows unrestricted access to the whole configuration database, in raw format—something like the Windows registry editor. Be warned that, like editing the Windows registry, trouble may follow if changes are made without a full understanding of what effect they may have—one wrong click can really ruin your day. The utility is available in two forms: a command-line version on the SmartCenter (**dbedit**), or a GUI included with SmartConsole: go to **\Program Files\CheckPoint\SmartConsole\R65\ PROGRAM** and run **GuiDBEdit.exe**.

Q: Is it not possible to manage the configuration of Connectra and Interspect devices directly from SmartDashboard? And what about Integrity server?

A: At present the SmartDashboard interface does not include the functionality to configure the settings in Interspect and Connectra—there is little overlap between the existing settings and those needed for these devices so this would require significant extensions to the UI. The exception is the SmartDefense database: this can now be managed centrally in SmartDashboard. The same limitations apply to the Integrity server product. However, one of Check Point's priorities is centralizing security configuration, so it seems likely that all these devices will become increasingly integrated into SmartDashboard over the life of NGX.

Q: When I log in to SmartPortal there is a Read Only checkbox—but I thought all access via SmartPortal was read-only anyway?

A: The Read Only option prohibits the Log Switch and Log Purge options on the Traffic Log page.

Chapter 4

Advanced Authentication

Solutions in this chapter:

- Authentication Overview
- Users and Administrators
- SmartDirectory
- User Authentication
- Session Authentication
- Client Authentication

☑ Summary

☑ Solutions Fast Track

☑ Frequently Asked Questions

Introduction

Using Check Point NGX R65, you can control the traffic coming into or going out of your networks. However, sometimes you will need or want to authenticate specific users that are accessing your resources. For example, an administrator might have to download privileged files from a restricted user's workstation, and would need special privileges for a short amount of time. With authentication, Check Point NGX's features are greatly expanded and complement already strong security with the ability to implement security on a per-user basis. Once you understand how NGX authentication works, you will probably find many uses for it in your environment.

Authentication Overview

Check Point NGX works based on the information it has to permit or deny a connection. To authenticate a particular user, the firewall needs additional information to match the user and a connection. The main topic of this chapter addresses the best way to authenticate users so that they can access privileged resources. Check Point Software has made few changes to the way authentication works since it released the NGX R60.

We will first address the issue of which users can authenticate. Check Point NGX is flexible enough to authenticate users created in various sources, databases, or external directory servers. We will then examine the different types of authentication that NGX allows, which are called user, session, and client authentication. We will also touch on SmartDirectory, Check Point's Lightweight Directory Access Protocol (LDAP) implementation.

Using Authentication in Your Environment

Using authentication involves additional configuration of the firewall and planning an environment that allows users to access the resources they need. Some of the environments that can benefit from authentication include:

- Using Dynamic Host Configuration Protocol (DHCP) without Internet Protocol (IP) reservations, while needing to give a few users access to special resources

- A support technician downloading drivers and antivirus programs on restricted machines

- Implementing an additional security layer on an extranet site

Users and Administrators

Think of a user as an entity: Bob, Peter, and so on. To recognize (or authenticate) him or herself, the user needs either to know something (a password) or to have something (a token or digital certificate). This chapter focuses on passwords. Most companies already have some sort of user database (Microsoft Active Directory, a Remote Authentication Dial-in User Service [RADIUS] server, etc.), and would like to integrate this database with their firewall, through the use of an Authentication Scheme.

Managing Users and Administrators

Before you can authenticate users, you need to define them, of course. Check Point NGX is very flexible in this sense. You can use NGX's built-in user database, as well as external user directories, including LDAP through Check Point SmartDirectory.

There are two ways you can access and edit the user database. You can access the **Manage Users and Administrators** dialog from the **Manage | Users and Administrators** menu (see Figure 4.1), or you can use the Object Tree (as in Figure 4.2). Both include a listing of all user-related objects: users, groups, templates, administrators, external user groups, LDAP, and so on. Each entity type is represented by a different icon: Administrators have crowns over them, groups are represented by two users, templates are outlines, and external users have a circle around them.

Figure 4.1 The Manage Users and Administrators Dialog

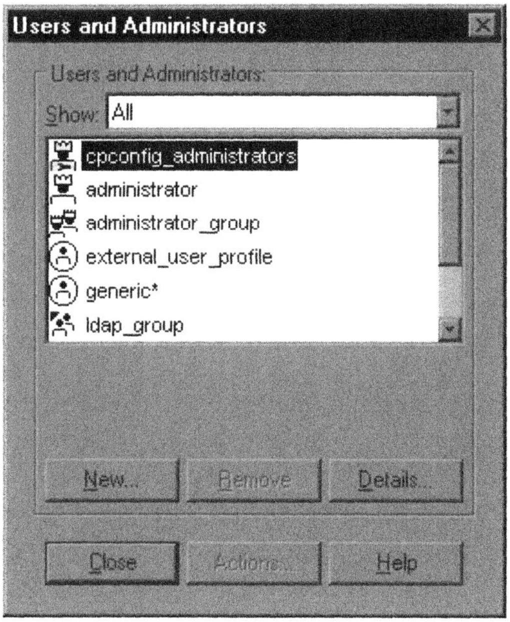

In the **Users** tab within the Object Tree, you can right-click on any entity class to add new objects.

Figure 4.2 An Object Tree Listing of User Entities and Their Icons

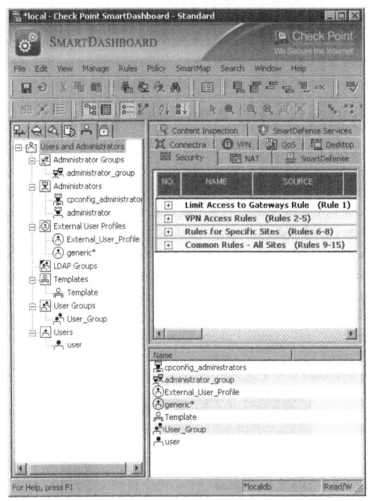

The first item you will see in the Manage Users and Administrators dialog box will be a yellow icon named cpconfig_administrators, which represents the administrator configured through the SecurePlatform Web interface or the cpconfig utility on a SmartCenter.

Permissions Profiles

Before you create an administrator, you need to create a Permissions Profile. Go to the **Manage | Permissions Profiles** dialog and select **New | Permissions Profiles**, as in Figure 4.3.

Figure 4.3 The Permissions Profiles Dialog

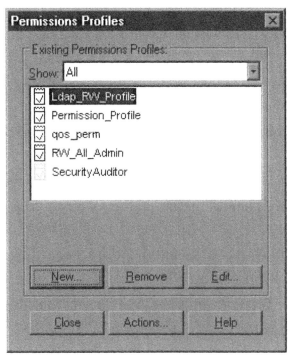

In the **General** tab, you can name the profile, select a color, and enter a comment. In the **Permissions** tab, you can select among the following:

- Allow access via:

  SmartPortal and Console Applications Administrators can access both the GUI and the Web interface.

  SmartPortal only Administrators can access only the SmartPortal Web interface.

- Permissions:

  None Disables an administrator's permissions.

  Read/Write All Allows full access to all NGX management applications.

  Manage Administrators Allows you to change other administrators' accounts and profiles.

  Read-Only All Grants access to all configurations, but administrators cannot change anything.

Customized Allows you to create a personalized profile for administrators with specific functions. The permissions for each option can be Disabled, or Enabled with Read Only and Read/Write. The specific functions you can select are:

SmartUpdate Using SmartUpdate for managing product updates and assigning licenses

Objects Database Working with the network objects (services, resources, and servers)

Check Point Users Database Working with the internal user database

LDAP Users Database Managing an external LDAP database through SmartDirectory

Security Policy Working with the security and network address translator (NAT) rules and installing a policy

QoS Policy Working with the QoS rules and installing a policy

Log Consolidator Working with Eventia Reporter's Consolidation Policy

Eventia Reporter Working with the Eventia Reporter tables and generating reports

Monitoring Accessing the SmartView Monitor database for statuses

UserAuthority Web Access Working with the UserAuthority Web Access product

ROBO Gateways Database Working with the SmartLSM (Large Scale Manager)

Eventia Analyzer Events Working with the Eventia Analyzer Events database

Eventia Analyzer Policy Working with the Eventia Analyzer database

Track Logs Accessing the Traffic Log and Active sessions in the SmartView Tracker

Audit Logs Accessing the Active sessions and Audit Logs in the SmartView Tracker

Integrity Server Managing the Integrity Server (see Figure 4.4)

Figure 4.4 The Permissions Tab of the Permissions Profile Properties Dialog

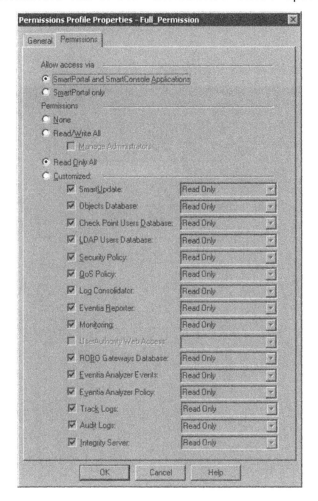

Administrators

The administrators are the users that have access to the configuration of the firewall. Depending on the Permissions Profile assigned to the administrators, they may or may not have permission to read and write to different parts of the security policy. Once you create or edit an administrator, you'll see the tabs outlined in the following sections.

General Tab

In the **General** tab of the Administrator Properties dialog, you can give a name to the administrator and select a previously created Permissions Profile. You can also click on

New and directly create a new profile. **View Permissions Profile** allows you to view and edit existing profiles (see Figure 4.5).

Figure 4.5 Creating a New Administrator

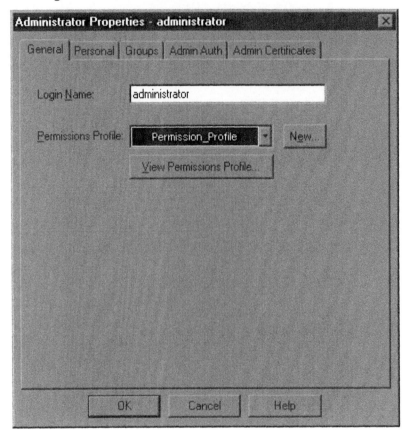

Personal Tab

You will find a **Personal** tab for both administrators and users. You use the **Expiration Date** field (in dd-mmm-yyyy format) to set a valid period for an administrator. By default in NGX, the expiration date is 31 December 2030.

Groups

You can select which administrator groups this administrator belongs to. You can **Add** and **Remove** administrators from the **Available Groups** and the **Belongs to Groups** boxes. Admin Groups are used in the Permission to Install field in Check Point objects.

Admin Auth

Here you can select what Authentication Scheme will be used for administrators—basically, what to check the password against. The options are Undefined, SecurID, Check Point Password, OS Password, RADIUS, and TACACS. If you select **Undefined**, the administrator will only be able to authenticate using a digital certificate.

Admin Certificates

One of the advantages of using SmartDashboard Administrators is that you can implement authentication via digital certificates generated by the Internal Certificate Authority (ICA). If there is no certificate for the administrator, you can click on **Generate and Save**. Enter and verify the certificate's password, and save the certificate file. Once you generate the certificate, you can revoke it from this tab.

Administrator Groups

You can create Administrator Groups and place administrators in them. You can use Administrator Groups by editing a Check Point gateway, using the **Advanced | Permissions to Install** tab. Here you can specify Administrator Groups to which you want to grant install access. Only administrators with Manage Administrators permission can modify these properties.

User Templates

Before you create users, you have to understand templates. There are many options to configure for users, and templates save you time by preconfiguring options at the time of user creation. Let's look at the different tabs you see once you select **New | Template**.

General

Select the **Name** the template will have, which you will use when selecting **New | User from Template**.

Personal

You use the **Expiration Date** field (in dd-mmm-yyyy format) to set a valid time period for users. By default in NGX R65, the expiration date is 31 December 2030. Enter a **Comment** for the template and select a **Color** for the display of its icon. These fields are for informational use only.

Groups

You can **Add** and **Remove** administrators from the **Available Groups** and the **Belongs to Groups** boxes.

Authentication

Here you can select what **Authentication Scheme** will be used for these users. The options are Undefined, SecurID, Check Point Password, OS Password, RADIUS, and TACACS. If you select **Undefined**, the user will not be able to authenticate using a password, only a digital certificate (for virtual private networks [VPNs] only).

Location

Location refers to the users' allowed sources and destinations. You will be able to select **Network Objects** and move them to either the **Source** or **Destination** box, or leave them as **Any**. The location then becomes a restriction as to where the users can connect from and connect to. When you configure an authentication rule, you can decide whether the rule has to intersect with the location of the users, or whether it can ignore it.

Time

You can select what day of the week and range of time the **User may connect at**. Although you can select more than one **Day in week**, you are limited to a single range for **Time of day**.

Encryption

Encryption is used for VPN Remote Access. If you select **IKE** for **Client Encryption**, the user will be able to participate in the Remote Access community.

User Groups

You can create user groups and place users in them. You can select a **Name**, **Comment**, and **Color** for the group, and **Add** and **Remove** them from the **Not in Group** box to the **In Group** box, as in Figure 4.6.

Figure 4.6 Creating a User Group

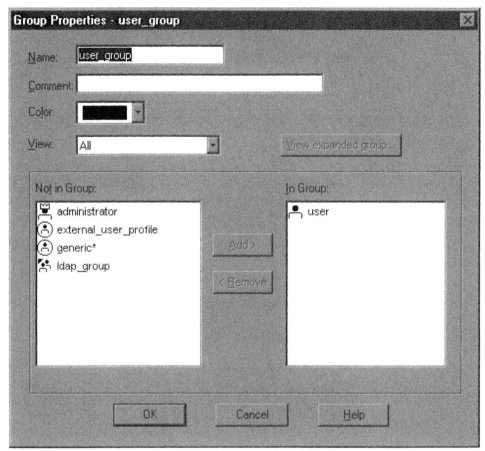

User groups can also contain other groups in a nested fashion. When you add a group to another group, NGX will ask **Would you like to add each member of the group separately?** and each group will be expanded in the new group. With nested groups, if you change a group the change will be reflected in the parent group, but that will not happen if you expand the group.

Check Point NGX does not reference individual users directly in rules or object properties, so if you have a user, you should place him or her in a group. If a user is not in a group, the user is still part of the All Users group.

Users

When you want to create a user you have to work based on an existing template. Once you select **New | User from Template** as in Figure 4.7, you can select the initial template you want and then you will see a dialog box with many tabs. Let's look at them.

Figure 4.7 Creating a User from a Template

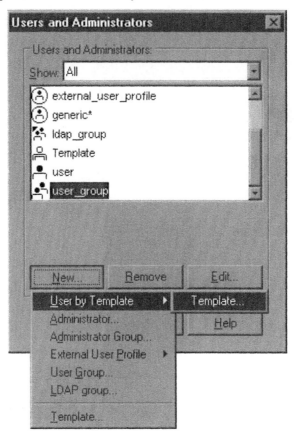

General

Select the **Login Name** for the user. The name can have special characters in it, as well as spaces and long names.

Personal

The **Expiration Date** field (in dd–mmm–yyyy format) is used to set a valid time period for a user. By default, in NGX R65 the expiration date is 31 December 2030. Enter a **Comment** and select a **Color** for the display of its icon. These fields will be prepopulated with information from the template.

Groups

You can select which user groups the user belongs to. You can **Add** and **Remove** them from the **Available Groups** and the **Belongs to Groups** boxes. The tab will be prepopulated according to the template.

Authentication

Here you can select which **Authentication Scheme** the user will have. The options are Undefined, SecurID, Check Point Password, OS Password, RADIUS, and TACACS. If you select **Check Point Password**, you can click **Enter Password** to assign and verify it. The passwords should be four to eight characters in length. If you select **RADIUS** or **TACACS**, you can select which server to use for verification.

Location

Here you can select specific **Source** and **Destination** locations for the users. The fields will be prepopulated from the template. Remember that when you configure an authentication rule, you can decide whether the rule has to intersect with the location of the users, or whether it can ignore it.

Time

You can select what day of the week and range of time **User may connect at**. Although you can select more than one **Day in week**, you are limited to a single range for **Time of day**. It will be prepopulated from the template.

Certificates

In this tab, you will see the **Certificate State** (**There is no certificate for this object**, or **Object has a certificate**), and the **Distinguished Name** if it has a certificate. Digital certificates for users apply only for Remote Access VPNs.

Encryption

Encryption is used for VPN Remote Access. If you select **IKE**, the user will be able to participate in the Remote Access community.

External User Profiles

If you're working with external directory servers (RADIUS, TACACS, OS Password, or SecurID) you can create an External User Profile. If users are recognized by an external directory server they will be granted permissions based on the appropriate External User Profile. Still, using OS Password usually is not a good option due to the complexity of managing passwords in the OS on which the Security Gateway is installed.

Match by Domain

This profile allows you to selectively query an external user database based on the domain the user enters. The important properties are in the General tab. If you use Distinguished Name (DN) format, you can select a specific organizational unit, organization, or country to authorize. Alternatively, you can use Free Format, in which case the domain will be separated from the username by a character such as @ or \ (for Microsoft), either before or after the username. In Free Format, you can choose **Any Domain is Acceptable**, or a specific **Domain Name**. See Figure 4.8 for details.

Figure 4.8 External User Profiles | Match by Domain

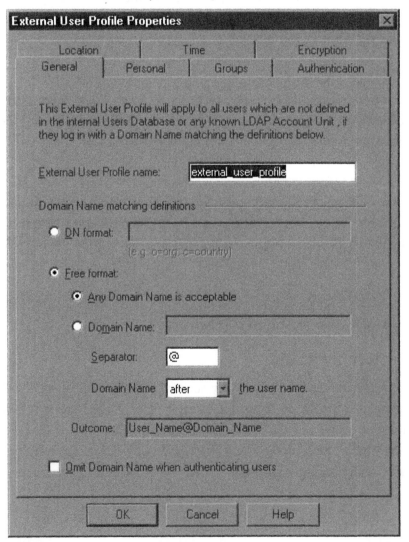

The other tabs in the External User Profile (Personal, Groups, Authentication, Location, Time, and Encryption) function like they do in the normal user entity. Remember that in this scenario, you're leaving authentication and authorization decisions to an external entity.

Match All Users

If you don't need to be selective regarding the domain with which users must log in, you can use the Match All Users External Profile. It is named *generic** and will match any user recognized by the external directory server. Remember that in this scenario, you're leaving authentication and authorization decisions to an external entity.

LDAP Group

We will look at LDAP Groups in the upcoming "SmartDirectory" section.

Understanding Authentication Schemes

Check Point NGX is flexible enough to work with several external directory servers, in which a user entity can be defined in the Internal Check Point database, but the password is verified from different sources. Check Point refers to these as Authentication Schemes.

Undefined

You use the Undefined Authentication Scheme to disable the user's ability to enter a password. This will force users to employ strong authentication with a digital certificate.

SecurID

Selecting SecurID as the Authentication Scheme will enable Check Point NGX to become an ACE/Agent for RSA's SecurID tokens. This integration will require use of a special sdconf.rec generated by the ACE server, and will allow you to enter new PINs and reauthenticate often to secure servers. However, it's a lot more difficult to configure than through SecurID's RADIUS interface.

Check Point Password

If you select Check Point Password (previously called VPN-1 & Firewall-1 Password), you will enter the user's password directly into NGX's internal database. Passwords can be four to eight characters in length. Be aware that the only way to assign or change passwords is through the SmartDashboard interface.

RADIUS

RADIUS is a standard protocol that can authenticate users with a RADIUS server that holds a database. The RADIUS protocol is very flexible and relatively secure. It uses a specific secret key to secure the authentication and only authorized clients can request authentication from the server. You can also set up backup servers in case one of them is out of service.

To configure RADIUS authentication, first create a RADIUS server from the **Manage | Servers and OPSEC Applications** dialog, as in Figure 4.9. Select **New | RADIUS** to create the server. Input the appropriate data in the **Name**, **Comment**, and **Color** fields, as in Figure 4.10. For **Host**, select the physical server that is running the RADIUS server. If you don't have the server created, use the **New** button to create a new node. Select the **Service** to use, either NEW-RADIUS (the official port number) or RADIUS (the most common port number used). The **Shared Secret** is a password used to secure the information sent between the Check Point Gateways and the RADIUS server(s). You can select the **Version** to use, either Version 1.0 or Version 2.0. Also select a **Priority**, to know which server to use first if more than one is available. You can also create **RADIUS groups** for high availability and load sharing.

Figure 4.9 The Manage Servers and OPSEC Applications Dialog

Figure 4.10 Creating a RADIUS Server

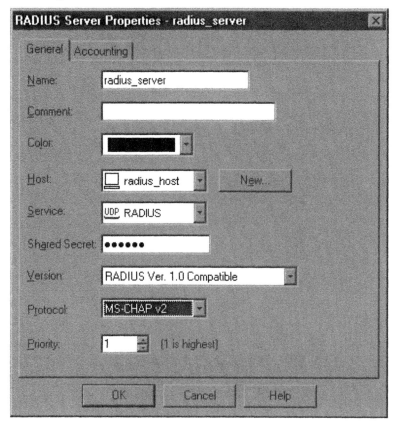

TACACS

The Terminal Access Controller Access Control System is a standard protocol that can authenticate users with an external user database. To configure TACACS authentication, first create a TACACS server from the **Manage | Servers and OPSEC Applications** dialog. Select **New | TACACS** and input the appropriate data in the **Name**, **Comment**, and **Color** fields, as in Figure 4.11. For **Host**, select the physical server that is running the TACACS server. If you don't have the server created, use the **New** button to create a new node. Select the **Type** of the server used, either TACACS, or TACACS+ which is more secure. If you select TACACS+ you can also enter a **Secret Key** for encryption. Finally, select the **Service** to use (UDP TACACS or TCP TACACSPLUS).

Figure 4.11 Creating a TACACS Server

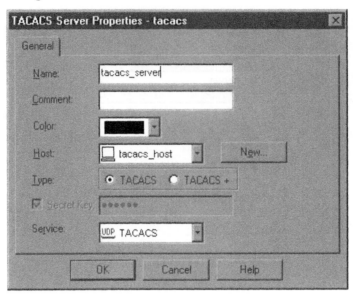

Tools & Traps...

Using Microsoft Internet Authentication Service (IAS)

Microsoft Windows servers (NT, 2000, and 2003) have a built-in component called the Internet Authentication Service (IAS). It is basically a RADIUS service integrated into the NT domain or Active Directory. RADIUS authentication does not require a Check Point SmartDirectory license. To make the connection between IAS and NGX follow these steps:

1. Create the appropriate RADIUS server in the SmartDashboard. In the **Start | Programs | Administrative Tools | Internet Authentication Service** management console, add a new **RADIUS client**. The IP address should be the firewall gateway's IP facing the RADIUS server. If you have a cluster, add a client for each cluster member. Input the same **Shared Secret** you defined when creating the RADIUS server in the SmartDashboard.

2. In the Remote Access Policies, edit one of the policies listed (in NT and **access servers**). **Edit the Profile** and go to the **Authentication** tab. Select either Unencrypted Authentication or Microsoft Encrypted

Continued

Authentication Version 2, which is more secure. In the **Advanced** tab of the profile, eliminate all attributes.

3. Modify the Active Directory users to allow connections. Go to **Start | Settings | Control Panel | Administrative Tools | Active Directory Users and Computers**, and edit the properties of the user you want to authenticate using RADIUS. In the **Dial-In** tab, select **Allow Access** and **Apply**.

4. In the SmartDashboard, create a generic∗ user (an external user profile that matches all users) with RADIUS authentication. Include the generic∗ user in user groups you insert in the rulebase.

5. You can differentiate among RADIUS users by setting the *add_radius_groups* property with the GUIdbEdit application, and then configuring the RADIUS server to send a *Class* attribute for different user groups. In SmartDashboard create groups named *RAD_<ClassAttribute>* and integrate them in the rulebase.

SmartDirectory

Most enterprises already have an existing user database that they want to integrate with their security infrastructure. LDAP is an open industry standard for directory access, supported by many vendors and applications including Microsoft Active Directory, Novell, Netscape, and others. Check Point's LDAP implementation is called SmartDirectory. It requires a separate license, but it's included in SmartCenter Pro and UTM-1 appliances. You can use SmartDirectory for user authentication and for certificate revocation list (CRL) retrieval.

LDAP elements include the LDAP servers, which hold the directory information; the LDAP tree, which is the hierarchy of the directory; and the LDAP schema, which is a description of the data within the directory. The LDAP tree is a strict hierarchy that can include countries, organizations, organizational units, groups, and common names. Each entity in the LDAP tree has a DN containing the entire path under which the entity exists. When dealing with the schema, take into consideration that standard LDAP servers will not have some of the information that Check Point requires for its users (e.g., VPN-related data, location data, etc.). There are two methods to overcome this limitation: extending the Active Directory schema, and applying a user template to LDAP users.

You can extend the LDAP schema to include the Check Point schema, although you should not undertake this lightly. Because it implies modifying the underlying schema of a production LDAP server, you should make a complete backup of the server prior to modifying the schema. You can find detailed instructions in the Check Point SmartCenter Administration Guide, under SmartDirectory (LDAP) Reference Information.

Configuring SmartDirectory

The first step in configuring SmartDirectory is to enable it from the Global Properties. From **Policy | Global Properties | SmartDirectory (LDAP)**, select **Use SmartDirectory (LDAP)**, as in Figure 4.12.

Figure 4.12 SmartDirectory (LDAP) Global Properties

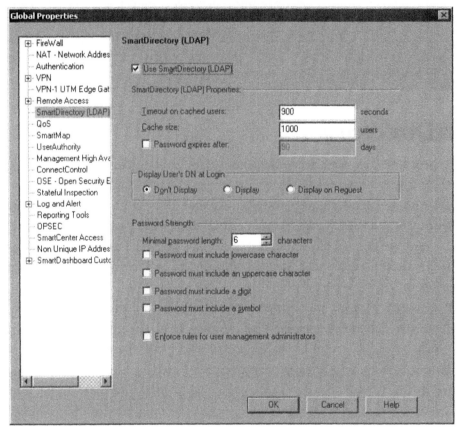

The settings you can configure here include:

- **Timeout on cached users** How long the cached users (i.e., the users' credentials after a successful authentication is made) are stored.

- **Cache size** How many user credentials to store in memory.

- **Password expires after** How long the user's password is valid. Older passwords won't be accepted.

- **Display User's DN at Login** Selects whether to display the DN once authenticated.

- **Password Strength** Selects the password length, and whether to require lowercase, uppercase, digits, and symbols.

- **Enforce rules for user management administrators** Applies the password strength rules for LDAP administrators.

Account Units

Check Point creates Account Units to connect the LDAP servers with Check Point VPN-1. The Account Unit holds servers that have the connection information to the LDAP servers. Create an Account Unit from **Manage | Servers and OPSEC Applications | New | LDAP Account Unit**, as in Figure 4.13.

Figure 4.13 LDAP Account Unit Properties: General

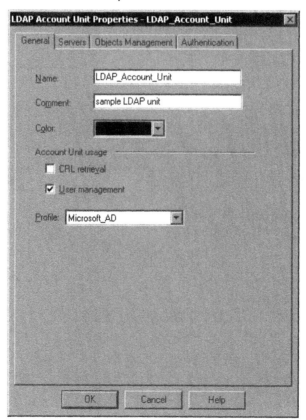

You should enter a **Name**, **Comment**, and **Color**, as well as making sure **User management** is selected. If that option is disabled, the SmartDirectory option in Global Properties has not been enabled. For **Profile**, the selection includes Microsoft_AD (Microsoft Active Directory), Netscape_DS (Netscape Directory Services), Novell_DS (Novell Directory Services), and OPSEC_DS (for OPSEC-certified LDAP servers). The profiles provide basic compatibility with the designated LDAP standard.

You need to configure the **Servers** tab with the list of LDAP servers that hold the Account Unit's information, as in Figure 4.14. You can use multiple servers for resiliency, and you need to select one of the servers for Pre-NG FP3 compatibility.

Figure 4.14 LDAP Account Unit Properties: Servers

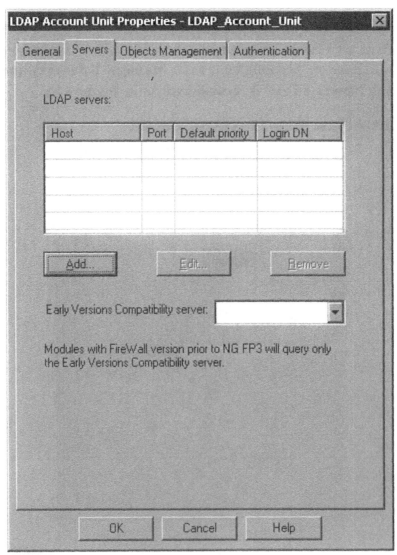

Click on **Add** to include an LDAP server for the Account Unit, as in Figure 4.15.

Figure 4.15 LDAP Server Properties: General

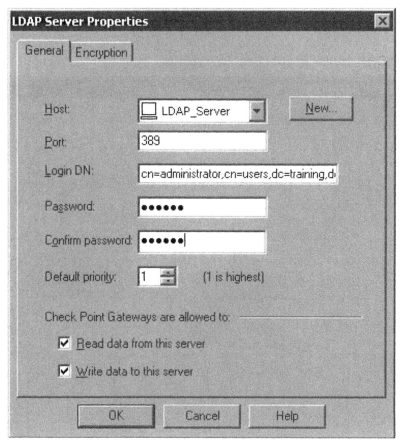

For **Host**, select an existing object or create a new object where the LDAP server is running. The default LDAP **Port** is 389; enter the **Login DN** (the DN that will be used to read and write from the LDAP server). For Microsoft Active Directory, the DN follows the format *cn=<username>, cn=groups, dc=<domainsection1>, dc=<domainsection2>*. For user LDAPAdmin in domain training.com, the DN would be *cn=LDAPAdmin, cn=groups,dc=training,dc=com*. Lastly, select whether the **Check Point Gateways are allowed to** read and/or write data on the server. You would need write permission to lock out a user after failed attempts.

For information as sensitive as user authentication, it is important to enable encryption in the **Encryption** tab, as in Figure 4.16. Enabling encryption activates port 636, the default LDAP encryption port. You must fetch the Fingerprint by pressing the **Fetch** button. For it to work in a Microsoft environment, the domain controller must have Certificate Services installed. Then select the minimum and maximum encryption strengths. Select **OK** to save the server configuration.

Figure 4.16 LDAP Server Properties: Encryption

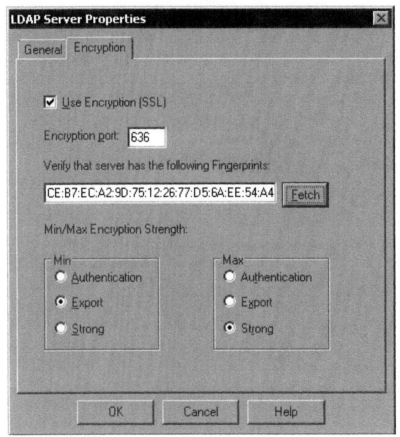

In the **Objects Management** tab, the LDAP branches can be fetched, which will be the first verification that the LDAP server is communicating with the SmartCenter (see Figure 4.17).

Figure 4.17 LDAP Account Unit Properties: Objects Management

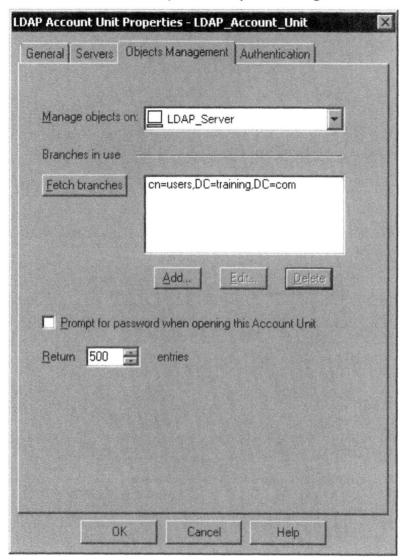

Lastly, the **Authentication** tab is crucial for enabling LDAP users in the Check Point rulebase (see Figure 4.18).

Figure 4.18 LDAP Account Unit Properties: Authentication

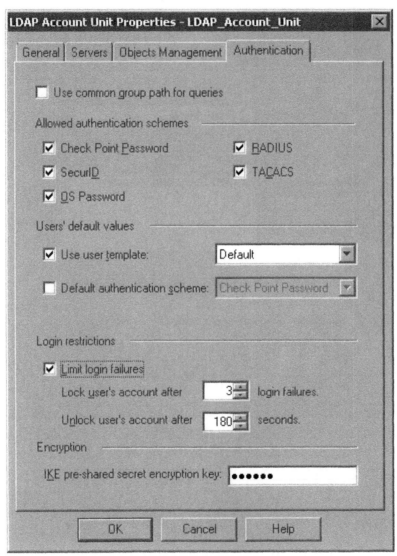

The **Allowed authentication schemes** define which schemes are approved for the LDAP users. The most important section is **Users' default values**. If the LDAP schema has not been extended to include the Check Point schema, these settings are used to fill in those properties missing for the Check Point LDAP schema. If a user template is selected, all of the template's properties are dynamically assigned to any LDAP user that authenticates to VPN-1. A default authentication scheme will only define which scheme to use, and nothing else. In both options, select **Check Point Password** for the authentication scheme.

If you have multiple LDAP servers, add them in the **LDAP Account Unit Properties**, until all servers are included. Select the highest-priority one, or the most robust, as the Early Compatibility server.

Accessing the LDAP Server

Once you have configured an Account Unit, the Users and Administrators Object Tree will show the Account Unit at the bottom, as in Figure 4.19. Double-click on the **Account Unit** and it should expand to show the LDAP tree; double-click on any of the branches to retrieve the LDAP entities within that branch.

Figure 4.19 The Users and Administrators Object Tree

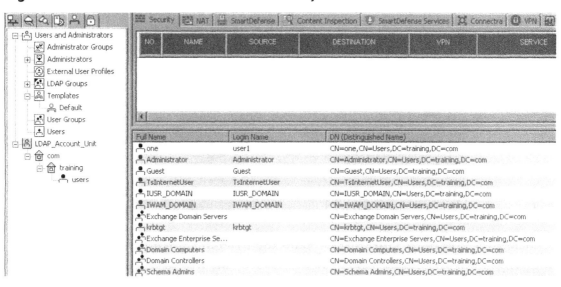

Within the branch information, if write permissions have been configured for the LDAP server, users and groups can be added, edited, and removed.

LDAP Groups

The preferred way to grant user access via SmartDirectory is to use LDAP groups. Figure 4.20 shows an example.

Figure 4.20 An LDAP Group

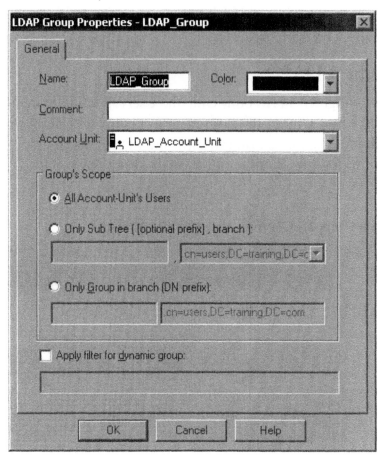

Select the **Account Unit** that contains the users to authenticate. In the **Group's Scope**, you can select to recognize all of the Account Unit users, or only those in a certain subtree, or a group in a branch. You can also apply a filter to create a dynamic group (e.g., all users in ou=Access).

Once created, an LDAP group behaves like any other user group in the object database. We will now examine the different types of authentication and how to integrate groups into the rulebase.

User Authentication

User authentication is simple to understand and configure. It works by intercepting connections that are passing through the firewall (Check Point calls this *folding* the connection), and modifying the traffic in such a way that the firewall asks the user to identify itself before allowing the connection to pass through. Because the user requests a connection to his or her final destination, user authentication is a type of *transparent* authentication; in other words, the user doesn't need to go through an intermediate process.

Because NGX needs to modify the traffic itself, it can do so only with specific services which it can understand well: HTTP/S, FTP, Telnet, and rlogin. These services belong to the *Authenticated* group in the predefined Check Point services. When one of these services is used to access a restricted resource, and a rule is configured to allow User Auth for that connection, the traffic is modified so that the user can enter a password to enable the traffic. For HTTP, Telnet, and rlogin, the user sees an intermediary prompt from the firewall, and once the user authenticates, a new connection to the final destination is made. In the case of FTP traffic, the username and password to authenticate to the FTP server need to be embedded in the user credentials.

User authentication is performed on each connection so that if a machine is being shared by different users (e.g., in a client/server or thin client environment), each user will authenticate his or her connection only, which is safe. Because the firewall needs to examine the traffic of these authenticated services, it requires more processing power from the firewall than either session or client authentication.

Configuring User Authentication in the Rulebase

To allow user authentication, create a new rule. In the **Source** field, select **Add User Access**, and add the user groups that will be able to authenticate using that rule. You can also restrict the origin of the connections. Add the appropriate **Destination** to that rule (if you want to authenticate all traffic to the Internet, leave it as **Any)**, select which **Services** you'll authenticate, select **User Auth** as the **Action**, and add appropriate **Track**, **Time**, and **Comment** configurations. Figure 4.21 shows a user authentication rule.

Figure 4.21 Creating a User Authentication Rule

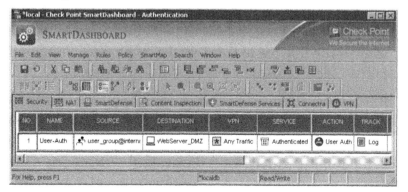

You should edit or verify the properties of the **Action** field in the user authentication rule, as in Figure 4.22.

Figure 4.22 Properties of the User Authentication Action

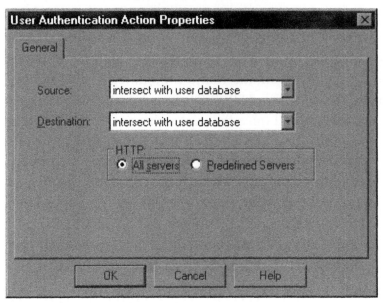

You can configure the following properties in the **Action** field:

- **Source** Controls whether the Restrict To location in the source of the rule has to intersect the configured location of the user in the database. Select **Ignore** to override the user database.

  For instance, if ruleX has a source of Internal_Net and userY has a source location of Alternate_Net, userX would never be authorized, because there is no intersection of Internal_Net and Alternate_Net. If the desired functionality is to allow userX to authenticate from Internal_Net, ignoring the user database will skip over checking the user's location properties.

- **Destination** Destination controls whether the Restrict To location in the destination of the rule has to intersect the configured location of the user in the database. Select **Ignore** to override the user database.

- **HTTP** Controls whether to allow authentication to a restricted number of servers, or to any accessible machines. When **Predefined Servers** is selected, users will be able to access only the list of servers that can be defined in the **Policy | Global Properties | Firewall-1 | Security Servers** dialog. To authenticate traffic to any destination on the Internet, select **All Servers**.

Interacting with User Authentication

Depending on the service you will authenticate (HTTP, FTP, Telnet, or rlogin) the way your users will authenticate is different. Let's see what the user experience is for these services.

Telnet and rlogin

User authentication for Telnet and rlogin is easy for the end-user to understand. When a user tries a command such as *telnet 172.29.109.1*, the firewall will intercept this command and present its own Telnet prompts, as in Figure 4.23. Once the user correctly authenticates, he or she will see the prompts from his or her original destination and can proceed accordingly.

Figure 4.23 Telnet User Authentication

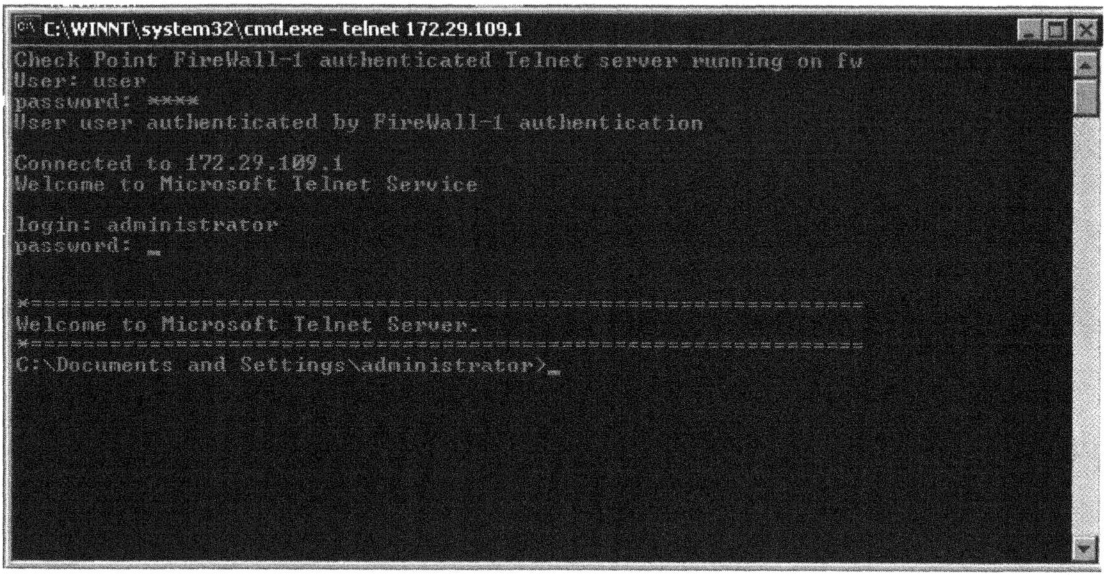

FTP

User authentication for FTP is a bit more complex to understand. The user will still use the command *ftp 172.29.109.1*, which will be intercepted by the firewall's FTP security server, but the username will have to reflect the user that is authenticating at the FTP server (i.e., the administrator), the user that is authenticating at the firewall (i.e., the user), and the final destination of the FTP connection (even though it was used in the original FTP command). For example, in this case, the username will be *administrator@user@172.29.109.1*, and the password will be the passwords of the FTP user separated by an @ sign from the password of the firewall user (i.e., *ftppassword@ fwpassword*). Then a connection to the FTP server will be established. Figure 4.24 shows the details.

Figure 4.24 FTP User Authentication

```
C:\WINNT\system32\cmd.exe - ftp 172.29.109.1

C:\Documents and Settings\Administrator>ftp 172.29.109.1
Connected to 172.29.109.1.
220 Check Point FireWall-1 Secure FTP server running on fw
User (172.29.109.1:(none)): administrator@user@172.29.109.1
331 password: you can use password@FW-1-password
Password:
230-User user authenticated by FireWall-1 authentication
230-Connected to server. Logging in...
230-220 Microsoft FTP Service
230-331 Password required for administrator.
230 230 User administrator logged in.
ftp>
```

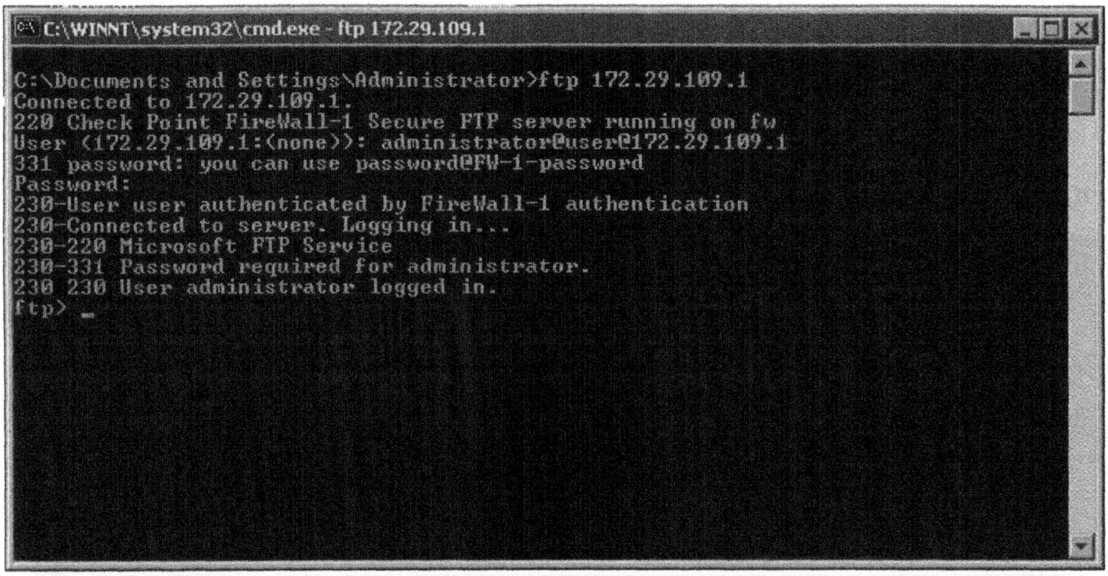

HTTP

User authentication for HTTP is simple to use. When activated, an HTTP connection that should be authenticated is modified by the firewall in such a way that the user's browser displays an authentication dialog box or prompt, using HTTP's authentication mechanism. The prompt reads *FW-1: No user*. Once the user authenticates with this prompt, the requested site is displayed in the browser. Figures 4.25 and 4.26 show examples that use Microsoft Internet Explorer and Mozilla Firefox.

WARNING

Selecting **User Authentication for HTTP traffic to the Internet** will mean that a user might need to authenticate as many as 10 times before seeing a single Web page, because current Web pages usually reference images or code from other sites, and the browsers need to reauthenticate for each different site.

Figure 4.25 HTTP User Authentication with Microsoft Internet Explorer

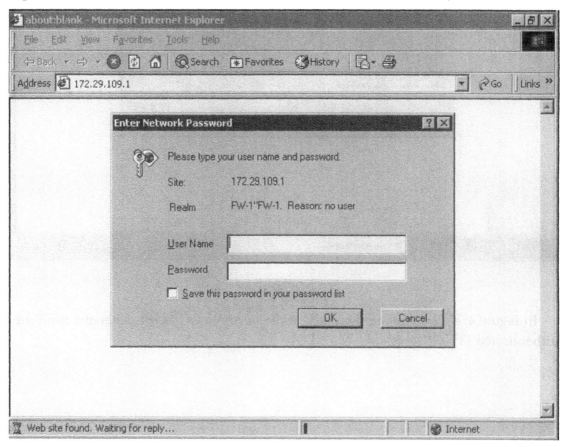

Figure 4.26 HTTP User Authentication with Mozilla Firefox

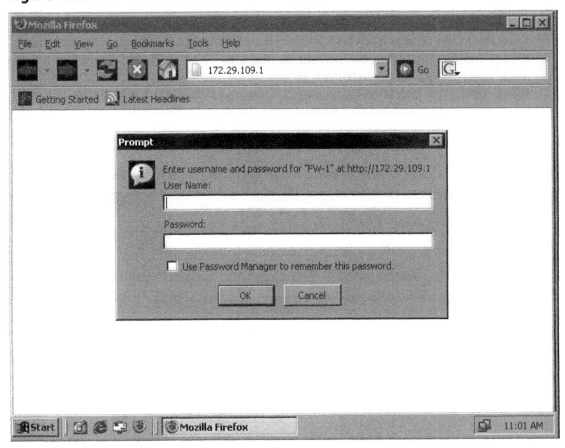

In Figure 4.27, you can see the entry in the SmartView Tracker generated from the authenticated HTTP access.

Figure 4.27 SmartView Tracker Entry for HTTP User Authentication

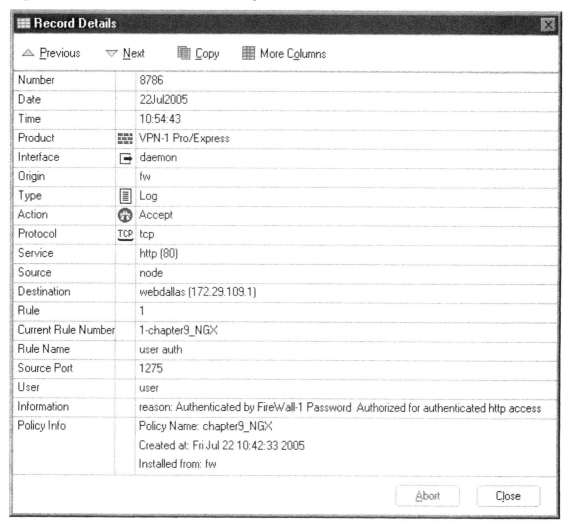

Record Details		✕
△ Previous ▽ Next 📋 Copy ▦ More Columns		
Number		8786
Date		22Jul2005
Time		10:54:43
Product	▦	VPN-1 Pro/Express
Interface	➡	daemon
Origin		fw
Type	🗒	Log
Action	🛡	Accept
Protocol	TCP	tcp
Service		http (80)
Source		node
Destination		webdallas (172.29.109.1)
Rule		1
Current Rule Number		1-chapter9_NGX
Rule Name		user auth
Source Port		1275
User		user
Information		reason: Authenticated by FireWall-1 Password Authorized for authenticated http access
Policy Info		Policy Name: chapter9_NGX
		Created at: Fri Jul 22 10:42:33 2005
		Installed from: fw
		Abort Close

TIP

If the requested site requests a password, users can enter the list of usernames and passwords in reverse order, separated by an @ sign (or even @@ if you're crossing multiple authentication daemons). You might need to use this for Outlook Web access.

Placing Authentication Rules

Check Point rules are sequential, which means that once a rule can be applied to traffic passing through the firewall, that rule is applied and the rest of the rulebase is ignored. However, there is one exception to this. If a rule allows traffic to a destination, even a rule that would require authentication before that rule, the traffic will pass through without the need for users to authenticate. Remember: An authentication rule accepts traffic that is authenticated, but doesn't block traffic that fails authentication.

Advanced Topics

Now we'll discuss some advanced topics.

Changing the Banner

Traffic that is intercepted by the firewall, be it FTP, Telnet, rlogin, or HTTP, displays a message from Check Point NGX requesting authentication. It is advisable to change this default message to a generic one that doesn't broadcast the firewall's identity, and that can include additional information for users. You can select a file to be presented instead of the regular banner for FTP, Telnet, and rlogin (not for HTTP) in the SmartDashboard's **Global Properties | Firewall | Security Servers** dialog box.

Use Host Header As Destination

If you are making HTTP connections, once the connection is authenticated the firewall needs to redirect the original query to the intended destination. It does so by looking at the original URL's IP address, and redirecting the user's browser to that IP. However, if the firewall resolves the destination URL to a nonroutable IP (i.e., the non-NATed IP), or if the Web server is configured to need the Host Header for access (i.e., a Web hosting service that shares one IP with multiple Web pages), the connection will fail. To solve this, enable the setting *http_use_host_h_as_dst* using **Policy | Global Properties | SmartDashboard Customization | Configure | Firewall-1 | Web Security | HTTP Protocol**, as in Figure 4.28.

Figure 4.28 Changing Advanced Properties with SmartDashboard Customization

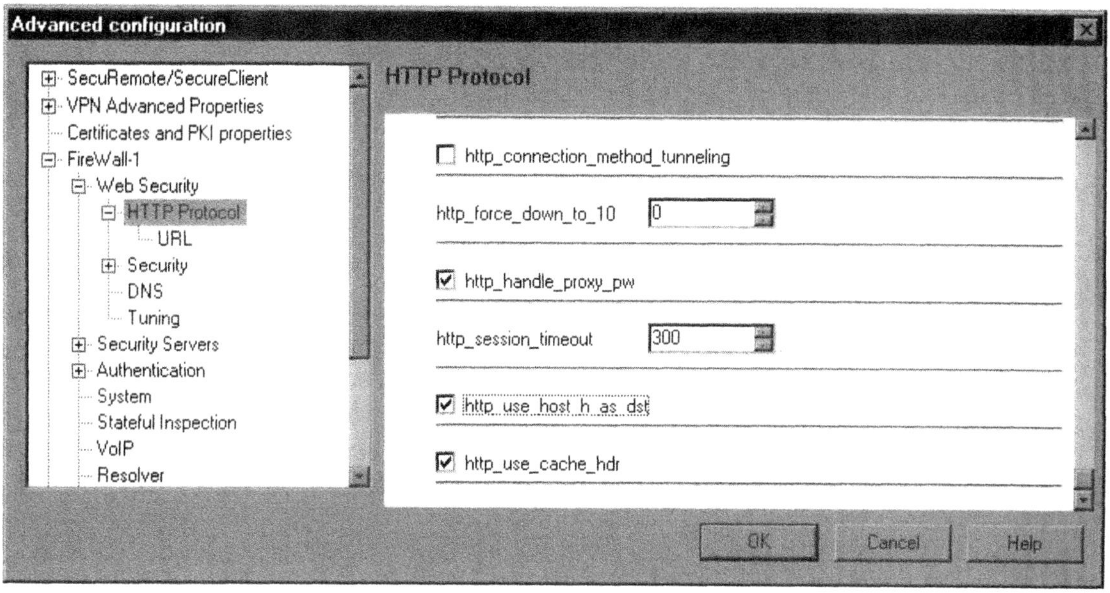

TIP

The best scenario for user authentication is when you need to grant authenticated access to a limited number of servers you control (i.e., your intranet, or servers you host in a data center). This is because you can control the HTML code of those servers so that they do not refer sites that are different from their own. Your users will have an easy-to-understand experience and will authenticate only once. User authentication for Telnet is also easy to understand and implement, as your users receive simple prompts to authenticate first to the firewall and then to their final destinations.

Session Authentication

Another method available for authentication in Check Point NGX is session authentication. This method uses a client program, called the Session Authentication Agent, which is usually installed in each machine that will be used for authentication. You can use the Session Authentication Agent for any service; it authenticates a particular session by the user. When the firewall encounters a rule with session authentication, it tries to query the appropriate machine using the FW1_snauth service on port 261. The agent will then automatically present the user with an authentication dialog. Session authentication combines user and client authentication, because it can authenticate per session for any service.

However, you need to consider that the Session Authentication Agent is a separate program that you have to install in each user's machine, and that it is a Windows-only program. Furthermore, the last available version is from NG Feature Pack 1 and there's no NGX version (as of this writing).

WARNING

The firewall will try to authenticate all sessions that fall under a session authentication rule. If you configure a rule for authenticating any service to any destination, you might end up authenticating every DNS query and NBT broadcast sent, overloading the firewall authentication mechanism and network. Limit the number of services that use session authentication.

Client Authentication

Client authentication is a versatile authentication method that you can use for most of your needs. Unlike user authentication, in which a connection is being authenticated, here you authenticate a machine or an IP (which the firewall considers the client). Client authentication is nontransparent by default, which means that the connection has to be directed to the firewall so that it can ask for the specific authentication. However, with partially or fully automatic sign-on methods, client authentication can be as transparent as user or session authentication. Some of the benefits of client authentication are that any service can be authenticated, and that the authentication can last for a specific period of time. Once a user achieves client authentication, traffic can flow freely with little intervention. Because the firewall doesn't have to interpret or modify the passing connections, is it faster than user and session authentication and doesn't intervene in the HTTP traffic passing through the gateway.

WARNING

Client authentication has some security disadvantages. In a multiuser environment (e.g., Citrix or Terminal Services), all requests originate from the same IP and will be given the same access. Also, if the user doesn't sign off, other users that log on at that machine will have the same permissions as the previously authenticated user until the authorization expires.

Configuring Client Authentication in the Rulebase

To allow client authentication, create a new rule above any rule that would block ports 900 and 259 to the firewall (usually the Stealth rule). In the source field, select **Add User Access**, and then add the user group that will be able to authenticate, and optionally restrict to a location from where that group can connect. Then, add the appropriate **Destination** to that rule (if you want to authenticate all traffic to the Internet, leave it as **Any)**, select which **Services** you'll authenticate (here you can use any service at all), select **ClientAuth** as the **Action**, and add appropriate **Track, Time**, and **Comment** configurations, as in Figure 4.29.

Figure 4.29 Configuring Client Authentication in the Rulebase

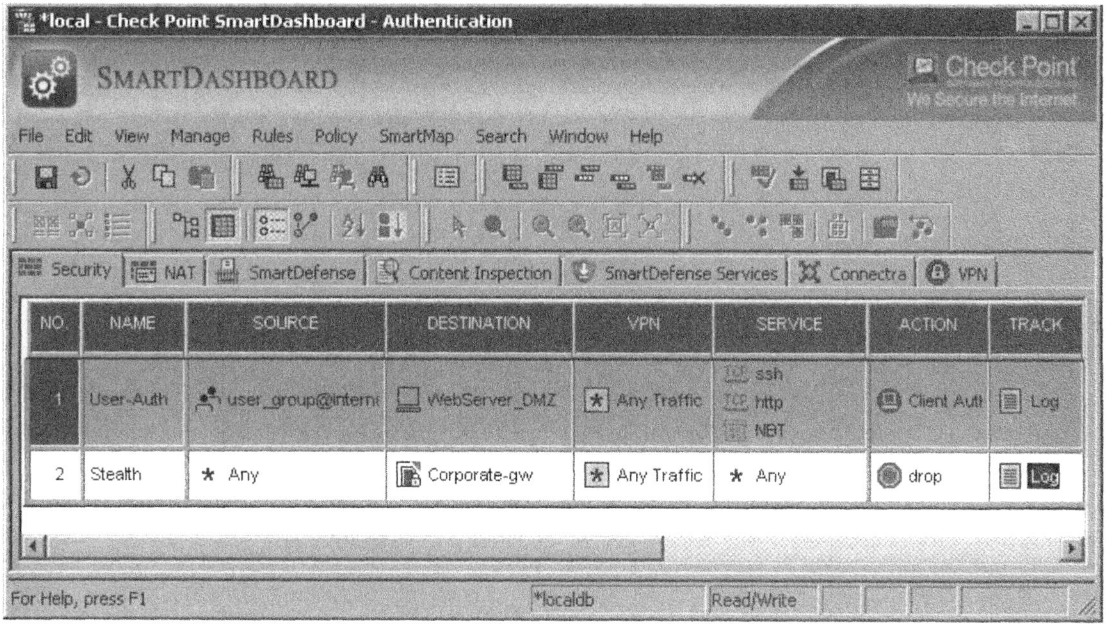

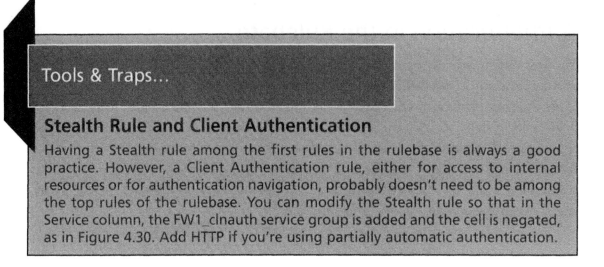

Tools & Traps...

Stealth Rule and Client Authentication

Having a Stealth rule among the first rules in the rulebase is always a good practice. However, a Client Authentication rule, either for access to internal resources or for authentication navigation, probably doesn't need to be among the top rules of the rulebase. You can modify the Stealth rule so that in the Service column, the FW1_clnauth service group is added and the cell is negated, as in Figure 4.30. Add HTTP if you're using partially automatic authentication.

Figure 4.30 A Stealth Rule

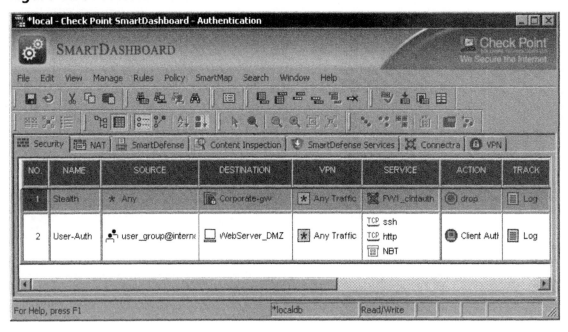

Let's take a look at the Action column of the Client Authentication rule. You can select many different behaviors according to your desired policy. Once you select **Client Auth** as the **Action**, right-click on the field and select **Edit Properties** to configure the setting, as in Figure 4.31.

Figure 4.31 Configuring Client Authentication General Properties

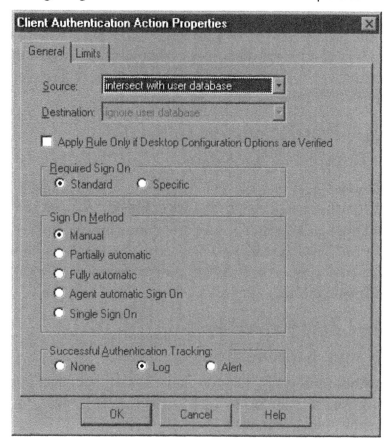

ClientAuth | Edit Properties | General | Source

As in other authentication actions, **Source** is used to control whether the source of the rule has to intersect the configured **Location** of the user, or whether it takes precedence. Select **Ignore** if you want to override the location configured for the user.

ClientAuth | Edit Properties | General | Destination

Client authentication cannot determine the final destination of a connection, because users are authenticating directly to the firewall. Therefore, the destination field is grayed out and cannot be selected.

ClientAuth | Edit Properties | General | Apply Rule Only if Desktop Configuration Options are Verified

Checking this box will allow the client to access resources granted in the rule, once the user authenticates, only if the user is using Check Point SecureClient and the Secure Configuration Verification (SCV) has succeeded.

ClientAuth | Edit Properties | General | Required Sign-On

If you select **Standard** sign-on, users will be able to access all resources permitted in the rule at which they authenticated. If you select **Specific** sign-on, users will have to explicitly specify, through a form or a sequence of prompts, the services and destinations allowed for the client. Specific sign-on is useful for a kiosk machine, where an administrator can authorize access to certain sites or services only, without interacting with the firewall administrator.

ClientAuth | Edit Properties | General | Sign On Method

The **Sign On Method** is one of the most important settings when using client authentication. Be sure you know how each method works so that you select the most appropriate to your environment.

Manual Sign-On

The **Manual** sign-on method activates two ports on the firewall gateway for receipt of the authentication. They are port 900 using HTTP and port 259 using Telnet. Because users need to access these ports on the firewall, you must place the Client Authentication rule above the Stealth rule (the one that drops all connections to the firewall module).

This method is nontransparent, meaning that users will know they are first authenticating to a firewall and then be able to access the appropriate resources.

If you want to HTTP to port 900, you can look at Figures 4.32 through 4.36.

Figure 4.32 HTTP Manual Client Authentication: Entering the Username

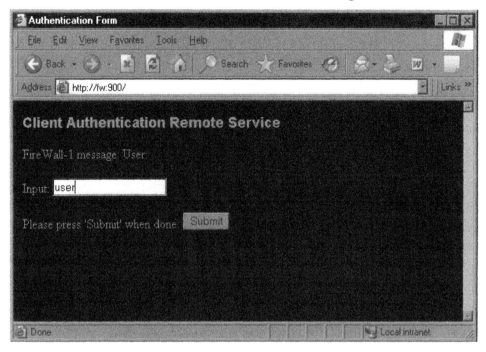

Figure 4.33 HTTP Manual Client Authentication: Entering the Password

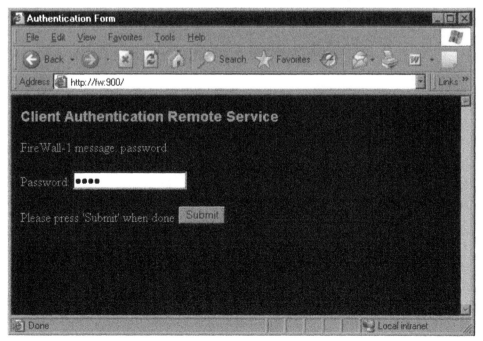

Figure 4.34 HTTP Manual Client Authentication: Selecting the Sign-On

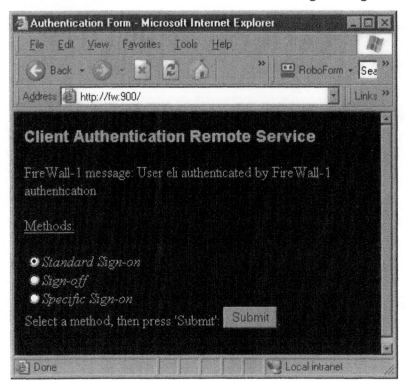

Figure 4.35 HTTP: Manual Client Authentication: Specific Sign-On

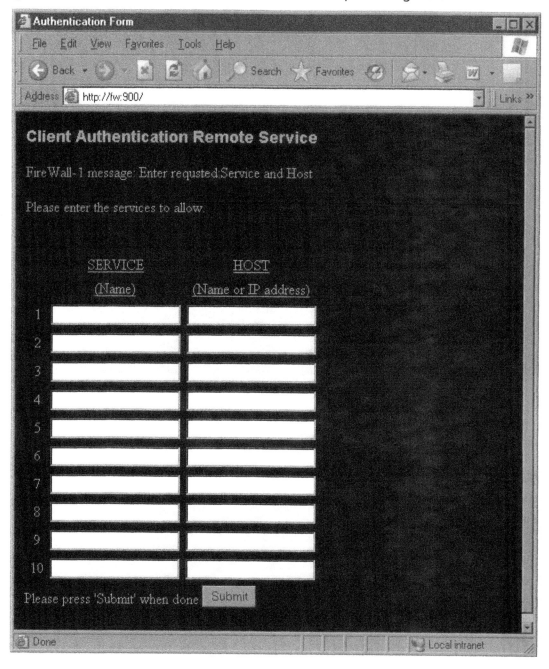

Figure 4.36 HTTP Manual Client Authentication: Successful Sign-On

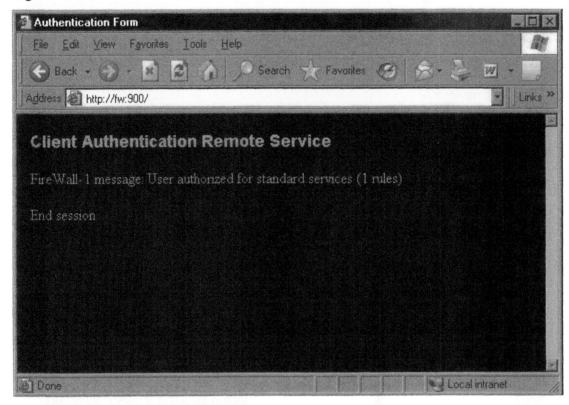

If you want to telnet to port 259, see Figures 4.37 through 4.40.

Figure 4.37 Telnet Manual Client Authentication: Standard Sign-On

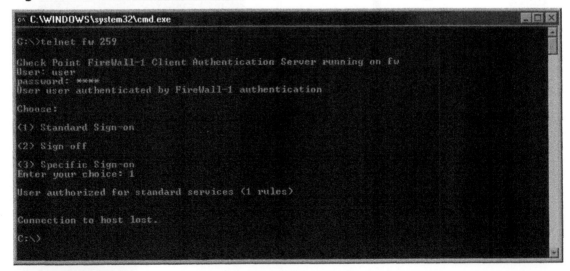

Figure 4.38 Telnet Manual Client Authentication: Specific Sign-On

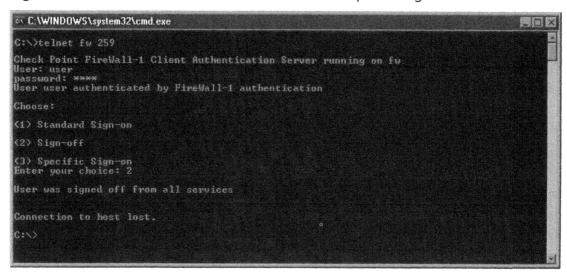

Figure 4.39 Telnet Manual Client Authentication: Sign-Off

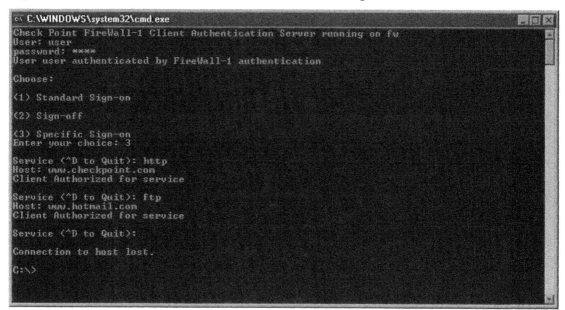

Partially Automatic Sign-On

With partially automatic authentication, if a user tries to access a resource for which he could authenticate using any of the authenticated services (HTTP, FTP, Telnet, or rlogin), the firewall will intercept the connection and request authentication from the user, as it would do with user authentication. Manual authentication may still be used.

Once the user enters the username and password, the firewall interprets the authentication as though it had been manually entered to the firewall, as in client authentication. This is extremely useful, because now users will be required to authenticate only once and can use any resource that the rulebase allows them to. Partially automatic authentication is one of the most used methods of authentication. One thing to keep in mind is that as with user authentication, it can be easy for an intruder sniffing the network to decipher usernames and passwords.

Fully Automatic Sign-On

With fully automatic authentication, you further extend the ways the firewall can request authentication from the user. If an authenticated service is used, the firewall intercepts the traffic and requests authentication, as in user authentication. For other services, it will try to invoke session authentication to authenticate the user at the connecting machine. Manual authentication may still be used.

Agent Automatic Sign-On

With agent automatic authentication, the firewall will try to authenticate connections only using the Session Authentication Agent at the connecting machine. Manual authentication may still be used.

Single Sign-On

If you select Single Sign-On, the firewall will try to contact a User Authority server to query the identity of the user logged in at the station. You need to have a User Authority system installed.

General | Successful Authentication Tracking

Here you can select whether you want information or alerts sent to the log when a user successfully authenticates. If you select **Alert** it will also write the information to the log.

Figure 4.40 Configuring Client Authentication Limit Properties

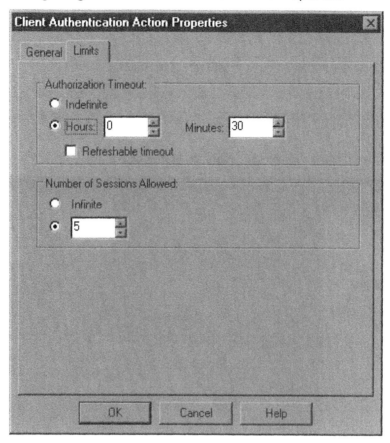

Limits | Authorization Timeout

Here you can select how long the user authorization will last. Select **Indefinite** to require an explicit sign-off from the user (via HTTP to port 900 or Telnet to port 259) to cancel the authorization. Select a specific time limit, in **Hours** and **Minutes**, if you want to require reauthentication after a time has lapsed. Select **Refreshable timeout** if you want the user to not be required to reauthenticate as long as the connection is being used. This is useful in that if a user leaves his machine, someone else can't sit down and use it.

Limits | Number of Sessions Allowed

This limits the number of open connections an authenticated user can make through the firewall. If you're using FTP, Telnet, or rlogin connections, you could limit the number of sessions through here. However, if you're using HTTP connections, you will need to select **Infinite** sessions because a browser will normally open many sessions.

Advanced Topics

Now let's discuss a few advanced topics.

Check Point Gateway | Authentication

There are some properties that you need to configure and verify per gateway, to fine-tune the authentication experience for your users, as in Figure 4.41.

Figure 4.41 Check Point Gateway | Authentication

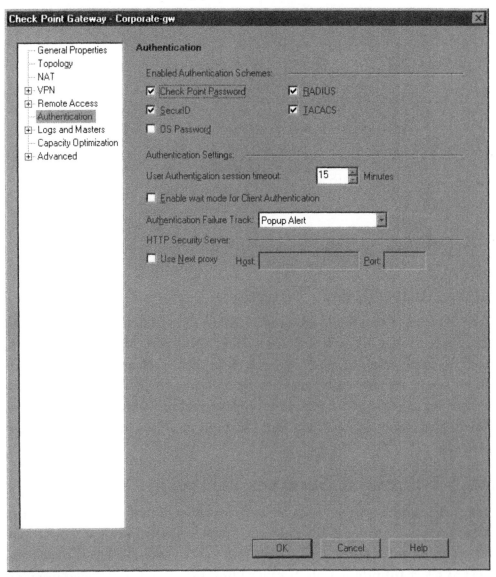

Enabled Authentication Schemes

It is very important that you select which Authentication Schemes the gateway will allow for its users. If a user authenticates with a scheme that the gateway does not accept, the user will not be granted access to resources on the gateway. You can select **Check Point Password** (previously VPN-1/Firewall-1 Password), **SecurID**, **OS Password**, **RADIUS**, or **TACACS**.

Authentication Settings

Here are brief descriptions of three authentication settings:

- **User Authentication session timeout** This setting (by default, 15 minutes) has two behaviors. For FTP and Telnet connections, connections with no activity are terminated after the timeout expires. For HTTP, it applies to the use of one-time passwords (i.e., SecurID tokens). Although the timeout hasn't expired, the server will not request another one-time password for access to a previously authenticated server.

- **Enable wait mode for Client Authentication** This setting applies to Telnet client authentication, whereby the Telnet session remains open, and when the user closes the session (by pressing **Ctrl+C** or through some other manner), the authentication expires. If this option is not selected, the user will have to manually sign off or wait for the session timeout.

- **Authentication Failure Track** Here you can define whether a failed authentication will generate an alert, a log, or no activity. We recommend that you at least log all failed authentications.

HTTP Security Server

If you use an HTTP Security Server, you can configure an HTTP Proxy Server behind the Security Server. Enter the host and port for the proxy server to activate it.

Global Properties | Authentication

Certain properties are configured globally for all authentication performed by the Check Point gateways. Appropriately enough, you access them from the **Global Properties | Authentication** tab, as in Figure 4.42.

Figure 4.42 Global Properties | Authentication

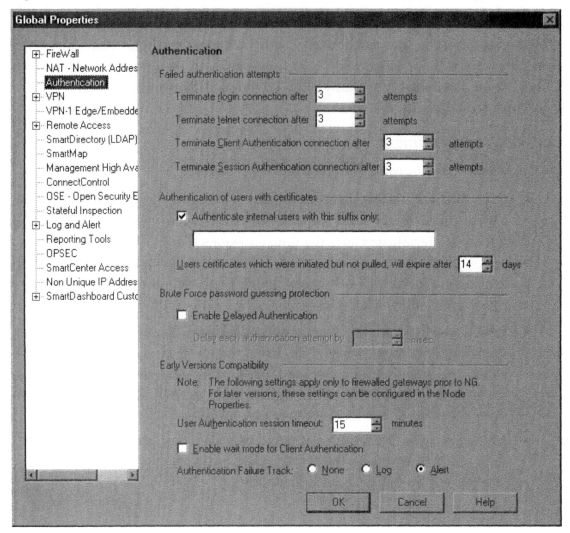

Failed Authentication Attempts

To prevent an intruder from brute-force-guessing your passwords, you can use the **Failed authentication attempts** setting to terminate connections after a set number of failed attempts (i.e., wrong passwords). You can set a different number of allowed tries for rlogin, Telnet, client authentication, and session authentication connections.

Authentication of Users with Certificates

For Remote Access VPNs, if you are using VPNs, you can restrict the gateway to accept only those users that have a specific suffix in their certificates. Also, if an administrator *initializes* a certificate in the Certificate Authority, you can define for how many additional days users can pull that certificate before it expires.

Brute Force Password-Guessing Protection

To prevent an intruder from brute-force-guessing your passwords, you can enable this protection, which is new for NGX. By setting a specific number of milliseconds to delay each authentication, you can dramatically affect any automatic password-guessing system, and a user will barely notice a difference.

Early Versions Compatibility

If you are managing gateways prior to NG, you can apply the following setting globally. For NG or later gateways, these settings are set per gateway. By the way, because you don't have an option to administer pre-NG gateways in NGX, you can probably ignore this section.

Registry Settings

Now we'll discuss registry settings.

New Interface

The default client authentication HTTP interface requires four pages for a successful login: the username page, password page, method page, and optional specific sign-on page. If you enable the *hclient_enable_new_interface* setting by selecting **Policy Menu | Global Properties | SmartDashboard Customization | Firewall-1 | Authentication | Client Authentication | HTTP**, the HTTP interface will combine the username and password pages into one, and will streamline the user experience, as in Figure 4.43.

Figure 4.43 Client Authentication HTTP New Interface

Use Host Header As Destination

If you're using partially or fully automatic sign-on with HTTP connections, once the connection is authenticated the firewall needs to redirect the original query to the intended destination. It does so by looking up the original URL's IP address and redirecting the user's browser to that IP. However, if the firewall resolves the destination URL to a nonroutable IP (i.e., the non-NATed IP), or if the Web server is configured to need the host header for access (i.e., a Web hosting service that shares one IP with multiple Web pages), the connection will fail. To avoid this, enable the *http_use_host_h_ as _dst* setting by selecting **Policy Menu | Global Properties | SmartDashboard Customization | Firewall-1 | Web Security | HTTP Protocol**.

Opening All Client Authentication Rules

When you begin to create a complex policy with different rules for granting user access to different resources, you need to consider the fact that the default behavior for client authentication is to grant access only for the rule where you authenticated. If you need to authenticate once and be granted access by all rules that would permit the user, you have to enable the *automatically_open_ca_rules* setting by selecting **Policy Menu | Global Properties | SmartDashboard Customization | Firewall-1 | Authentication | Client Authentication**.

Configuration Files

Now we'll discuss configuration files.

Enabling Encrypted Authentication

Because Telnet and HTTP are not encrypted, client authentication is inherently less secure than session authentication. However, you can configure NGX to enable HTTPS manual authentication, which will give you the encryption you want when using the built-in HTTP server at port 900 for authentication. See the "Are You 0wned?" sidebar for details.

Are You Owned?

Securing Client Authentication

Although client authentication is a great tool, is flexible, and is easy to understand, you have to be aware of its security implications. When you enable client authentication and place the rule above the Stealth rule, you're opening ports 259 and 900 to the firewall. Remember that neither of these services is encrypted, so you're vulnerable to sniffing attacks. Never allow client authentication from *any* sources, as it's easy for a scanner to detect these ports running on your firewall and try to brute-force a username and password combination (use the NGX Brute Force Protection feature to minimize this).

It's a good idea to change the HTTP server on port 900 to an encrypted HTTPS server, and to disable Telnet authentication to port 259. Edit the $FWDIR/conf/fwauthd.conf file and change this line:

```
900     fwssd   in.ahclientd   wait   900
```

Continued

to this:

900   fwssd   in.ahclientd   wait   900   ssl:defaultCert

Then eliminate the following line:

259   fwssd   in.aclientd   wait   259

You could also change the default 900 and 259 ports to other port numbers, and edit the fw1_clnauth_http and fw1_clnauth_telnet services to reflect the new ports.

Custom Pages

If you plan to use client authentication's HTTP interface, you will probably want to change its appearance and include your company's logo, an unauthorized use warning, and some nice graphics. You can do this by editing the HTML files in the $FWDIR/conf/ahclientd directory. Remember to leave the % commands intact, as NGX uses them to insert the information it needs.

Summary

Many security rulebases do not need individual user rights, and they work with hosts, gateways, networks, groups, ranges, and servers. However, for both security and tracking purposes, you might need to integrate authentication with your security policy. You'll be able to identify users' navigation, and grant privileged users access to restricted resources or connections with specific services.

You have a choice of how to recognize a user: by accessing external directory servers with RADIUS or TACACS, or by using the internal user database. You can integrate with Microsoft Active Directory through the Microsoft Internet Authentication Service, or get the SmartDirectory license for LDAP integration.

You can choose among user, client, and session authentication, depending on your needs and a balance of security, ease of use, and flexibility. User authentication is easy to use and is transparent, but it is not flexible, has no security, and can be cumbersome for accessing external Web sites. Client authentication is flexible and can be secure, but it is not transparent to the user and it is less secure than other methods. Session authentication is flexible, secure, and easy to use, but installing the agent on each machine will be something you have to consider.

Check Point NGX gives you many options. You just have to choose which to implement.

Solutions Fast Track

Authentication Overview

☑ With authentication you can grant specific permissions to groups of users that might have different IPs and might be moving around different computers.

☑ Users in DHCP environments are suitable for implementing authentication, as well as roaming administrators that need to access special files.

☑ Authentication rules have to be placed carefully so that a nonauthentication rule does not override the need for a user to authenticate.

Users and Administrators

☑ Several schemes are available to authenticate users, from both the internal database and external directories such as RADIUS, TACACS, LDAP, and SecurID.

☑ Administrators are created in the SmartDashboard and assign Permissions Profiles to limit their actions within the configuration applications.

☑ Users are created based on templates, and should be placed in groups to be integrated with the rulebase.

SmartDirectory

☑ SmartDirectory is Check Point's LDAP implementation, which allows connections to external user databases such as Microsoft Active Directory.

☑ SmartDirectory requires the creation of an LDAP Account Unit, which can connect to multiple LDAP servers. The LDAP Account Unit is used for creating LDAP user groups.

☑ Within the LDAP Account Unit, you can select a user template that will be applied to LDAP authenticated users when the LDAP schema has not been extended to include Check Point fields.

User Authentication

☑ User authentication is transparent to the user and doesn't require configuration of client machines.

☑ Only the four authenticated services—HTTP, FTP, Telnet, and rlogin—can work with user authentication.

☑ User-authenticated HTTP access to the Internet will require users to authenticate multiple times for a single Web page.

Session Authentication

☑ Session authentication can authenticate each session from the client, and can have encryption enabled for security.

☑ Session authentication requires a Session Authentication Agent installed in the authorizing machine.

Client Authentication

☑ Client authentication works with any defined service available.

☑ Manual authentication is performed by an HTTP connection to port 900 or by a telnet to port 259.

☑ Other sign-on methods integrate user, session, and SSO authentication into client authentication.

Frequently Asked Questions

Q: How can I enter a single user in a rule instead of a group?

A: You can only enter groups in a rule. However, you can create a group that contains only one user.

Q: Can I use Check Point NGX as a Web proxy?

A: Yes, you can. However, NGX is not a cache and the connections using NGX as a proxy will go through the HTTP Security Server, which carries a performance penalty.

Q: Which authentication should I use?

A: For HTTP intranet access, try user authentication. For accessing the Internet, try encrypted manual client authentication. Try redirecting nonallowed traffic to the client authentication page using a resource. The answer will depend on your needs and your security policy.

Q: We came back from our New Year's celebration and no one could authenticate to the firewall. What can I do?

A: Check the expiration date of the users.

Q: We need to authenticate our users in Active Directory, but we have a strict separation of duties between the security administrators and the user manager. How do we maintain this strict separation?

A: Use a template for applying settings to the LDAP users. In the LDAP Account Unit, access the LDAP server with a read-only user. This setup will be able to authenticate with the LDAP password, but it won't modify any of the LDAP data.

Q: We want to limit LDAP users that can authenticate to VPN-1. They are not within a particular group, but they have a common field in the LDAP database. How can we limit the authentication to these users?

A: Create an LDAP group, set the scope as all the users in the Account Unit, and apply a filter to create a dynamic group based on the common field.

Q: I would like to give external access to an internal Web site. What authentication method should I use?

A: Try user authentication, because you have a controlled environment (your Web site) and you should authenticate every session, for increased security.

Chapter 5

Advanced VPN Concepts and Tunnel Monitoring

Solutions in this chapter:

- Encryption Overview
- VPN Communities
- Policy-Based VPN
- Route-Based VPN

☑ Summary

☑ Solutions Fast Track

☑ Frequently Asked Questions

Introduction

VPNs (virtual private networks) have emerged as a technology due to their ability to leverage an organization's existing infrastructure (including the Internet) to both create and augment existing communication links securely. Checkpoint VPNs are based on standard secure protocols defined in the Internet RFCs. This enables the creation of secure links between selected categories of network nodes such as the VPN-1 Power module. VPN implementations may be created as site-to -site VPNs to ensure secure links between gateways, or as remote access VPNs to ensure that the links between gateways and remote access clients are secured.

Check Point's VPN-1 Power is an integrated software solution that provides secure connectivity to corporate networks, remote and mobile users, branch offices and business partners on a wide range of open platforms and security appliances.

VPN-1 Power is composed of:

- VPN endpoints, including gateways, gateway clusters, and remote client software for mobile systems. These are the systems that negotiate the VPN link parameters.

- VPN trust entities such as the CheckPoint Internal Certificate Authority (ICA). ICA is a component of the VPN-1 Power suite and it is used in order to establish trust between SIC connections. It supports deployment from gateways, authenticating administrators, and third-entity servers. ICA supplies certificates for both internal gateways and remote access clients involved in the negotiation of a VPN link.

- VPN management tools such as SmartCenter Server and SmartDashboard make the implementation of VPNs using CheckPoint products relatively simple. SmartDashboard is the console used to manage the SmartCenter Server Management module. The SmartDashboard module includes the VPN Manager giving administrators the capability to define and deploy intranet and remote access VPNs across their organization.

Encryption Overview

Symmetric cryptographic systems use the same key for the encryption and decryption of data between the entities that are communicating. The material used to construct these keys needs to be exchanged securely. Information can be exchanged in a secure manner only if the key is held and used solely by the communicating entities and no other.

Internet Key Exchange (IKE) is used to allow both entities to produce the same symmetric key in parallel. The symmetric key then encrypts and decrypts the accepted IP packets that make up the bulk transfer of data between the VPN-1 Power peers. IKE constructs a VPN tunnel between the peers by authenticating the systems on both sides of the VPN tunnel and reaching an agreement on the encryption and integrity scheme to be used. A successful IKE negotiation results in a security association (SA) between the systems.

The accord resulting from exchanging keys and encryption methods needs to be performed in a secure manner. As such, IKE is comprised of two phases. IKE Phase I puts down the practicalities required for the second phase. Diffie-Hellman (DH) is used by the IKE protocol to exchange the material that the systems use to construct the symmetric keys. The Diffie-Hellman algorithm constructs an encryption key known as a "shared secret" from the private key of one entity and the public key of the system. Since the symmetric keys used in IPSec are derived from the DH key that is shared between the VPN peers, the symmetric keys are never in point of fact exchanged over the network.

IKE Overview

The IKE suite of protocols permits a pair of security gateways to:

- Dynamically establish a secure tunnel through which the security gateways are able to exchange tunnel and key information.

- Assemble user-level tunnels or Security Associations (SAs) that incorporate tunnel attribute negotiations and key management. SAs are able to be refreshed or concluded utilizing the same secure channel.

IKE is founded on the Oakley and SKEME key determination protocols. The ISAKMP framework for key exchange and security association establishment is used by VPN-1 and implemented by IKE to provide:

- Automatic key refreshment using a configurable timeout

- Support for public key infrastructure (PKI) authentication systems

- Anti-replay defense

IKE utilizes UDP port 500 to exchange IKE data across the security gateways. UDP port 500 packets are required to be permitted through any IP interface concerned in the connection of a security gateway peer.

Main Mode and Aggressive Mode

IKE Phase I negotiations are implemented in order to establish IKE SAs. The SAs shield the IKE phase II negotiations from an eavesdropping attack. IKE implements one of two possible modes in phase I negotiations, either main mode or aggressive mode. The selection of main or aggressive mode is a subject of substituting costs and benefits in either case. The primary makeup of the two modes is:

- Main mode
    - Is more secure because it protects the identities of the peers during negotiations
    - Provides superior proposal flexibility with more options than aggressive mode
    - Uses more resources and takes more time than aggressive mode because a greater number of messages are exchanged between peers
    - Exchanges six messages
- Aggressive mode
    - Exposes identities of the peers to eavesdropping, making it less secure than main mode
    - Is quicker than main mode because a smaller number of messages need to be exchanged between peers
    - Exchanges three messages

Renegotiating IKE and IPSec Lifetimes

IKE phase I uses more resources (especially the processor) than IKE phase II. In phase I, the Diffie-Hellman keys need to be created and the peers need to authenticate each time the setup occurs. As a consequence, IKE phase I is carried out less regularly than phase II. The IKE SA remains valid for only a definite period, following which the IKE SA needs to be renegotiated. An IPSec SA is legitimate for an even smaller period than phase I. As a result, numerous IKE phase II exchanges take place for each phase I exchange.

The timeframe between each IKE renegotiation is known as the lifetime. In most cases, a shorter lifetime will result in a more secure IPSec tunnel. The trade-off is that the cost associated with the amount of processor intensive IKE negotiations is greater. By using a longer IKE lifetime, VPN connections may be brought up quicker. IKE phase I occurs once a day by default; IKE phase II occurs every hour by default (the time-out for each phase is configurable and may be changed). The IPSec lifetime is configurable based on the number of kilobytes that are transmitted using DBedit to edit the objects_5_0.c file. The pertinent properties are included within the community set:

- ike_p2_use_rekey_kbytes. Change from false (default) to true.

- ike_p2_rekey_kbytes. Modify to include the required rekeying value (default 50,000).

Perfect Forward Secrecy

The keys produced by peers during IKE phase II and used by IPSec are formulated from a series of random binary digits. These are exchanged among peers and are based on the DH key computed during IKE phase I negotiations.

The DH key is calculated once. This is then used multiple times by the IKE phase II negotiations. Because the keys that are used during IKE phase II are derived from the DH key calculated within the IKE phase I negotiations, a mathematical association is created between the DH keys. Consequently, reusing a single DH key will deteriorate the strength of any subsequent keys that are exchanged. This means that the compromise of a single key will make the compromise of all subsequent keys easier.

Perfect Forward Secrecy (PFS) covers the situation where the compromise of a current session key or long-term private key will not result in a compromise of previous or successive keys in cryptography. VPN-1 Power supports PFS with a PFS mode. Enabling PFS will result in a fresh DH key being constructed for the period of an IKE phase II negotiation, and being renewed for every subsequent key exchange. Since a new DH key is constructed for the duration of each IKE phase I negotiation, no dependency exists between these keys and those produced in subsequent IKE phase I negotiations.

Checkpoint recommends that you permit PFS in IKE phase II only in cases where the security requirements are large due to the increased overhead and latency. The DH group employed throughout PFS mode is configurable among groups 1, 2, 5, and 14, with group 2 (1042 bits) set as the default.

IP Compression

IP compression is a process that decreases the size of the data segment of the TCP/IP packet. This reduction can significantly improve performance on a VPN-1 device. IPSec as implemented in VPN-1 provides support for the Inflate/Deflate IP compression algorithm. Deflate is an elegant algorithm that adjusts how the compression of data is conducted based on the data contents. The choice of using IP compression is negotiated as a part of the IKE phase II negotiations. Although it can improve the efficiency of the VPN tunnel, IP compression is not enabled by default.

IP compression is essential for systems that use SecuRemote and SecureClient across with slow or high latency network links such as dialup modems. It can add compression in order to make the link seem faster. VPN-1 Power encryption scrambles TCP/IP packets in an irregular manner. The result is that encrypted data cannot be compressed and consequently bandwidth is reduced. Where IP compression is enabled, VPN-1 will compress the packets ahead of encryption. This effectively recovers the reduced bandwidth that can result from encryption.

IKE DoS Attacks

The IKE protocol necessitates that the receiving gateway allocate memory from the initial IKE phase I request packet that is received. The gateway replies, and accepts an additional packet, which is subsequently processed using the information collected from the initial packet.

An attacker can transmit numerous IKE initial packets that have a forged and invalid source IP address for each packet. The receiving gateway is required to reply to each of these packets, assigning memory for each new initial packet. This can devour all resources of the CPU preventing additional connections from being allocated to legitimate users.

The attacker transferring IKE packets can spoof a host that is permitted to initiate IKE negotiations. This is referred to as an identified source. The attacker can also spoof an IP address that is unknown to the receiving gateway (such as a SecuRemote or SecureClient, or VPN-1 Power gateway that uses a dynamic IP address). This is referred to as an unidentified source.

IKE Phase I

During IKE phase I:

- The peers authenticate using either certificates or via a preshared secret. Other authentication methods are accessible if one of the peers is a remote access client.

- A Diffie-Hellman key is produced. The makeup of the Diffie-Hellman protocol results in each peer being able to autonomously create the shared secret. The shared secret is a key that is known only to the peers in the negotiation.

- *Key material*, which is composed of random bits and other mathematical data, is sent with a concurrence between the peers as to the methods that the IKE phase II negotiation will use, which are exchanged among the peers.

The generation of the Diffie Hellman Key is slow and uses a lot of resources, causing degradation in performance. The result of IKE phase I is an IKE SA. This is an agreement on keys and methods that will be used in IKE phase II. Figure 5.1 illustrates the process that occurs throughout IKE phase I. It does not inevitably reproduce the actual order of events due to a variety of real-world occurrences (such as packet loss and retransmits).

Figure 5.1 IKE Phase I (IKE Gateway Exchange)

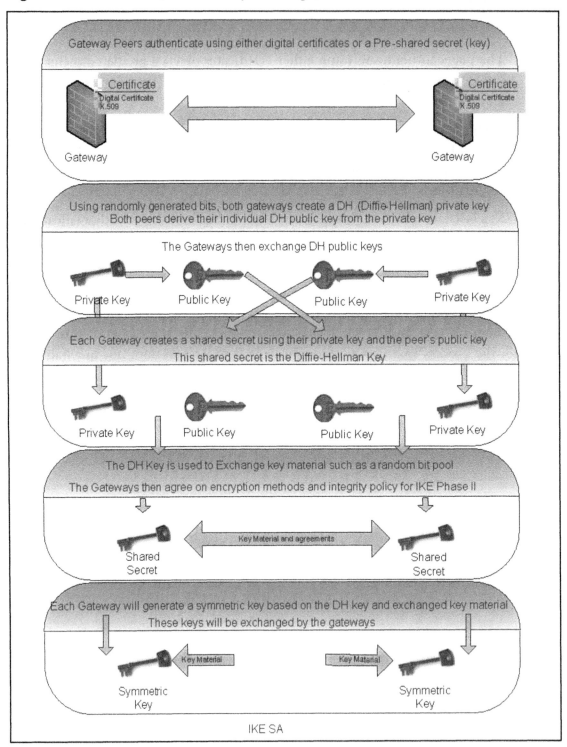

IPSEC Phase II

IKE phase II is encrypted based on the keys and methods agreed upon during the IKE phase I negotiation. The key material exchanged through IKE phase II is used for constructing the IPSec keys. The conclusion of phase II negotiations results is the IPSec Security Association (SA) being created. The IPSec SA is an agreement on the keys to be used and methods that are to be implemented in the IPSec communications. IPSec takes place based on the keys and methods agreed upon in the IKE phase II negotiations (see Figure 5.2).

Once the IPSec keys have been produced and exchanged by the gateways, the systems can begin the transfer of encrypted data (see Figure 5.3).

Figure 5.2 IKE Phase II Negotiations

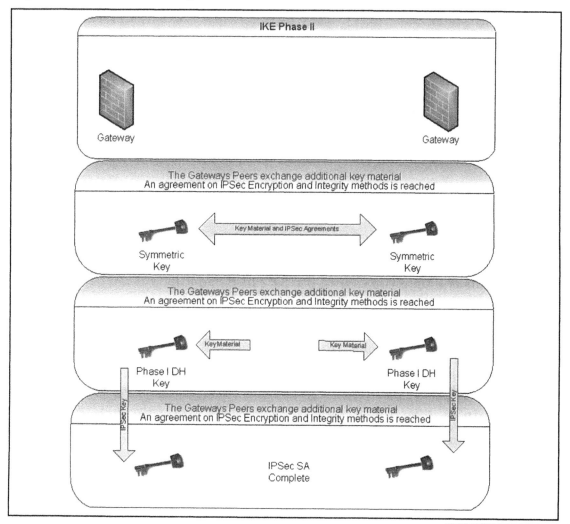

Figure 5.3 IPSec and the VPN Tunnel

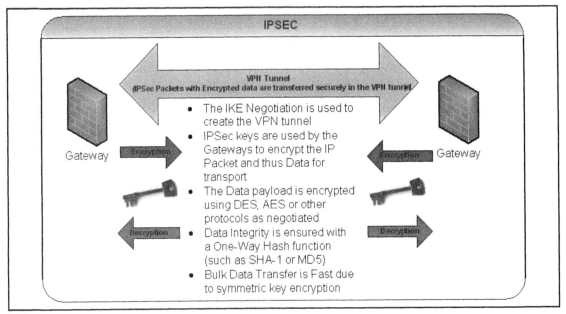

Configuring Advanced IKE Properties

IKE is configured in two places:

- On the VPN community network object (for IKE properties)
- On the gateway network object (for subnet key exchange).

1. On the VPN Community Network Object VPN Properties page, select:

   - Encryption methods used by IKE phase I and II
   - Integrity methods used by IKE phase I and II

2. On the Advanced Settings > Advanced VPN Properties page, select:

   - The Diffie-Hellman group to use
   - How often to renegotiate the IKE Security Associations
   - Whether the system will use aggressive mode (the default is to use Main mode)
   - Whether Perfect Forward Secrecy will be used, and which Diffie-Hellman group would require it.

- The frequency at which the IPSec security associations are to be renegotiated

- The option to use Support IP compression

3. On the Gateway Network Object

4. On the VPN Advanced page, deselect Support Key exchange for subnets if the SA is to be calculated for each host or peer. The option to support key exchange for subnets is the default.

IKE Policies

The IKE policy defines the combination of security parameters that are to be used during the IKE SA negotiation. IKE policies are configured on the communicating security gateway peers with the requirement that there has to be at minimum one policy on the local peer that matches at least one policy on the remote peer. If this is not the case the two peers are not able to negotiate an IKE SA successfully. Without an IKE SA no data transfer can occur between the peers.

IKE policies are global to the system. Each IPSec tunnel uses the same set of policies when negotiating IKE SAs. The agreed-on IKE SA between the local system and a remote security gateway may fluctuate due to a dependence on the IKE policies used by each remote peer. The initial set of IKE policies the peer uses is always the same and independent of the peer with which the VPN-1 system is negotiating.

During negotiation, VPN-1 may skip IKE policies that require parameters that are not configured or available for the remote security gateway with which the IKE SA is being negotiated.

It is possible to define multiple IKE policies, with each policy having a different combination of security parameters. A default IKE policy that contains default values for every policy parameter is possible. This policy is used only when IKE policies are not configured and IKE is required.

The following sections describe each of the parameters contained in an IKE policy.

Priority

Priority allows more secure policies to be given preference throughout the negotiation process. During IKE negotiation all policies are scanned, one at a time, starting from the highest priority policy and ending with the lowest priority policy. The first policy that the peer security gateway accepts is used for that IKE session. This procedure is repeated for every IKE session that needs to be established.

Encryption

A specific encryption transform can be applied to each IKE policy.

Hash Function

An individual hash function can be specified for an IKE policy.

IKE also uses an authentication algorithm during IKE exchanges. This authentication algorithm is automatically set to the HMAC version of the specified hash algorithm. Therefore, you cannot have the hash function set to MD5 and authentication algorithm set to HMAC-SHA.

Authentication Mode

As part of the IKE protocol, one security gateway needs to authenticate the other security gateway to make sure that the IKE SA is established with the intended entity.

Digital Certificates (Using RSA Algorithms)

For digital certificate authentication, an initiator signs message interchange data using his private key and a responder uses the initiator's public key to verify this signature. Classically, the public key is exchanged via messages containing an X.509v3 certificate that provides a level of assurance that the peer's identity as represented in the certificate is associated with a particular public key.

Preshared Keys

With preshared key authentication mode, the same secret string needs to be configured on both security gateways before the gateways can authenticate each other. It is not advisable to share a preshared key among multiple pairs of security gateways as this will reduce the security level of all gateways using this key.

Diffie-Hellman Group

An IKE policy must specify which Diffie-Hellmann group is to be used during the symmetric key generation phase of IKE.

Lifetime

Similar to a user SA, an IKE SA does not (and should not) last ad infinitum. Consequently, VPN-1 gives the capability to specify a lifetime parameter for an IKE policy. The timer for the lifetime parameter begins when the IKE SA is established using IKE.

IKE SA Negotiation

As the initiator of an IKE SA, VPN-1 sends its IKE policies to the remote peer. If the peer has an IKE policy that matches the encryption, hash, authentication method, and Diffie-Hellmann group settings, the peer returns the matching policy. The peers use the lesser lifetime setting as the IKE SA lifetime. In the event that no match is established, the IKE SA will not succeed, and a log entry is constructed.

When acting as the responder to an IKE negotiation, VPN-1 receives all IKE policies from the remote security gateway. VPN-1 will then examine its own list of IKE policies to confirm whether a matching policy is present, beginning from the highest priority down. If it finds a match, that policy can be successfully negotiated. The SA lifetime is negotiated to the lesser of the two lifetimes, and failures are logged.

VPN Communities

Creating VPN tunnels between gateways is simplified using the configuration of the VPN communities feature. A VPN community is a collection of VPN-enabled gateways and peers that are able to communicate using a VPN tunnel. In order to understand VPN communities, several terms need to be defined:

- **VPN community member** refers to the gateway that resides at one end of a VPN tunnel (see Figure 5.4).

- **VPN domain** refers to the hosts behind the gateway. The VPN domain can be the entire network that lies within the protected segment of the gateway or just a segment of that network.

- **VPN site** includes the community member plus VPN domain; an archetypal VPN site would be the branch office of a corporation with multiple locations.

- **VPN community** refers to the collection of VPN tunnels/links and their attributes.

- **Domain-based VPN** covers the process of routing VPN traffic based on the encryption domain behind each gateway in the community. A star community permits satellite gateways to communicate with all others through center gateways.

- **Route-based VPN** occurs when traffic is routed within the VPN community based on the static or dynamic routing information that is configured on the operating systems of the gateways.

Figure 5.4 Terminology Used with Checkpoint VPNs

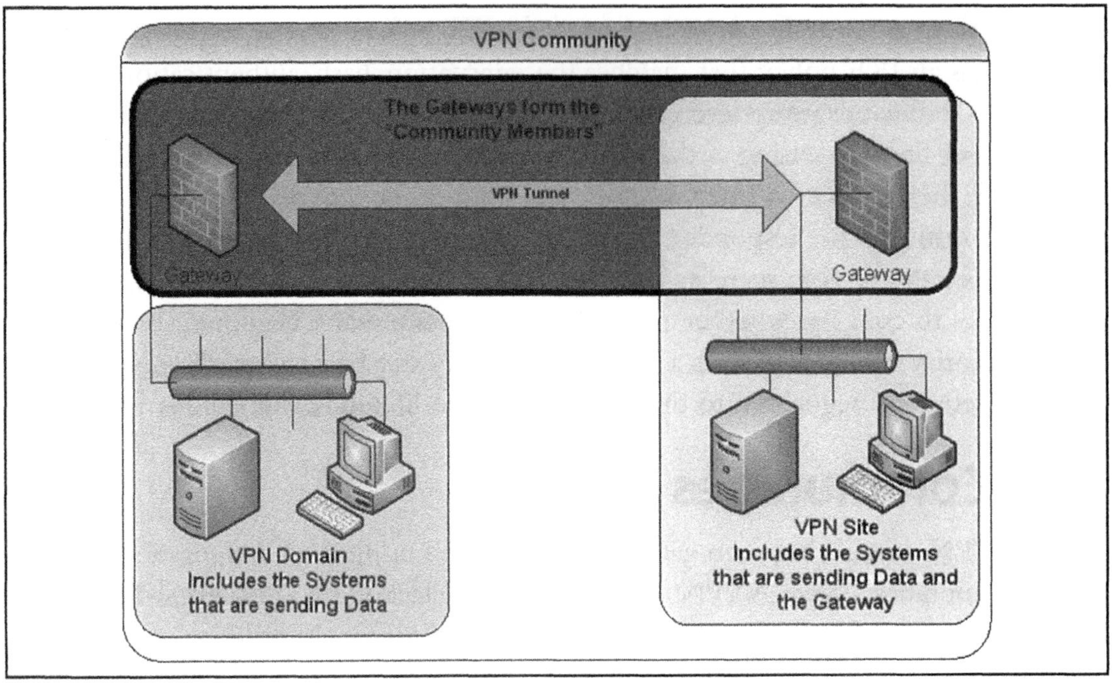

A Checkpoint SmartCenter Server can manage multiple VPN communities allowing communities to be created and organized according to their particular needs.

Remote Access Community

A Remote Access Community is a category of VPN community created particularly for users that typically work from remote locations, defined as those places that are outside of the corporate LAN. These kinds of community make certain secure communication occurs between users and the corporate LAN.

REMOTE ACCESS COMMUNITY CHANGES

Defining services in the clear in the community (available in gateway-to-gateway communities) is not supported if one of the internally managed members is an earlier version than NG FP3.

Mesh Topology

A mesh topography is a VPN community in which a VPN site can construct a VPN tunnel with any other VPN site in the community (see Figure 5.5).

Figure 5.5 Checkpoint VPN-1 Basic Mesh Community

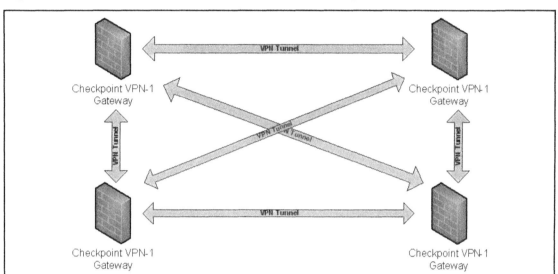

Star Topology

A star topography is a VPN community consisting of central or hubs gateways that are connected with satellite or spokes gateways (see Figure 5.6). A satellite system can create a tunnel only with other sites whose gateways are defined as central in this kind of community.

Figure 5.6 Checkpoint VPN-1 Star VPN Community

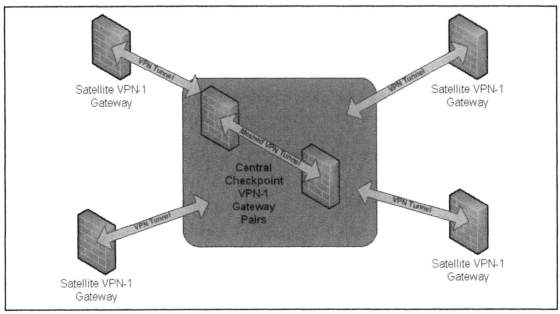

A satellite gateway is unable to generate a VPN tunnel with a gateway that is also defined as a satellite gateway. Central gateways can generate VPN tunnels with other central gateways only if the Mesh Center Gateways option has been selected on the Central Gateways tab for the Star Community Properties window on the VPN-1 Policy.

VPN Routing

VPN routing connections are subject to the equivalent access control rules as any other connection. When VPN routing is appropriately configured but a Security Policy rule is also configured to not allow the connection, the connection will be dropped by VPN-1. For instance, if a gateway has a rule set to reject all SMTP traffic from inside the internal network to a network exterior to the VPN-1 host, if a peer gateway opens an SMTP connection on the blocked network with this gateway, the connection is still rejected.

If VPN routing is to be successful, at least one rule in the Security Policy rule base must cover traffic in both directions, inbound and outbound, and on the central gateway.

In order to be able to route traffic to a host behind a gateway, an encryption domain must be configured for that gateway. The configuration for VPN routing is executed either directly through SmartDashboard or by editing the VPN routing configuration files on the gateways.

VPN routing cannot be configured between gateways that are not contained within a VPN community.

Configuring VPN Routing for Gateways via SmartDashboard

For uncomplicated hub or spoke networks and in circumstances where there is only a single hub, the easiest method is to configure a VPN star community in SmartDashboard (see Figure 5.7). The following steps demonstrate how this is done:

1. On the Star Community properties window, Central Gateways page, select the gateway that is to function as the hub.

2. On the Satellite Gateways page, select gateways as the spokes, or satellites.

Figure 5.7 Configuring a Satellite Community Using a Star Topography

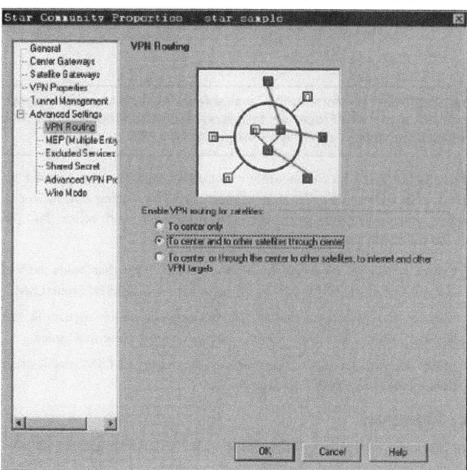

3. On the VPN Routing page, select the Enable VPN routing for satellites option and then select one of the following options:

- To center and to other satellites through center. This allows connectivity between the gateways, for example if the spoke gateways are DAIP gateways, and the hub is a gateway with a static IP address.

- To center, or through the center to other satellites, to Internet and other VPN targets. This allows connectivity between the gateways as well as the ability to inspect all communication passing through the Hub to the Internet.

4. Create a suitable access control rule in the Security Policy Rule Base remembering that one rule must cover traffic in both directions.

5. NAT the satellite gateways on the hub if the hub is used to route connections from satellites to the Internet.

> **NOTE**
>
> Disabling NAT in the community (available in Star and Meshed communities in the Advanced VPN Properties tab) is not supported if one of the internally managed members is an earlier version than NG FP3.

The two DAIP gateways can securely route communication through the gateway with the static IP address. In order to configure the VPN routing option to center and to other satellites through center with remote office branch office (RO_BO) gateways the following steps must be completed:

1. Create a network object in the VPN-1 policy editor that holds the VPN domains of all the VPN-1 RO_BO gateways managed by SmartLSM.

2. Edit the vpn_route.conf file, so that this network object appears in the Router column. This is the center gateway of the star community.

3. Install the vpn_route.conf file that was created on all LSM profiles that participate in the VPN community.

Route Injection

A Route Injection Mechanism (RIM) enables a VPN-1 Power gateway to use dynamic routing protocols to disseminate the encryption domain of a VPN-1

Power peer gateway to the internal network and then instigate back connections. RIM updates the local routing table of the VPN-1 Power gateway to incorporate the encryption domain of the VPN-1 Power peer when a VPN tunnel is formed.

It is only possible to enable a RIM when permanent tunnels are configured for the community. Permanent tunnels are kept alive by tunnel test packets. This tunnel will be considered and marked as being down if it fails to reply to the test packet. Consequently, the RIM will delete the route to the failed link from the local routing table, triggering the neighboring dynamic routing enabled devices to update their routing information. This will redirect all traffic destined to travel across the VPN tunnel to a predefined alternative path.

There are two possible methods to configure RIM:

- **Automatic RIM**. RIM can automatically inject the route to the encryption domain of the peer gateways.

- **A Custom Script**. A script can be used to specify tasks that RIM will execute according to particular needs.

Route injection can be integrated with MEP functionality in order to route return packets back through the same MEP gateway. With SecurePlatform installed on the gateway or if the operating system is IPSO or Linux, automatic RIM can be enabled using the GUI. A custom script can be used on these systems but custom-written scripts are not required.

Permanent Tunnels

As companies have become more dependent on VPNs for communication to other sites, uninterrupted connectivity has become more crucial than ever before. Therefore it is essential to make sure that the VPN tunnels are kept up and running. Permanent tunnels are constantly kept active and as a result, make it easier to recognize malfunctions and connectivity problems. Administrators can monitor the two sides of a VPN tunnel and identify problems without delay.

Each VPN tunnel in the community may be set to be a Permanent tunnel. Since Permanent tunnels are constantly monitored, if the VPN tunnel is down, then a log, alert, or user-defined action can be issued. A VPN tunnel is monitored by periodically sending tunnel test packets. As long as responses to the packets are received the VPN tunnel is considered "up." If no response is received within a given time period, the VPN tunnel is considered "down." Permanent tunnels can be established only between

Check Point gateways. The configuration of Permanent tunnels takes place on the community level and can be specified for:

- An entire community. This option sets every VPN tunnel in the community as permanent.

- A specific gateway. Use this option to configure specific gateways to have permanent tunnels.

- A single VPN tunnel. This feature allows configuring specific tunnels between specific gateways as permanent.

Wire Mode

Wire Mode was intended to improve connectivity by permitting existing connections to fail over effectively by bypassing firewall enforcement. By definition, traffic within a VPN community is private and if correctly implemented, secure. In a lot of cases, the firewall and the rule on the firewall concerning VPN connections is redundant. The firewall can be bypassed by VPN connections by defining internal interfaces and communities as "trusted" using Wire Mode.

When a packet reaches a gateway, the gateway asks itself two questions about it:

- Is this information coming from a "trusted" source?

- Is this information going to a "trusted" destination?

If the answer to both questions is yes, the VPN-1 Stateful inspection will not be enforced at the gateway and the traffic between the trusted interfaces bypasses the firewall if the VPN community to which both gateways are associated is designated as Wire Mode enabled.

As stateful inspection does not occur, there is no possibility of packets being discarded. The VPN connection is no different from any other connection along a dedicated wire. This is the meaning of Wire Mode. With stateful inspection not being conducted, the dynamic routing protocols that do not endure state verification from a nonwire mode configuration may currently be deployed. Wire mode thus assists Route-based VPNs.

Consider a scenario where:

- Gateway M1 and gateway M2 are both *wire mode enabled* and have trusted internal interfaces

- The community where gateway M1 and gateway M2 reside is wire mode enabled

- Host 1 residing behind gateway S1 is communicating through a VPN tunnel with Host 2 residing behind gateway M1

- MEP is configured for gateway M1 and gateway M2 with gateway M1 being the primary gateway and gateway M2 as the backup

In this scenario, if the gateway M1 fails, the connection fails over to the gateway M2. Any packet leaving Host 2 will be redirected by the router behind gateway M1 to gateway M2 given that gateway M2 is designated as the backup gateway. Without wire mode, stateful inspection would be enforced at gateway M2 and the connection is dropped since packets that come into a gateway whose session was initiated through a different gateway are regarded by VPN-1 as out-of-state packets. Given that gateway M2's internal interface is "trusted," and wire mode in enabled on the community, no stateful inspection is executed and gateway M2 will successfully maintain the connection without losing any information.

Consider a scenario where:

- Wire mode is enabled on Center gateway C without an internal trusted interface being specified

- The community is wire mode enabled

- Host 1 is residing behind Satellite gateway A and wants to open a connection through a VPN tunnel with Host 2, which is located behind Satellite gateway B.

In a Satellite community, Center gateways are used to route traffic between Satellite gateways within the community.

In this scenario, traffic from the Satellite gateways is only rerouted by gateway C and cannot pass through gateway C's firewall. Consequently, stateful inspection does not need to take place at gateway C. Given that wire mode is enabled, making them trusted on the community and on gateway C, stateful inspection is bypassed. Stateful inspection does take place on gateways A and B in this example.

In an alternate scenario:

- Gateway A belongs to Community 1

- Gateway B belongs to Community 2

- Gateway C belongs to Communities 1 and 2

- Wire mode is enabled on Center gateway C set without an internal trusted interface being specified

- Wire mode is enabled on both communities

- Host 1 resides behind Satellite gateway A, which wants to open a connection through a VPN tunnel with Host 2, which is behind Satellite gateway B

Wire mode can be enabled for routing VPN traffic involving two gateways that are not members of the same community. Because Gateway C is a member of both communities, it hence recognizes both communities as trusted. When Host 1 behind gateway A commences a connection to Host 2 behind gateway B, gateway C is used to route traffic between the two communities. As the traffic is not in reality entering gateway C, there is no need for stateful inspection to occur at that gateway. Stateful inspection does take place on gateways A and B.

PKI Solutions

X.509-based PKI solutions present the infrastructure that enables organizations to establish trust relationships connecting each other based on their mutual trust of the Certificate Authority (CA). The trusted CA issues a certificate for an entity, which includes the entity's public key. Peer entities that trust the CA can trust the certificate since they can verify the CA's signature, and then can rely on the information in the certificate. The most important information in the certificate is the association of the entity with the public key.

IKE standards advocate the use of PKI in VPN environments where strong authentication is necessary. A VPN-1 Power module taking part in a VPN tunnel establishment must have an RSA key pair and a certificate issued by a trusted CA. The certificate holds details about the module's identity, its public key, CRL retrieval details, and is signed by the CA.

As soon as two entities attempt to establish a VPN tunnel, each system supplies its peer with random information signed by its private key and with the certificate that contains the public key. The certificate facilitates the establishment of a trust relationship linking the gateways. Each gateway uses the peer gateway's public key to confirm the source of the signed information and the CA's public key to confirm the certificate's authenticity. As a result, the corroborated certificate is used to authenticate the peer.

Every deployment of Check Point SmartCenter server includes an Internal Certificate Authority (ICA) that can issue VPN certificates for the VPN modules it controls. These VPN certificates simplify the creation of VPNs connecting the modules.

Difficulties can occur when integration with other PKI solutions is required; for instance:

- A VPN must be established with a VPN-1 Power module administered through an external SmartCenter server. For instance, the peer gateway belongs to another organization that makes use of Check Point products, and its certificate is signed by its own SmartCenter server's ICA.

- A VPN must be established with a non-Check Point VPN entity. In this instance, the peer's certificate is signed by a third-entity CA.

- An organization may settle on, using a third-entity CA to generate certificates for its VPN-1 Power modules.

PKI Deployments and VPN

Following are some sample CA deployments:

- Simple Deployment—internal CA
- CA of an external SmartCenter Server
- CA services provided over the Internet
- CA on the LAN

Policy-Based VPN

Common VPN routing scenarios can be configured using a VPN star community. Not all VPN routing configuration may be handled through SmartDashboard. VPN star or mesh routing between gateways can be also be configured by editing the configuration file $FWDIR\conf\vpn_route.conf.

VPN routing cannot be configured between gateways that do not belong to a VPN community.

vpn_route.conf

For further control above VPN routing, edit the *vpn_route.conf* file in the *conf* directory of the SmartCenter Server. The configuration file, *vpn_route.conf*, is a text file that contains the name of network objects. The format is defined by Destination, Next hop, Install on Gateway. It uses tabs to separate the elements.

Think about a simple VPN routing scenario consisting of a hub and two spokes where all systems are controlled by the same SmartCenter management Server, and all VPN-1 Power enforcement modules are members of the matching VPN community.

Only Telnet and FTP services are to be encrypted between the spokes and routed through the hub. Although this could be done easily by configuring a VPN star community, the same objective can be accomplished by editing vpn_route.conf (see Table 5.1):

Table 5.1 Editing vpn_route.conf

Destination	Next Hop Router Interface	Install On
Spoke_B_VPN_Dom	Hub_C	Spoke_A
Spoke_A_VPN_Dom	Hub_C	Spoke_B

In this instance, Spoke_B_VPN_Dom is the name of the network object group that contains spoke B's VPN domain. Hub C is the name of the VPN-1 Power gateway enabled for VPN routing. Spoke_A_VPN_Dom is the name of the network object that represents Spoke A's encryption domain.

Route-Based VPN

The use of VPN Tunnel Interfaces (VTI) introduces a new method of configuring VPNs called Route-based VPN. This method is based on the concept that initiating a VTI between peer gateways is reminiscent of connecting them directly.

A VTI is an operating system level virtual interface that can be used as a gateway to the encryption domain of the peer gateway. Every VTI is associated with a single tunnel to a VPN-1 Power peer gateway. The tunnel itself with all its properties is defined by a VPN community connecting the two gateways. The peer gateway should also be configured with an analogous VTI. The native IP routing mechanism on each gateway can then direct traffic into the tunnel as it would for any other type of interface.

All traffic destined to the encryption domain of a peer gateway will be routed through the associated VTI. This infrastructure allows dynamic routing protocols to use VTIs. A dynamic routing protocol daemon running on the VPN-1 Power gateway can swap routing information with a neighboring routing daemon running on the other end of an IPSec tunnel that looks as if it is a single hop away.

Route-based VPN is supported using SecurePlatform and Nokia IPSO 3.9 (and greater) platforms and can be implemented only between two gateways within the same community.

Virtual Tunnel Interfaces

A VPN Tunnel Interface is a virtual interface on a VPN-1 module that is linked with an existing VPN tunnel and is used by IP routing as a point-to-point interface directly associated to a VPN peer gateway (see Figure 5.8).

The VPN routing process of an outbound packet can be described as follows:

- An IP packet with destination address X is matched against the routing table.

- The routing table indicates that IP address X should be routed through a point-to-point link, which is the VPN Tunnel Interface that is related by way of peer gateway Y.

- VPN-1 kernel captures the packet as it goes into the virtual tunnel interface.

- The packet is encrypted using the appropriate IPSec Security Association parameters with peer gateway Y as defined in the VPN community, and the new packet receives the peer gateway Y's IP address as the destination IP.

- Based on the new destination IP, the packet is rerouted by VPN-1 into the physical interface, according to the proper routing table entry for Y's address.

The opposite is done for inbound packets:

- An IPSec packet enters the system coming from gateway Y.
- VPN-1 intercepts the packet on the physical interface.
- VPN-1 identifies the originating VPN peer gateway.
- VPN-1 decapsulates the packet, and extracts the original IP packet.
- VPN-1 detects that a VPN Tunnel Interface exists for the peer VPN gateway, and reroutes the packet from the physical interface to the associated VPN Tunnel Interface.
- The packet enters the IP stack through the VPN Tunnel Interface.

Figure 5.8 Virtual Interface Routing

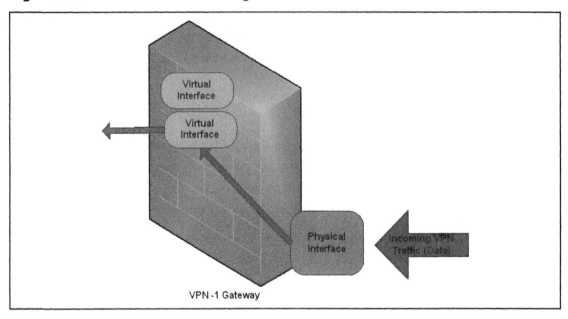

In a Route-based VPN, VTIs are created on the local gateway (see Figure 5.9). Each VTI is associated with a corresponding VTI on a remote VPN-1 Power peer. Traffic routed from the local gateway via the VTI is transferred encrypted to the associated VPN-1 Power peer gateway.

Figure 5.9 Route-Based VPNs

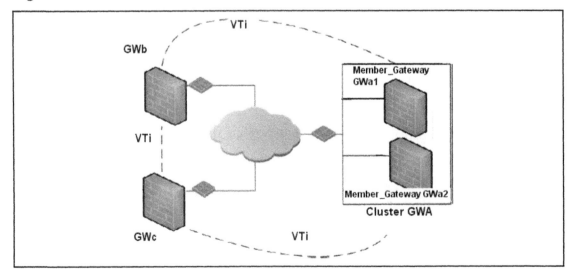

In a scenario demonstrated in Figure 5.9:

- There is a VTI connecting Cluster GWA and GWb

- There is a VTI connecting Cluster GWA and GWc

- There is a VTI connecting GWb and GWc

A virtual interface performs similar to a point-to-point interface directly linked to the remote VPN-1 Power peer. Traffic between network hosts is routed into the VPN tunnel using the IP routing mechanism of the operating system. Gateway objects are still necessary, as well as VPN communities and access control policies to describe which tunnels are accessible. Nevertheless, VPN encryption domains for each individual peer gateway are no longer required. The assessment as to whether or not to encrypt data is dependent on whether the traffic is routed through a virtual interface. The routing changes dynamically if a dynamic routing protocol such as OSPF or BGP is offered on the network.

Notes from the Underground...

Changes in Dynamic Routing

For NGX (R60) and above, the dynamic routing suite has been incorporated into SecurePlatform Pro. The administrator runs a daemon on the gateway to publish the changed routes to the network.

When a connection that originates on GWb is routed through a VTI to GWc (or a server behind GWc) and is accepted by the implied rules, the connection leaves GWb in the clear with the local IP address of the VTI as the source IP address. If this IP address is not routable, return packets will be lost. The solution for this issue is:

- Configuring a static route on GWb that redirects packets intended to GWc from being routed through the VTI.

- Not including it in any published route

- Adding route maps that filter out GWc's IP addresses

After excluding the IP addresses from a route-based VPN, it is still possible to have other connections encrypted to those addresses by using domain-based VPN definitions. An example would be when not passing on implied rules. The VTI may be configured in two ways:

- Numbered
- Unnumbered

Numbered VTI

If the VPN Tunnel Interface is numbered, the interface is assigned a local IP address and a remote IP address. The local IP address will be the source IP for the connections originating from the gateway and going through the VTI. VTIs may share an IP address but cannot use a previously existing IP address associated with a physical interface. Numbered interfaces are supported only by the SecurePlatform operating system.

Unnumbered VTI

If the VTI is unnumbered, local and remote IP addresses are not configured. Unnumbered VTIs must be assigned a proxy interface. The proxy interface is used as the source IP for outbound traffic. Unnumbered interfaces do away with the need to allocate and manage an IP address per interface. Unnumbered interfaces are supported only on the Nokia IPSO 3.9 platform and above.

Nokia IPSO interfaces may be physical or loopback.

Dynamic VPN Routing

VTIs allow the ability to use Dynamic Routing Protocols to exchange routing information between gateways. The Dynamic Routing Protocols that are supported include:

- BGP4
- OSPF
- RIPv1 (SecurePlatform Pro only)
- RIPv2 (SecurePlatform Pro only)

VPN Directional Match

To configure Directional VPN within a community:

1. In Global Properties > VPN page > Advanced > Select Enable VPN Directional Match in VPN Column.

2. In the VPN column of the appropriate rule, right-click on the VPN community. From the pop-up menu, select Edit Cell....
   The VPN Match Conditions window opens.

3. Select Match traffic in this direction only, and click Add...
   The Directional VPN Match Condition window opens.

4. In the Match on traffic reaching the Gateway from: drop-down box, select the object for internal_clear. (the source).

5. In the Match on traffic leaving the Gateway to: box, select the relevant community object (the destination).

6. Add another directional match in which the relevant community object is both the source and destination.
   This allows traffic from the local domain to the community, and within the community.

7. Click OK.

To configure Directional VPN between communities:

1. In Global Properties > VPN page > Advanced > Select Enable VPN Directional Match in VPN Column.

2. Right-click inside the VPN column of the right rule. From the pop-up menu, select Edit Cell or Add Direction.
   The VPN Match Conditions Window will open (see Figure 5.10).

Figure 5.10 VPN Match Conditions Window

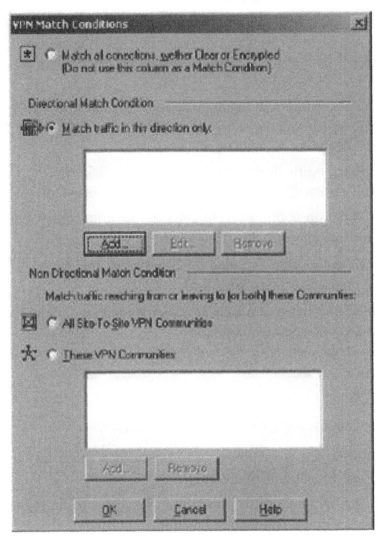

3. Click Add. The Directional VPN Match Window will open (see Figure 5.11).

Figure 5.11 Directional VPN Match Window

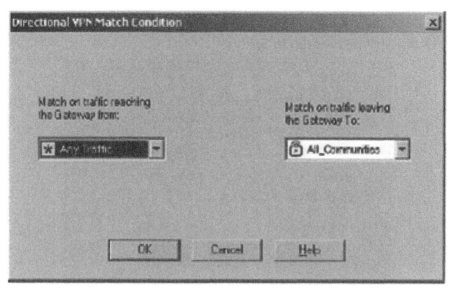

4. From the drop-down box on the left of Figure 5.11, pick the source of the connection.

5. From the drop-down box on the right of Figure 5.11, pick the connection's destination.

6. Click OK.

Nokia Configuration

A Route-based VPN is supported only by SecurePlatform and Nokia IPSO 3.9 (or above) platforms and can be implemented only when two gateways within the same community are involved.

Local and remote IP addresses are not configured if the VTI is unnumbered. Unnumbered VTIs must be allocated a proxy interface. The proxy interface is used as the source IP for outbound traffic. Unnumbered interfaces do away with the need to allocate and manage an IP address per interface. Unnumbered interfaces are supported only by the Nokia IPSO 3.9 (or greater) platform.

Nokia IPSO interfaces may be physical or loopback.

When a VTI connects a Nokia machine and a SecurePlatform host, a loopback interface has to be configured and defined in the Topology tab of the gateway. In Nokia Network Voyager:

1. Login and the window in Figure 5.12 will appear.

Figure 5.12 Initial Nokia Screen in Browser

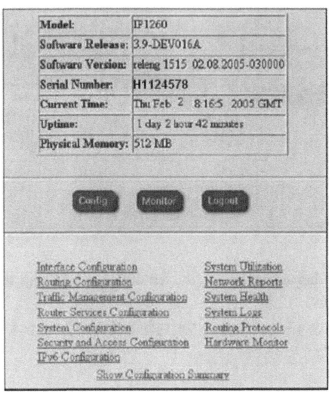

Model:	IP1260
Software Release:	3.9-DEV016A
Software Version:	releng 1515 02.08.2005-030000
Serial Number:	H1124578
Current Time:	Thu Feb 2 8:16:5 2005 GMT
Uptime:	1 day 2 hour 42 minutes
Physical Memory:	512 MB

Config   Monitor   Logout

Interface Configuration   System Utilization
Routing Configuration   Network Reports
Traffic Management Configuration   System Health
Router Services Configuration   System Logs
System Configuration   Routing Protocols
Security and Access Configuration   Hardware Monitor
IPv6 Configuration
                    Show Configuration Summary

2. Click Interface Configuration.
3. On the Configuration page, click Interfaces (see Figure 5.13).

Figure 5.13 Nokia Configuration Window

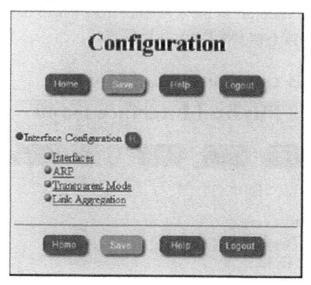

4. On the Interface Configuration page, click loop0 (see Figure 5.14).

Figure 5.14 Interface Configurations on a Nokia VPN-1

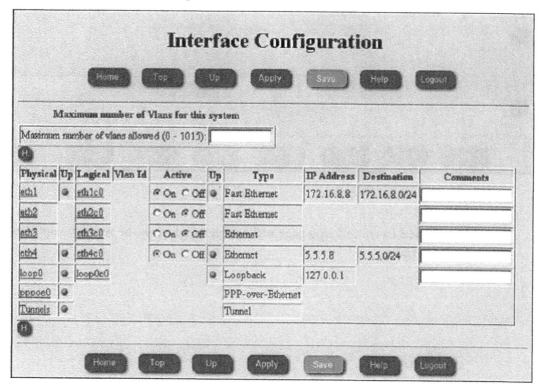

5. Enter an IP address in the Create a new loopback interface with IP address field and the value '30' in the Reference mask length field On the Physical Interface loop0 page (see Figure 5.15).

Figure 5.15 Loopback Configurations on a Nokia VPN-1

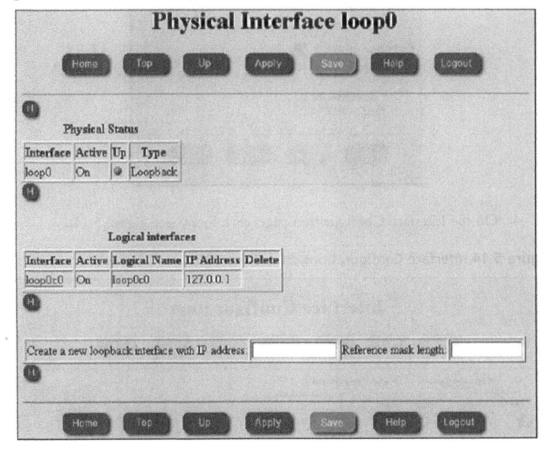

6. Click Apply.
   The Physical Interface loop0 page will refresh and displays the recently configured loopback interface.

7. Click Save.

Secure Platform Configuration

First Time Setup Using the Command Line is conducted after the installation from the CD has been completed and the computer has been rebooted. A first time setup is required in order to:

- Configure the network settings
- Apply the license
- Select which products will be installed
- Perform the SmartCenter initial setup, if selected

Perform the first time setup, as follows:

1. Run the sysconfig command from the console to configure SecurePlatform, using a text interface.
2. The command line setup wizard begins, and guides you through the first-time configuration.
3. Select "n" to proceed to the next menu, or "q" to exit the Wizard, and press Enter.
4. If you selected "n" and pressed Enter, the Network Configuration menu options are displayed. They are:
   - Host Name (Set/Show Host Name)
   - Domain Name (Set/Show Domain Name)
   - Domain Name Servers (Add/Remove/Show Domain Name Servers)
   - Network Connections (Add/Configure/Remove/Show Connection)
   - Routing (Set/Show Default Gateway)
5. You must configure the following:
   - The system's hostname
   - The domain name, and up to three DNS servers
   - The system's network interfaces
   - The default gateway for the system

6. Enter the preferred option number and press Enter.
   The Choose an action menu operation options will display.

7. Enter the preferred operation option number and press Enter.

HERE ARE SOME TIPS ON HOW TO GO BACK

- Select "e" and press Enter to return to the previous menu.
- Select "p" and press Enter to return to the previous menu, or select "q" and press Enter to exit the Wizard.

8. When you have completed the Network Configuration, choose "n" and press Enter to advance to the next menu, Time and Date Configuration. In the Time and Date Configuration menu it is possible to enter and set the current date and time and to set the time zone for the system.

Routing

This page enables you to manage the routing table on your device. It is possible to add a static or default route, or delete them.

NOTE

You cannot edit an existing route. To modify a specific route, delete it and create a new route in its place. Be careful not to delete a route that allows you connect to the device.

To delete a route, select the specific route checkbox and click Delete.

To configure routing, on the Routing Table page, click New. The Add Route drop-down box is displayed.

The options are:

- Route

- Default Route

To add a new route:

1. Select Route. The Add New Route page appears. Supply the following:

   ■ Destination IP Address

   ■ Destination Netmask

   ■ Interface (from the drop-down box)

   ■ Gateway

   ■ Metric

2. Click Apply.

To add a default route:

1. Select Default Route. The Add Default Route page appears. Supply the following:

   ■ Gateway

   ■ Metric

2. Click Apply.

Summary

This chapter described the process of connecting Check Point Firewall-1/ VPN-1 using an IPSec Virtual Private Network (VPN). With the ability to share facilities and reduce costs when compared to traditional routed networks over dedicated facilities, VPNs have become an integral component of many organizations' infrastructures. When the ability to rapidly link enterprise offices, small and home offices, and mobile workers in both gateway peer connections and as mobile hosts is added this benefit only increases.

CheckPoint VPN-1 allows network administrators to customize their security and quality of service requirements as needed for specific applications. VPN-1 can scale to meet sudden demands, especially when provider-provisioned on shared infrastructure, and is able to reduce the operational expenditure associated with network support and facilities.

In this chapter we have discussed the benefits and capabilities of Checkpoint VPN-1 including IPSec and the associated IKE negotiation phases. Deployment of VPNs in the enterprise DMZ is done primarily through the following three models. All these models are supported using Checkpoint VPN-1:

- VPN termination at the edge router

- VPN termination at the corporate firewall

- VPN termination at a dedicated appliance

Each of these deployment models presents its own complexities that must be addressed for the VPN-1 topology to be successfully implemented.

Solutions Fast Track

Encryption Overview

☑ VPNs are able to afford Privacy, authenticity, data integrity.

☑ In IPSec, the Key exchange is public (asymmetric) and the session encryption is symmetric to provide the best level of performance.

☑ In IKE Phase I, the peers authenticate using either certificates or via a preshared secret. Other authentication methods are accessible if one of the peers is a remote access client. A Diffie-Hellman key is produced. The makeup of the Diffie-Hellman protocol results in each peer being able to autonomously create the shared secret. The shared secret is a key that is known only to the peers in the negotiation.

☑ IKE Phase II is encrypted based on the keys and methods agreed upon during the IKE Phase I negotiation. The key material exchanged through IKE Phase II is used for constructing the IPSec keys.

☑ Perfect Forward Secrecy (PFS) covers the situation where the compromise of a current session key or long-term private key will not result in a compromise of previous or successive keys in cryptography.

☑ Double-check encryption rule properties on each gateway to ensure they are identical.

☑ Make sure key exchange rules (if any) are above your stealth rule.

☑ The four topologies supported by VPN-1 include mesh (fully and partially), star topology, hub-and-spoke, and remote access.

☑ The distinction between a star topology and a hub-and-spoke topology is that in a star topology, the branch or stub networks are not able to communicate with one another and are limited to communications with the central hub.

☑ There are three main choices for the symmetric key encryption schemes in IPSec with VPN-1. These are DES, 3DES, and AES.

☑ Message integrity is provided using the MD5, SHA-1, or HMAC hash algorithms. When using a HMAC algorithm, it is not possible to mix separate hash and HMAC algorithms (for instance by using MD5 and HMAC-SHA-1 together).

☑ Before an IPSec VPN tunnel can be established, the session parameters must be negotiated using Internet Key Exchange.

☑ IPSec security policies define the traffic permitted to enter the VPN tunnel.

Configuring SecuRemote/SecureClient VPNs

☑ SecuRemote/SecureClient can be used with dial-up or Ethernet adapters.

☑ Secure Domain Login is possible with SecuRemote/SecureClient.

☑ Several methods exist for automatically updating site topology.

VPN Tunnel Interfaces (VTI)

☑ The VTI may be configured in two ways: numbered or unnumbered.

☑ If the VPN Tunnel Interface is numbered, the interface is assigned a local IP address and a remote IP address.

☑ VTIs may share an IP address but cannot use a previously existing IP address associated with a physical interface.

☑ Numbered interfaces are supported only by the SecurePlatform operating system.

☑ If the VTI is unnumbered, local and remote IP addresses are not configured.

☑ Unnumbered VTIs must be assigned a proxy interface and do away with the need to allocate and manage an IP address per interface.

☑ The proxy interface is used as the source IP for outbound traffic.

☑ Unnumbered interfaces are supported only by the Nokia IPSO 3.9 platform and above.

Frequently Asked Questions

Q: Why can't I connect to a host in my peer's VPN domain?

A: This may not be allowed by policy. Ensure your policy allows the connection to and from the host and that traffic is allowed in both directions. Just because a VPN domain has been configured does not mean that you have set up the rules to allow the connection.

Q: What does it signify when "No response from peer: Scheme IKE" occurs in VPN-1's logs and you cannot initiate a VPN?

A: Confirm that fwd and isakmpd are both running on your peer gateway. Isakmpd listens on UDP port 500 to negotiate the IKE parameters. The netstat command may be used to check whether the port is listening. If the port is listening and you are still receiving the error, check that UDP 500 has not been blocked in the VPN-1 rules.

Q: What does it mean when you receive the error "No proposal chosen" in the logs and no VPN is initiated by the firewall?

A: The encryption rule properties diverge on the peer gateways. One gateway may support an encryption method that another doesn't. When VPN-1 is negotiating the IKE phase I parameters, it needs to have a common set of encryption methods with its peer gateway or the negotiation will fail. For instance, if one gateway supports only DES and the other supports only AES, then no VPN may be completed.

Q: Why is the VPN slow when I check Enable PFS?

A: Perfect Forward Secrecy (PFS) covers the situation where the compromise of a current session key or long-term private key will not result in a compromise of previous or successive keys in cryptography. Enabling PFS will result in a fresh DH key being constructed for the period of an IKE phase II negotiation, and being renewed for every subsequent key exchange. As new DH keys are constructed for the duration of each IKE phase I negotiation, no dependency exists between these keys and those produced in subsequent IKE phase I negotiations. This process increases the load on the VPN-1 gateway making the VPN slower. Checkpoint recommends implementing PFS only where there is a critical security need.

Q: How do I know that the key exchange is secure? Couldn't an attacker just sniff the key exchange and compromise the process?

A: IPSec key exchanges are based on a calculation of the symmetric keys, whereas the session is protected using the Diffie-Hellman (DH) protocol. In this negotiation, the keys are never sent over the network, but are created separately on each gateway.

Chapter 6

Advanced VPN
Client Installations

Solutions in this chapter:

- **SecuRemote**
- **SecureClient**
- **SSL Network Extender**

- ☑ **Summary**
- ☑ **Solutions Fast Track**
- ☑ **Frequently Asked Questions**

Introduction

Virtual private networks (VPNs) have been around for a long time, and with time, they have increased in popularity. If you haven't configured remote VPN access on your Check Point NGX R65 FireWall-1/VPN-1 yet, this chapter will take you through the different methods and configuration options. Several different methods currently exist; however, SecuRemote, SecureClient, and SSL Network Extender (SNX) are the most popular.

SecuRemote is a client-side application that allows authenticated users to enter the network to work as though they were directly connected at the office. SecuRemote offers split tunneling by default, so when a user is connected to the LAN, he can also connect to the Internet through his Internet service provider (ISP). SecuRemote comes free of charge with the purchase of a FireWall-1/VPN-1 license.

SecureClient offers the same functions as SecuRemote, but adds more flexibility and configuration options. With SecureClient, you can install a client-side desktop security policy that will protect the remote client while connected on the VPN. This desktop security policy will ensure that when a user is connected to the NGX R65 FireWall-1, the client will be protected from any possible hackers on the Internet. SecureClient can also prohibit Internet access from users' ISPs and have them route all traffic through the corporate firewall according to customizable desktop security rules. When the client disconnects from the VPN, Internet activity is returned to normal and the user can route traffic through his ISP.

SNX allows remote VPN users to connect without a client installed on their PC, as was the requirement for SecuRemote and SecureClient. SNX is Check Point's clientless VPN solution which works on Windows and most flavors of Linux. The popularity of a clientless solution is rampant and is often a common choice for users connecting from shared computers where they cannot install applications with administrator privileges.

NOTE

In this chapter, we will use a stand-alone configuration of NGX R65 for all configuration examples, and the SmartConsole demo mode for all screenshots.

SecuRemote

SecuRemote is a Check Point IPSec client-side application that permits you to connect to your network in a secure manner once you've been authenticated. The supported encrypted levels range from the Data Encryption Standard (DES) to AES-256 (the higher encryption algorithm is recommended). However, it is more CPU intensive, thus creating a heavier load on the gateway and client. SecuRemote will permit split tunneling while connected to the corporate firewall and will not secure the client PC from any external unauthorized access attempts.

The first step in using SecuRemote is to decide where you want to allow your remote VPN users to connect. This may be a network(s) or a single host that your gateway protects. Check Point uses a VPN encryption domain for VPN site-to-site and remote user access. Each VPN method can have a different VPN domain, which is strongly recommended. The definition of a VPN domain is essential for ensuring that the client is aware of the networks to which it can connect. When a user connects to the gateway and is authenticated, the gateway will send to the remote user the VPN domain information through the Secure Sockets Layer (SSL) protocol. The VPN domain information is stored on the client PC in a file named userc.C. When a remote client tries to reach inside the protected network of the gateway, the SecuRemote routing daemon will verify against this file before the PC's network interface card (NIC) to see whether it is the destined network. If the destined network resides behind a known site or gateway, it will ask for authentication.

To enable your firewall to start using SecuRemote, you must ensure that your firewall is VPN-enabled (see Figure 6.1).

Figure 6.1 Enabling VPN on a Gateway

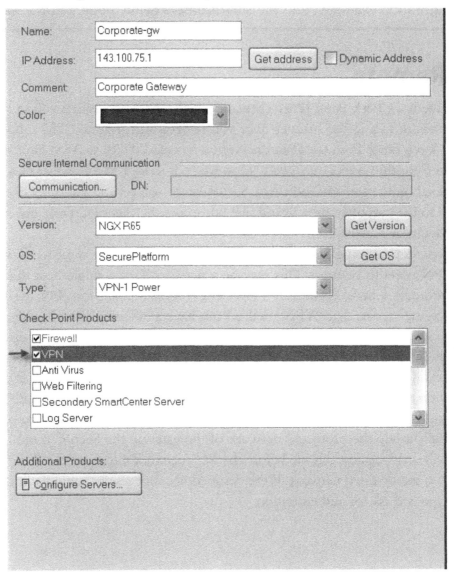

Once you have VPN-enabled your firewall, you must make your gateway a member of a VPN remote community. A community is a set of global properties that can be shared among several gateways. Select **Your gateway object | VPN | Add | Add This Gateway To Community | RemoteAccess**, as shown in Figure 6.2.

Figure 6.2 Adding a Gateway to a Remote Access Community

The VPN domain is essential to the inner workings of your remote access configuration. Without the VPN domain, the end-user will never know which network(s) or host(s) is behind the gateway. By default, Check Point enables the VPN domain using the Internet Protocol (IP) addresses behind the gateway based on the topology information. This means that if the gateway has only one internal interface with an IP address of 10.1.1.1 and a subnet of 255.255.255.0, remote users will be allowed to connect to all 10.1.1.*x* addresses. The VPN domain in Figure 6.2 would comprise all 255 possible addresses.

Tools & Traps…

VPN Domains

You must ensure that you define the VPN domain manually for your remote users. Don't let the system automatically create it for you. Create a simple group and place all network(s) or host(s) within this group. Then, define the group in the **Specify VPN domain** field for the remote access community (see Figure 6.3). By default, the VPN domain for the remote access community inherits the same values from the site-to-site VPN; create two different groups if needed, one for each.

Figure 6.3 Setting the VPN Domain per Remote Access Community

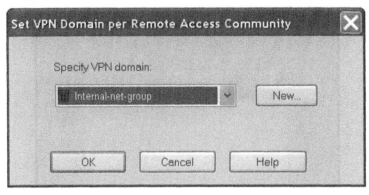

The remote access community must be configured and should now include your gateway object. The other two options required for the remote access community are the user groups and a general description of the remote access community. Assuming your users are already defined and are part of a user group, you must now create a rule within the security policy that will permit the connection. The rule base must specify the source as being a group of user(s) toward a destination which must be part of your VPN domain and part of the remote access community. The services permitted for the remote users should be defined; however, any service may be used temporarily for testing purposes. The remaining options within the security rule are optional, and once completed, you must install them on the gateway. Figure 6.4 shows an example rule permitting a user within the Mobile-VPN-user group to reach the Internal-net-group with any services. We will use the rule example in Figure 6.4 throughout this chapter.

Figure 6.4 Security Rule for Remote Users

NO.	NAME	SOURCE	DESTINATION	VPN	SERVICE	ACTION	TRACK	INSTALL ON	TIME	COMMENT
1	remote users	Mobile-vpn-user@Any	Internal-net-group	RemoteAccess	★ Any	accept	Log	Corporate-gw	★ Any	Allow Remote VPN Users within the Mobile-vpn-users group. They may go towards the Internal-net-group with any service.

Once you have installed the security policy, the end-user must install the SecuRemote software and follow a few steps to establish communication with the gateway. You can find the latest version of SecuRemote at www.checkpoint.com/downloads; SecuRemote and SecureClient are part of the same package and differ only by an option during the installation process (see Figure 6.5).

Figure 6.5 SecuRemote Installation Options

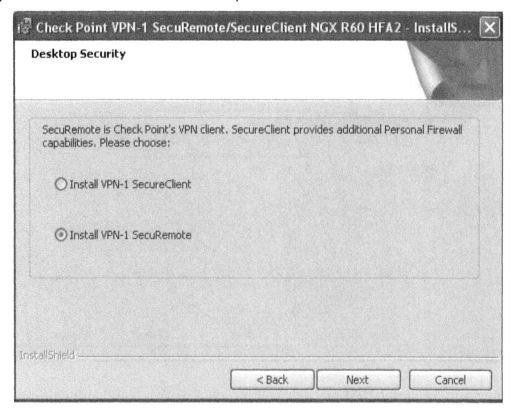

Toward the end of the SecuRemote/SecureClient installation, the computer requires a reboot. If the installation was successful, you should see an icon in the taskbar that resembles a yellow key. To start the client connection, you can double-click the icon in the taskbar and follow the initial setup instructions. The first step in configuring the SecuRemote client is to define a site (see Figure 6.6). A site is the IP address of the corporate gateway. You can decide to record the routable IP address of your gateway in your domain name system (DNS) record to allow easier site configuration for your clients. Your clients would then have to input only the DNS name instead of an IP address, which clients often forget. Examples of DNS settings include vpn.abc.com; remote.ab.com, and gatekeeper.abc.com. However, a drawback to obvious name conventions is that they may allow hackers to pinpoint the entry point into your VPN network. Something subtler such as syngress.abc.com may be suitable.

Figure 6.6 SecuRemote Site Definition

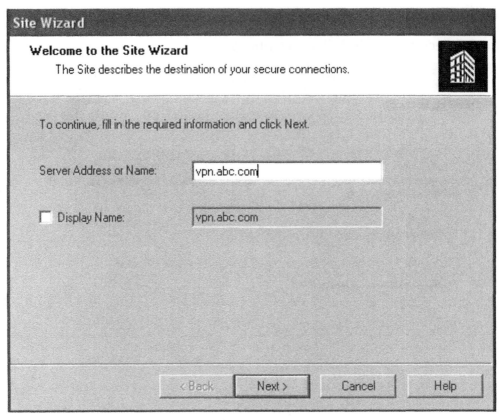

After you create the VPN site, you will be asked what type of authentication method you are using, and then you will be asked for your username and password. If you authenticate properly, the gateway will send the VPN domain topology through SSL to your client PC. Remember to look at this file, for it is the core of Check Point's client VPN solution. Once the site is created, you will be able to reach the internal VPN domain which will be encrypted from your client PC to the gateway. Once the packet reaches the gateway, it will be decrypted and sent in the clear toward the VPN domain destination. The return packet will arrive in clear text until it reaches the internal interface of the firewall, where it will be encrypted and then sent back to the client.

IP Pool NAT

Sometimes remote users have the same internal network IP scheme that you are using within the VPN domain, which may cause problems with the gateway. Home networks will often be configured with a network IP range of 192.168.1.0–192.168.1.255. You can resolve this configuration by enabling the use of IP Pool NAT for remote VPN connections. You enable IP Pool NAT through **Global Properties | NAT – Network Address Translation | Enable IP Pool NAT**. Once you have enabled IP Pool NAT, you will have the configuration options on your gateway object under **NAT | IP Pool NAT**. Figure 6.7 shows the various options available for IP Pool NAT.

Figure 6.7 IP Pool NAT Options

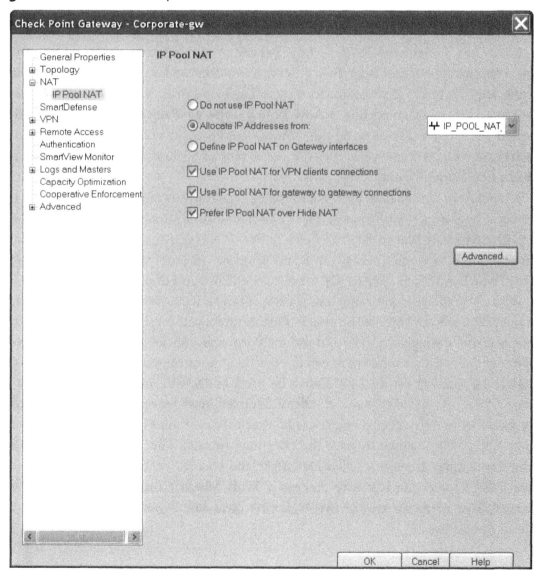

Prior to enabling the use of IP Pool NAT, you must create a network object with a subnet that is different from any other subnets you may encounter. Then you must select the newly created network object to identify which IPs the gateway will lease to its remote clients, and possibly even gateway-to-gateway connections should you encounter the same problem. When identifying the connections in SmartView Tracker, the source IP of the remote user should now be one from the IP Pool NAT network.

SecureClient

As noted earlier, SecureClient includes all the features of SecuRemote, plus some additional features and flexibility. To activate some of the SecureClient features, you must activate the **SecureClient Policy Server** on the gateway object. Once you have activated the SecureClient Policy Server, you must add a policy package to the current security policy if you want to use the Desktop Policy if it wasn't already there. You can do this by selecting **File | Add Policy Type to Package | Desktop Policy** through the SmartDashboard. At this point, a Desktop tab will appear within the SmartDashboard. Not everyone uses the full extent of SecureClient with the Desktop policy often being left out.

SecureClient also enables users to assign an IP address to remote users statically by username, by the internal Dynamic Host Configuration Protocol (DHCP) server, or via Office Mode, similar to IP Pool NAT in SecuRemote. An optional parameter for Office Mode is to assign internal DNS and Windows Internet Name Service (WINS) servers, which comes in very handy for network shares and domains.

With SecureClient, split tunneling is now optional. Remote users no longer have to use their own ISP for Internet browsing. Furthermore, you can force remote users to route all traffic through the VPN and use the corporate policies and security measures to protect the end-user while connected. Four conditions must apply to route all traffic through the gateway: Office Mode must be used, Hide NAT must be done on the Office IP Pool Range allocated, the **Allow SecureClient to route traffic through this gateway** option must be enabled, and a security rule must be enabled to allow the source Office Mode range to leave the corporate firewall. The process of routing all traffic through the gateway is called *Hub Mode*, and you can enable it on the gateway object itself by selecting **Remote Access | Hub Mode Configuration | Allow SecureClient to route traffic through this gateway**. Figure 6.8 shows where to activate the feature.

Figure 6.8 Hub Mode Configuration

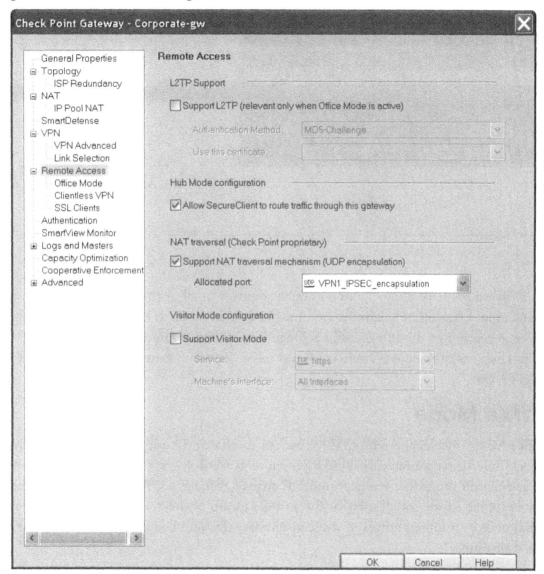

Desktop Policies

Desktop policies, which resemble the familiar look of security policies, are easy to create. You can configure them through the Dashboard on the Desktop tab. The Desktop tab has two sections: Inbound and Outbound. Inbound refers to all traffic destined to the remote user PC, and outbound refers to anything leaving the client PC. Figure 6.9 shows a desktop policy with three inbound rules and four outbound rules.

Figure 6.9 Desktop Policy

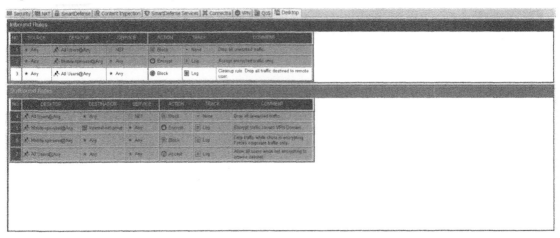

Desktop security policies allow granular control to all SecureClient users who are connecting. Logging mechanisms are built-in on the client so that any desktop policy that is accepting or dropping traffic is logged and easily audited. On the client side, right-click on the SecureClient icon and select **Tools | Launch SecureClient Log Viewer**.

Office Mode

Office Mode enables the remote VPN user to receive an IP address designated by the Check Point gateway, internal DHCP server, or RADIUS server. Office Mode options are located on the gateway object under **Remote Access | Office Mode**. You can enable Office Mode for all users or for a single group of users. By default, the IP lease duration is 15 minutes; however, you can increase this number to a more reasonable one over time.

It is possible to assign static Office Mode IPs to users. However, this requires that you modify the ipassignment.conf file located on the gateway at $FWDIR/conf. Always back up your files prior to modification in case you make a mistake and you have to roll back the configuration. Here is an example of how to assign the user *syngress* an IP address of 192.168.137.40:

```
Corporate-gw      addr     192.168.137.40     syngress
```

The first item, *Corporate-gw*, is the gateway name as it appears in the Dashboard. Instead of using this, you can use the gateway IP address or an asterisk (*).

The second item, *addr*, is the descriptor; this can also be *range* or *net*. In the preceding example, we wanted to assign a static IP to a specific user, so we used *addr*.

The third item is the IP address that will be assigned to the user. The last item is the username to which we are reserving the IP address. Note that using the ipassignment. conf file isn't very user-friendly and you must modify it manually every time you want to add a reservation as well as a policy install.

Notes from the Underground…

Assigning IP Addresses

Assigning IP addresses to users is not very common. Rather, it is more a feature that is activated for administrators who require access to specific devices or applications that may be protected by gateways. This is a mechanism that permits administrators to add the allocated source IP to any access control list (ACL) that may be preventing administrator access.

Advantages to using Office Mode are the ability to receive a routable IP address from your LAN, and the fact that you may receive internal DNS and WINS servers. Browsing the network neighborhood also becomes a lot easier, as all the names are resolved automatically from the client's perspective. This advantage may also bring some disadvantages, because it will add a load to the VPN. If you plan to roll out a large number of SecureClient users, try to benchmark the load this may bring to your firewall. You may want to add a faster machine or add software accelerators.

Another advantage of using Office Mode is that it allows you to route the Office Mode range internally. From within the LAN, you can reach an Office Mode Secure Client user. This is practical when using soft phones or whenever your administrators want to debug remote VPN users.

Visitor Mode

Visitor Mode allows remote SecureClient users to connect to the gateway over SSL on port 443. Often when a remote user is traveling and trying to connect through a hotel, many ports are blocked and only a select few are open. Transmission Control Protocol (TCP) port 443 is almost always open, as it is a commonly used port for secure Web browsing. Visitor Mode for remote SecureClient access must be enabled directly on the gateway object, as shown in Figure 6.10.

Figure 6.10 Visitor Mode

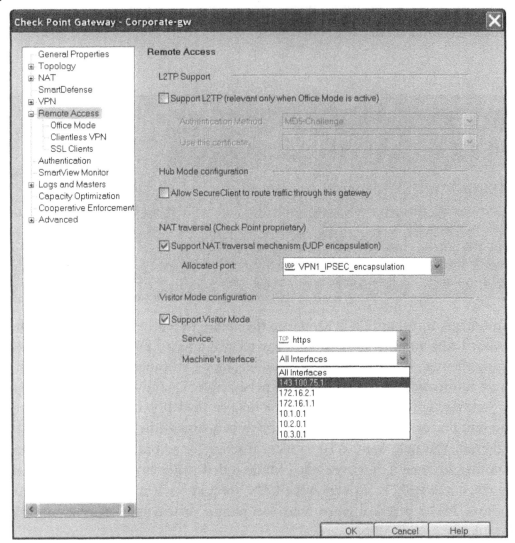

Visitor Mode configuration allows you to select on which interface it will listen for incoming connections. If you have several external interfaces, you may want to select only one, or you may want to select all interfaces, which is the default. Once you have enabled Visitor Mode, the client will have to decide whether to connect using Visitor Mode or via the default IPSec mode by using connection profiles.

Connection Profiles

With SecureClient, you can use connection profiles to give your users even more flexibility by allowing them to choose which type of profile to use. Several connection profile combinations are available, including Visitor Mode, Hub Mode, Policy Server, Multiple Entry Points (MEPs), and Backup Gateways. You can create a connection profile by selecting **Manage | Remote Access | Connection Profiles** through the Dashboard. Figure 6.11 shows the initial configuration option for a connection profile that will be configured to use Visitor Mode.

Figure 6.11 Connection Profile: General Tab

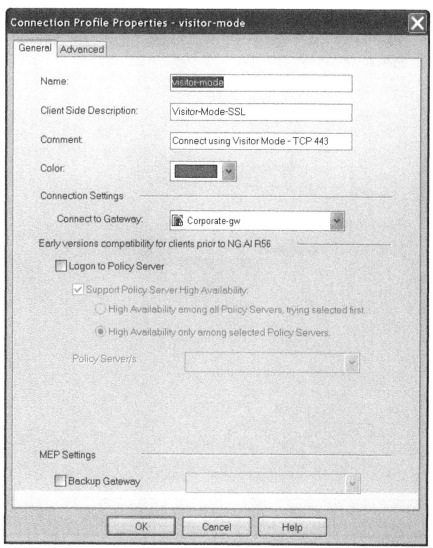

We will discuss the remaining options in Figure 6.11 later in this chapter. For now, note that it is important to enter a client-side description that all users will understand when they are selecting profiles. Using a difficult name will generate support calls, so give an obvious profile name to your remote users. The advanced options for connection profiles are **Support Office Mode**, **Connectivity enhancements** (NAT traversal tunneling or Visitor Mode), and **Hub Mode configuration** (route all traffic through gateway), as shown in Figure 6.12.

Figure 6.12 Connection Profile: Advanced Tab

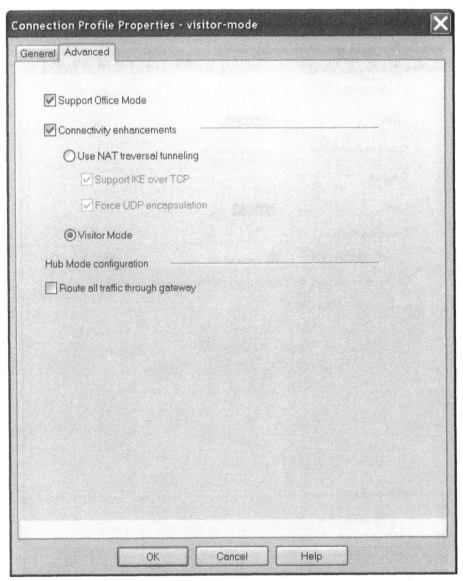

When the user will be creating a site and connecting to the corporate gateway, it will receive new topology information through SSL and will now be able to select which profile it can use. Figure 6.13 shows a SecureClient that has successfully created a site and has received the options to select from two different connection profiles.

Figure 6.13 SecureClient Connection Profile Selection

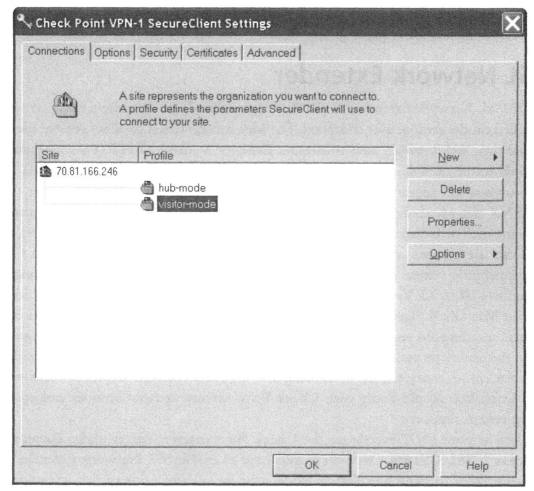

If you want to create several different profiles for users, ensure that you have educated your remote users on the different types of profiles available.

Windows L2TP Integration

Installing client-side applications to grant remote users VPN access may be a troublesome task for many organizations. Most of the PC population is still Windows-based, and therefore, Check Point has to support the built-in VPN client from Microsoft, which complies with the Layer 2 Tunneling Protocol (L2TP). You can configure L2TP support directly on the gateway object under **Remote Access**. On the general Remote Access page of the gateway object, you must enable support for L2TP, and it's only applicable when Office Mode is active. Once enabled, you have two authentication method options: MD5-Challenge and Smart Card (certificates). When you have activated the support for L2TP, don't forget to install the security policy. Security policies must always be installed for changes to take effect.

SSL Network Extender

SNX (SSL Network Extender) is a VPN solution that doesn't require a client to be installed on the remote user computer. The idea behind this is to allow remote users to use their Web browser, such as Internet Explorer, to make an HTTPS connection directly to the firewall. Once they make the HTTPS connection to the firewall, a pop-up box will appear and they are prompted to enter their credentials.

SNX is supported on various operating systems and browsers. Some operating systems such as Ubuntu are not officially listed as a supported OS; nevertheless, you can use Ubuntu, and we will discuss later how to activate SNX with this OS. The operating system prerequisite for clients using SNX is one of the following: Windows 2000, XP, Vista, Linux RHEL 3.0, Linux Suse 9 or later, Red Hat Linux 7.3, or Mac OS X Tiger. Although SNX does not officially support many flavors of Linux, an advanced end-user can configure such support. Remote clients must have the ability to use ActiveX or a Java applet because SNX will download either one for connectivity. Check Point officially supports Internet Explorer, Firefox, and Safari. You should verify with Check Point for any updated browser and operating system support.

You activate SNX directly on the Check Point gateway object under **Remote Access | SSL Clients**. Once there, you have to enable SSL Network Extender; however, keep in mind that Visitor Mode must be enabled prior to this activation. Once SSL Network Extender is activated and the proper rules are in place, the client is ready to open an HTTPS session directly on the corporate-gw interface. Remember that you can activate all interfaces through Visitor Mode, or you can select just the external interface. Figure 6.14 shows the pop-up box from Internet Explorer once the remote client has made the HTTPS connection toward the gateway.

Figure 6.14 SNX Authentication Window

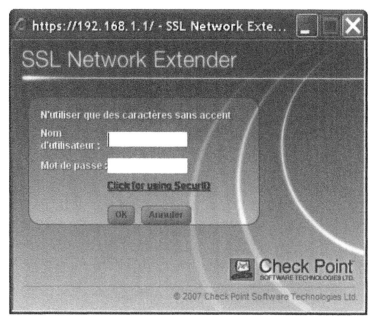

Notice that Figure 6.14 is in French; Check Point supports multiple languages for any remote offices that you may have. In addition to French, SNX also comes bundled with the following languages: Brazilian Portuguese, English, German, Hebrew, Italian, Japanese, simplified Chinese, Spanish, and traditional Chinese. The languages are defined in /opt/CPsuite-R65/fw1/conf/extender/language/chkp. Switching to French from the default language of English requires the following manual change to the index.html file located on the gateway under the /opt/CPsuite-R65/fw1/conf/extender directory:

```
function set_initial_cookie()
{
      try {
            if(getCookie("language") == null)
                  setCookie("language", "french");
            if(getCookie("skin") == null)
                  setCookie("skin", "skin1");
} catch (e) {}
}
```

Once the user has successfully authenticated to the gateway, the SNX Connection Details window will appear and will look similar to Figure 6.15 (depending on your operating system). Notice that the Office Mode IP is displayed and that this user has a reserved IP address which was defined in the ipassignment.conf file.

Figure 6.15 SNX Connection Details

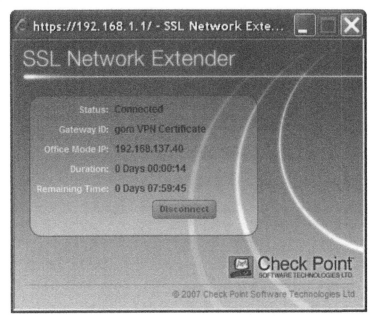

You can find other options for SNX in the Global properties by selecting **Policy** | **Global Properties** | **Remote Access** | **SSL Network Extender**. From here, you can select **User Authentication method**, **Supported encryption methods**, **Client upgrade upon connection**, **Client uninstall upon disconnection**, and **(ICS) Integrity Clientless Security**. Changing the default values and supporting higher encryption methods is recommended. By default, the **Client upgrade upon connection** option is set to ask the user; it is recommended that you set this to **Always Upgrade**. With this option, the client is not bothered by possible errors when connecting.

Notes from the Underground…

Ubuntu Support

The recent 7.10 release of Ubuntu has gained massive popularity for its general ease of use, so here we will explain how to configure Ubuntu 7.10 to work with SNX.

Continued

First, install the Linux SSL Network Extender client, snx_install.sh, which you can find on the Check Point Web site (www.checkpoint.com/downloads):

```
$ sudo -s -H
# bash ./snx_install.sh
Installation successful
```

Your system may indicate that installation was not successful, so test to see if it's working:

```
# snx
snx: symbol lookup error: snx: undefined symbol: cerr
```

If it's not working, install libstdc++2.10-glibc2.2:

```
$ sudo apt-get install libstdc++2.10-glibc2.2
```

Now, override libc with the following command:

```
# LD_PRELOAD=/usr/lib/libstdc++-libc6.2-2.so.3 snx -s corporate-gw -u
username
Check Point's Linux SNX build 541600050
Please enter your password: ********
SNX authentication: ********
Please confirm the connection to gateway: sept19 Root CA fingerprint: LINK
ASKS HOOF OF FINK DIN BLAB TEN HOOT BALM OUCH SHED Do you accept?
[y]es/[N]o: y
SNX - connected.
Session parameters:
=====================
Office Mode IP : 192.168.137.40
Timeout        : 8 hours
#
```

Configuring Ubuntu to work with SNX may seem painless for an administrator; however, for the general user, it may not be that simple. Linux clients still have some time to go, and with time, this process will surely get easier.

There are plenty of advantages to using a clientless VPN solution, including SNX; however, be advised that there are some disadvantages as well. With SNX you cannot use connection profiles, Hub Mode, or desktop policies, as you can with SecureClient. SNX will also create a heavier load for traffic; in addition, you can expect to see a longer delay.

Backup Gateways

The demand to have a backup entry point for remote VPN access has risen over time and is possible with NGX R65. Backup gateways can be used to access internal corporate information if the primary gateway is not available. The backup gateway should be on a different ISP and managed by the same SmartCenter Server (SCS) for better backup plans. The backup gateway should have its own VPN domain defined, as there shouldn't be an overlap between the two gateways; otherwise, you will not be able to install the security policy.

You must enable the backup gateway feature through **Global Properties** | **VPN** | **Advanced**. Once enabled, the backup gateway should be represented in each VPN community in which the primary gateway is currently being used. On the primary gateway object under the **VPN**, a new feature will appear. At the bottom will be an option to select **Use Backup Gateways**. Once this feature has been selected, you may select the backup gateway from the pull-down menu. Asymmetric routing may become an issue when using backup gateways, so IP Pool NAT must be defined on each gateway participating in the VPN. If you are configuring backup gateways for SecureClient users, you should use Office Mode for ease and simplicity.

Multiple Entry Point VPNs

Multiple Entry Point (MEP) VPNs are an addition to the backup gateway configuration. However, clients will now be using a probing method to select through which gateway it will be connecting. With a backup gateway, there is always a primary and a backup. MEP enhances VPN clients to determine by which entry point they will choose to come in. SecureClient can use three different mechanisms to determine with which gateway it will choose to end its encryption: first to respond, Primary-Backup, or Load Distribution.

The mechanism that responds first must have at least two gateways, and these gateways should be configured to have the same VPN domains. If all participating members have the same VPN domain, SecureClient will use the first-to-respond method to determine with which one it will encrypt.

Primary-Backup requires the configuration of a connection profile. The connection profile will consist of a primary gateway and, at the lower part of the connection profile setting, a backup gateway. Figure 6.16 shows a primary gateway object, *Corporate-gw*, with *syngress* defined as the backup.

Figure 6.16 Connection Profile: Primary Backup

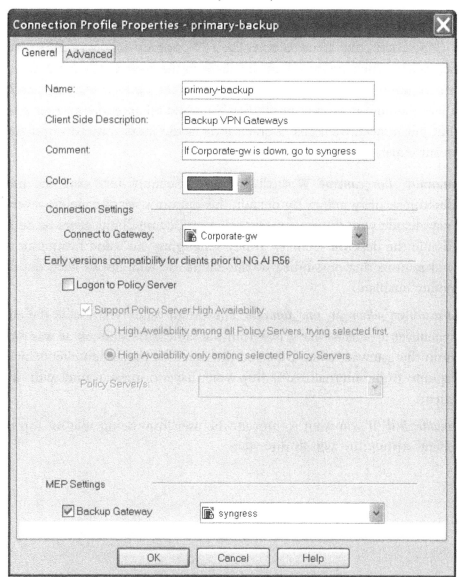

MEP Load Distribution will dynamically set remote clients to randomly select the active gateway to set up the VPN. To activate Load Distribution, select **Global Properties | Remote Access | VPN – Basic | enable the Load Distribution option**.

Userc.C

As described earlier in this chapter, whenever a remote client connects to the gateway to start a VPN session, the client receives the VPN domain topology information and many other values which are stored on the client in the userc.C file. By default, this file is in clear text; however, when compiling a VPN client package with the Packaging tool, you have the option to encrypt the file. We could fill an entire chapter discussing this one file, but instead, we'll take a quick look at the most common options we've seen from our experience:

- *manual_slan_control* With this option a SecureClient user can disable the desktop security policy. By default, this option is set to true; however, you may decide you don't want your remote SecureClient users to be able to disable the desktop security policy. Changing the value from true to false will remove that possibility, so the client PC will always have the desktop policy enabled.

- *disconnect_when_in_enc_domain* This useful value will disable the client whenever it detects that it is within the same VPN domain as was received from the gateway when it created the site. This way, when clients bring their laptops to the internal LAN, they won't have to mess around with the VPN client.

- *enable_kill* If you want to prevent the user from being able to stop the client, setting this will do the trick.

Summary

NGX R65 has several different options that allow remote connectivity for your users or partners. SecuRemote is the standard client which Check Point has been offering from day one. It allows you to connect to your network and do basically anything you want while you are connected. Split tunneling with SecuRemote is permitted and the client doesn't have any protection. SecureClient is based on SecuRemote, but adds a few more bells and whistles. Some of its strongest points include the ability to receive and protect the client by receiving a desktop policy which is user-defined on the gateway, and the ability to use Office Mode as well as internal corporate WINS and DNS servers, making network shares readily available. The most recent addition to NGX R65 is the clientless solution offered by SNX. SNX alleviates the burden of having to install and debug remote clients of possible issues; however, doing so decreases the security of your corporate network and end client.

Solutions Fast Track

SecuRemote

☑ SecuRemote offers remote users the ability to connect to the internal corporate network in a secure way using AES-256 as the highest level of encryption.

☑ It is possible to allow SecuRemote users the ability to query an internal DNS server by defining a SecuRemote DNS within the Dashboard. You can add several different domains for the client to query.

☑ Split tunneling is the default when using SecuRemote. No additional security mechanisms are in place to protect the client when connecting.

SecureClient

☑ You can use SecureClient to download a desktop policy from the Policy Server which is configured through the Dashboard. The desktop policy rules are divided into two sections: inbound toward the client and outbound from the client.

☑ You can configure SecureClient to route all traffic through the corporate network when connected. This means the client will be using the corporate

ISP when browsing on the Internet and all security mechanisms in place will be protecting the client.

☑ You must take anti-spoofing into consideration when activating Office Mode. You must define the Office Mode range on the gateway's interface.

SSL Network Extender

☑ SSL Network Extender (SNX) is a clientless VPN solution that is often used when installing client software becomes cumbersome.

☑ You can use SNX on several different operating systems and browsers. However, many people find Internet Explorer to be the easiest to use.

☑ SNX supports the same authentication mechanisms in place for your security gateway.

Frequently Asked Questions

Q: How can I use the internal corporate DNS and WINS server?

A: To use the internal DNS and WINS server, you must use Office Mode. Ensure that you have created the objects that represent your internal servers, and then select the **Advanced** options found on your corporate gateway by choosing **Remote Access | Office Mode | Optional Parameters**. Ensure that a rule within the security policy permits the Office Mode range selected to query the appropriate servers.

Q: Can I use SecureClient and connect to a site that doesn't have it?

A: Sure. All the features of SecureClient will be disabled and it will become a SecuRemote client.

Q: You mentioned the ability to change languages in SNX. Is this available in SecuRemote/Client?

A: Absolutely. You can change languages on the client side; however, you must restart the application.

Q: Can two SecureClient Office Mode users talk to each other?

A: Yes. If two VPN users are currently connected with Office Mode, they can talk to each other. They must know what IPs they currently have if they are not static.

Q: I lost all Internet activity when I connected with SecureClient for the first time. What should I do?

A: Ensure that you have been assigned an Office Mode IP and that you have enabled a rule to permit your Office Mode users to access the Internet. Also, don't forget to put NAT on your Office Mode.

Q: Can I force SecuRemote users to access an internal DNS server for my domain?

A: Yes. You have to create a SecuRemote DNS which would have your internal DNS object and domain(s) in question.

Q: Can I use the desktop policy with SSL Network Extender?

A: No. Unfortunately, you cannot use the desktop policy when using SNX.

Q: Is it possible to authenticate my remote VPN users with my corporate Active Directory server?

A: Yes. As long as Active Directory is LDAP-compliant, NGX R65 is able to communicate with the Active Directory server.

Chapter 7

SmartDefense

Solutions in this chapter:

- Configuring SmartDefense
- Network Security
- Application Intelligence
- Web Intelligence

☑ Summary

☑ Solutions Fast Track

☑ Frequently Asked Questions

Introduction

SmartDefense is a compilation of technologies built into the Check Point enforcement point to add extra fortifications against attacks. The technologies include:

- Network Security, which encases Transmission Control Protocol/Internet Protocol (TCP/IP)-level attack security

- Application Intelligence, which presents fortifications against Layer 7 attacks by inspecting the data segment of a packet

- Web Intelligence, which offers protection to Web services from particular Hypertext Transfer Protocol (HTTP)-based attacks

This chapter covers best practices in terms of implementing and handling these features. You can disable SmartDefense or use it in a monitor-only mode if enhanced protection is not advantageous. A number of features, including buffer size, cannot be disabled but may be modified.

SmartDefense not only protects against a range of known attacks, varying from different classes of Microsoft networking worms to distributed denial of service (DDoS) attacks, but it also incorporates intelligent security technologies that protect against entire categories of emerging and unknown attacks.

SmartDefense is built on Check Point's Stateful Inspection and Application Intelligence technologies. These enable an administrator to block specific attacks and complete classes of attacks while allowing legitimate traffic to pass. Application Intelligence is a collection of technologies that identify and thwart application-level attacks by integrating a deep conception of application behavior into network security fortifications. The primary functions of Application Intelligence are to:

- Validate compliance to standards

- Corroborate expected usage of the network and associated protocols

- Block malicious data

- Control hazardous operations that occur in applications

Configuring SmartDefense

To configure SmartDefense follow these steps:

1. In the SmartDashboard window, click the **SmartDefense** tab. The SmartDefense Settings window opens.

2. In the SmartDefense Settings window, select the **SmartDefense category** on which you want to view information.

3. To view details of a specific attack, click + to expand the subdivision and then select the desired attack.

4. Determine from which attacks you need to protect your site, and select **Settings** to configure the various attack classes as well as the specific attacks.

5. Install the security policy. You must reinstall the security policy to put into operation changes to the SmartDefense configuration.

Updating SmartDefense with the Latest Defenses

To receive updates of the most recent defenses from the SmartDefense Web site, select **SmartDefense Settings | General** and then click **Update SmartDefense**.

Network Security

In this section, we will discuss the best-practice network security provisions of SmartDefense. The Network Security and Application Intelligence technologies are free with SmartDefense. Updates are issued by paid subscription. Check Point clients may gain a benefit from the SmartDefense service, as it provides real-time updates and advisories with additional protection against new and rising threats.

SmartDefense is a management component of Check Point FW-1 and VPN-1 that is designed to allow administrators to organize their network in a manner that allows them to practically defend it from both known and unknown (zero-day) attacks. It presents administrators with the most network and application-level security protection for dynamic Internet threats, including the Cisco IOS Malformed OSPF Denial of Service Attack that resulted in a vulnerable system not being able to respond to ordinary requests.

Check Point SmartDefense is a collection of Active Defense products that actively protect organizations from known and unknown network attacks by using intelligent security technology. SmartDefense blocks attacks by type and class using Check Point's patented Stateful Inspection technology and provides a single, centralized console to deliver real-time information regarding attacks as well as attack detection, blocking, logging, auditing, and alerting.

The following features are included in Check Point's SmartDefense:

- Centralized, type-based attack prevention designed to provide a single location for the control and blocking of both known and unknown attacks using a novel attack-type classification technology.

- Online updates and Web worm prevention which allows for online updates from Check Point's SmartDefense attack center to thwart new classes of attacks such as Web worms.

- Real-time attack information using Check Point's online attack information center, which provides security administrators with updated information on each attack class.

- DoS and DDoS attack protection for the most frequent and damaging classes of Internet attacks that result from attempts to flood networks or servers with fake traffic to prevent legitimate traffic. Check Point's SmartDefense mitigates risk and loss from DoS and DDoS attacks through the following:

  - TCP Reservation, which allows a site's network administrators to reserve a fraction of FW-1 capacity for TCP connections. This shields mission-critical TCP traffic from User Datagram Protocol (UDP) and Internet Control Message Protocol (ICMP)-based DoS attacks designed to flood the link.

  - Client Quotas, which allow administrators to define limits on the number of connections that originate from a single Internet Protocol (IP) address. This effectively detects suspicious traffic so that the administrator can act against a DoS attack prior to it escalating beyond control.

  - Server Quotas, which allow administrators to define quotas for each corresponding connection to a single system and respond if the quotas are reached. This enables a more thorough recognition and, hence, defense against DDoS attacks.

You can find additional information regarding SmartDefense at www.checkpoint.com/products/protect/smartdefense.html.

Denial of Service

A DoS attack is intended to interrupt the normal functioning of a system, site, or service. This disruption is characteristically achieved either by overpowering the target with forged packets such that it may no longer answer legitimate requests, or by exploiting operating systems and application and system vulnerabilities to crash the system remotely. DoS attacks are commonly used to remove hosts so that an attacker can start a man-in-the-middle (MITM) attack.

Check Point SmartDefense provides reinforcement capabilities that aid in defending against many common classes of DoS attacks.

Aggressive Aging

Aggressive Aging manages the connections table capacity and the memory expenditure of the firewall to increase durability and stability. Aggressive Aging uses small timeouts that Check Point designates as "aggressive timeouts." If an established connection is determined to be idle for longer than the defined (by protocol) aggressive timeout, the inspection engine will mark it *eligible for deletion* from the state table. As soon as the connections table or memory consumption attains a user-defined threshold (or high-water mark), Aggressive Aging is initiated. You can configure Aggressive Aging timeouts on a per-service basis.

When the set threshold is surpassed, the start of a new incoming connection triggers the deletion of 10 connections from the eligible for deletion table. An additional 10 connections are deleted for each fresh connection until the memory consumption or the connections capacity drops under a predefined low-water mark.

In the event that no eligible for deletion connections exist, the firewall will not delete connections. The table is verified following every subsequent connection that surpasses the high-water mark. The timeout configuration is a primary aspect of memory consumption configuration. Low timeout values will result in connections being removed earlier from the table to make it easier for the firewall to process additional connections at the same time. When memory consumption surpasses the threshold, using shorter timeouts can preserve the connectivity of a majority of the traffic through the firewall.

The chief advantage of Aggressive Aging is that is begins to function when the firewall has existing memory and prior to the connections table becoming completely filled. This feature diminishes the likelihood of connectivity issues that can occur due to circumstances involving low resources.

Aggressive Aging allows the firewall gateway to process an increased volume of unanticipated network traffic as may occur during a DoS attack.

Teardrop Attacks

In implementing the TCP/IP protocol stack, a number of systems fail to correctly deal with the reassembly of overlapping IP fragments (see http://insecure.org/sploits/linux.fragmentation.teardrop.html for details).

Conveying multiple IP fragments to the target that are created with overlapping fragment offsets where one fragment is completely enclosed inside the offset of the other can result in the host incorrectly allocating memory. This would remotely crash the vulnerable system that received the packets. Teardrop is a widely available attack tool that exploits this vulnerability. Teardrop is closely related to syndrop, a modified version that exploits a Microsoft SYN sequence bug.

SmartDefense blocks attacks that rely on overlapping IP fragment offsets. The default action is to block attacks and log them as *Virtual defragmentation error: Overlapping fragments*. Check Point SmartDefense blocks such attacks by default and provides the administrator with the ability to construct alerts, e-mail notices, Simple Network Management Protocol (SNMP) traps, and user-defined actions when these attacks occur.

The Ping of Death

The Ping of Death is a malformed *PING* request that is sent in a series of fragment packets, which when reassembled by the target exceeds the maximum IP packet size (65,535 octets). This results in a system that is vulnerable to crashing (see http://insecure.org/sploits/ping-o-death.html for details).

SmartDefense blocks this type of attack by default. The firewall logs blocked attacks with *Virtual defragmentation error: Packet too big*. SmartDefense provides the administrator with the ability to construct alerts, e-mail notices, SNMP traps, and user-defined actions when these attacks occur.

LAND Attacks

A LAND attack involves the attacker sending a TCP SYN packet (a connection initiation), giving the target with the source and destination addresses set as the target's address. It also uses the same port on the target host as both source and destination. Land.c is an easily obtainable attack tool designed to exploit this vulnerability (see http://insecure.org/sploits/land.ip.DOS.html for further information).

Check Point SmartDefense blocks this attack by default and provides the administrator with the ability to construct alerts, e-mail notices, SNMP traps, and user-defined actions when these attacks occur.

Non-TCP Flooding

An attacker sometimes directly targets security devices such as firewalls. In advanced firewalls, state information regarding connections is maintained in a state table. The state table includes connection-oriented TCP and connectionless non-TCP protocols. Attackers can send high volumes of non-TCP traffic in an effort to fill up a firewall's state table. This results in a denial of service by preventing the firewall from accepting new connections. Unlike TCP, non-TCP traffic does not provide mechanisms to "reset" or clear a connection.

SmartDefense can restrict non-TCP traffic from occupying more than a predefined percentage of a Check Point enforcement point's state table. This eliminates the possibility of this class of attack.

IP and ICMP

Check Point provides a wide-ranging series of tests to ensure the integrity of connections at the network layer. A Check Point enforcement point executes stateful inspection on IP and ICMP connections to identify distinct protocol types, ensuring that they are inspected, monitored, and managed as per the packet flow security definitions. Check Point enforcement points categorize defined IP or ICMP packets by protocol type before executing a protocol header analysis. This process includes protocol flag analysis and verification.

Packet Sanity

The Packet Sanity option executes a number of Layer 3 and Layer 4 "sanity" checks. These incorporate substantiating packet size, an inspection of UDP and TCP header lengths, dropping IP options, and verifying the TCP flags to ensure that packets have not been selectively crafted by a malicious user. This process also checks that all packet parameters are accurately defined as per standards (such as the RFCs). This validation is always enforced. However, administrators can configure whether logs and/or alerts will be delivered for packets that violate these requirements.

Max PING Size

PING (ICMP echo request) is a protocol that is commonly used to confirm whether a remote system is available. The client sends an echo request, and the server responds with an echo reply. This packet also encapsulates the initial client's IP data. A malicious user can issue an ICMP echo request to a target host with an oversize echo data field to compromise the security and availability of the client's system. This could cause a buffer overflow. This is different from the Ping of Death, in which the *PING* request is malformed through a manipulation of IP fragments.

The Max PING Size check can restrict the maximum requested data echo size. The default maximum is 548 bytes as defined from the maximum size in the protocol definition. Administrators can also configure whether logs and/or alerts will be issued for offending packets.

IP Fragments

When an IP packet exceeds the allowed size transported on a particular network, it is divided into a number of smaller IP packets and transmitted as fragments. In an attempt to conceal an attack or exploit, an attacker might break the data section of a single packet into several fragmented packets. Without reassembling the fragments, it is not always possible to detect such an attack. Consequently, malicious content that is split across fragments can traverse some firewalls. In contrast, a Check Point enforcement point collects and reassembles all the fragments of a given IP packet, verifying that the options for the fragments are consistent (e.g., that Time To Live [TTL] is the same for all fragments) so that security checks can be run against the complete packet contents.

The IP Fragments page allows an administrator to configure whether fragmented IP packets can traverse Check Point gateways. It is also possible to allow fragments, setting a limit on the number of fragments allowed, and to set a timeout period for holding unassembled fragments before discarding them. These measures help to protect against DoS attacks that seek to overwhelm the resources of perimeter security devices by flooding them with spurious packet fragments.

Network Quota

Network Quota enforces a limit on the number of connections that are allowed to the same source IP address. When a certain source exceeds the number of allowed connections, Network Quota can either block all new connection attempts from that source, or track the event. This capability is useful in protecting against DoS attacks, and it can help to limit worm propagation by recognizing an inappropriate increase in traffic from an infected source.

The Network Quota protection enforces a limit on the number of connections that are allowed from the same source IP address. When the number of connection requests from a certain source exceeds the configured limit, Client Quota generates an alert and/or blocks all new connections from that source. This feature is particularly useful for preventing DDoS attacks from overwhelming a server.

TCP

The majority of traffic on the Internet today uses TCP as its protocol. Web applications rely on TCP for the reliable transmission of data. SmartDefense is able to inspect TCP segments and examine a packet to verify that it contains only the allowed options. To verify that TCP packets are legitimate, the following tests are conducted:

- Protocol type verification
- Protocol header analysis
- Protocol flags analysis and verification

SYN Attack Configuration

TCP is a connection-oriented protocol with a defined "handshake" process. To begin a connection, a client sends a SYN (Synchronize) connection request to a target host. The host then replies with an ACK (Acknowledge) response. Finally, the client responds back with a SYN-ACK reply. This process is essential to TCP communications and is used to synchronize the two hosts before communications can begin.

SYN flood attacks consist of initiating a TCP handshake (SYN) and not sending the final reply (SYN-ACK) to the server's response (ACK) in the handshaking sequence. This results in the server maintaining an open record in its pending connection queue. As a server's pending connection queue is limited in size, it is relatively simple to completely fill the queue with a flood of fake SYNs. As a result, the server is unable to accept valid TCP connections, resulting in a denial of service.

SmartDefense protects against SYN flood attacks on both protected servers and the Check Point enforcement point. This control keeps attackers from overwhelming servers with false SYN requests. SmartDefense provides two varieties of defense modes against SYN attacks and routinely switches between them as needed:

- Passive defense, which is the default behavior
- SYN Relay Defense (logged as Active Defense), which automatically activates as soon as a SYN attack is detected

The Passive SYN Gateway control is the default action for SYN protection. Using this mode, the Check Point enforcement point monitors TCP handshake progression. All SYN requests are passed to the target server, and a timer is tracked for each request. If the requesting client does not reply to the target host's ACK response inside the configured time frame, a TCP reset is delivered to the server, making it drop the connection from the server's pending connection queue.

As the timeout period is shorter than the pending connection table, this reduces the quantity of pending TCP sessions. This mode provides increased SYN protection at an optimized performance.

When SmartDefense detects a predefined number of unanswered SYN requests per given time period, it switches to SYN Relay Defense. SYN Relay Defense counters the attack by making sure the three-way handshake is completed (i.e., that the connection is valid) before sending a SYN packet to the target host. SYN Relay Defense also ensures that the protected server does not receive any invalid connection attempts, which is advantageous if the server has limited memory or often reaches an overloaded state. In these ways, SYN Relay Defense is a high-performance kernel-level process, which acts as a relay mechanism at the connection level.

Small PMTU

The maximum transmission unit (MTU) of a given network link specifies the largest permissible size of an IP packet on that link. PMTU, or "path" MTU, refers to the smallest MTU in the path (i.e., all of the links) from one device to another.

In a small PMTU attack, the attacker deceives a server into transporting large quantities of data using very small packets by setting the PMTU to a very small value. As each packet has a relatively large related overhead in the IP and other headers, the target server can be filled to capacity. The **Minimal MTU size** configuration option sets a minimum permissible size for packets in a data stream, allowing FireWall-1 to deny connections that attempt to set this size unreasonably low. You should be careful when configuring this option because an exceedingly small value will not prevent an attack, whereas an unnecessarily large value might result in legitimate requests being dropped.

Sequence Verifier

The Sequence Verifier matches the current TCP packet's sequence numbers against a state kept for that TCP connection. Packets that match the connection in terms of TCP session but have sequence numbers that do not make sense are either dropped or stripped of data.

Fingerprint Scrambling

Fingerprinting is a technique by which a remote host gathers information about a host or network by inspecting the unintentional side effects of benign communications. Techniques entail *active fingerprinting*, by which the attacker sends slightly off-protocol packets and tries to gather information from the responses (or lack thereof), and *passive fingerprinting*, by which the attacker either generates no traffic at all (or relies on passively received traffic) or generates no more than standard traffic. These controls deal chiefly with scrambling the passive fingerprints of hosts inside the firewall perimeter.

SmartDefense can jumble some of the fields generally used for fingerprinting, disguising the original characteristics of hosts behind the firewall. Completely preventing fingerprinting is nearly impossible, but this control makes it more difficult for the attacker. Also note that although this feature makes it more difficult to fingerprint the hosts protected by the firewall, it does little to hide the fact that there is a firewall here (i.e., fingerprinting the firewall's existence is still possible).

ISN Spoofing

The first thing that happens when a TCP connection is established is a synchronization of numbers linking the client and the server. This occurs in a process called the *TCP three-way handshake*. In this progression, the client notifies the server about the sequence numbers for the client side of the connection, and the server notifies the client about the sequence numbers for the server side of the connection. The sequence of numbers chosen during the three-way handshake stage is called the Initial Sequence Number (ISN).

The mere fact that there is dissimilarity among the various algorithms for the different operating systems creates a unique fingerprint for every system. By sending successive SYN requests and checking the difference between the ISNs, a potential attacker can determine the operating system that the server is running. SmartDefense prevents this kind of reconnaissance from occurring by creating a difference between the sequence numbers used by the server and the sequence numbers perceived by the client.

TTL

Each IP packet has a field called Time To Live (TTL). Each router along the path or route decrements this value by one. When a router decrements this value to zero it drops the packet and sends an ICMP notification (destination unreachable) to the source. Usually, when a host sends a packet, it sets the TTL to a value that is large enough that the packet can reach its destination under ordinary circumstances.

Different operating systems use different default initial values for TTL. Because of this, an attacker can speculate as to the number of routers between it and the sending machine by making an informed postulation concerning the original TTL.

Further, knowledge of the initial TTLs used offers additional information concerning what operating system the host is running. SmartDefense can amend the TTL field of all packets (or selectively on only all outgoing packets) to a given number. Using this approach it is not possible to know how many internal routers (hops) are between the target and the listener, and the listener cannot utilize any knowledge of the default TTL value to speculate as to the operating system of the source host.

IP ID

IP packets have a 16-bit field called the ID, which is used when an IP packet is fragmented. The ID allows the receiving machine to know which virtual packet the fragmented packets belong to. Although two IP packets must have two distinct IP IDs, there is no official specification as to how to assign the IP ID to each packet.

Different operating systems use different algorithms for assigning IP IDs to packets. Consequently, an attacker can use this information to understand what operating system generated a particular packet. SmartDefense can replace the original IP ID with one generated by the Check Point enforcement point, thus disguising the algorithm used by the original operating system and consequently disguising the operating system's characteristics from prospective attackers.

Successive Events

Successive Events Detection (formerly known as Malicious Activity Detection) provides a method for detecting malicious or suspicious events and alerting the security administrator.

Successive Events Detection runs on the SmartCenter Server and analyzes logs from Check Point enforcement points by correlating log entries to attack profiles. The security administrator can adjust attack detection parameters, turn detection on or off for particular attacks, or disable the Successive Events feature entirely. Logs that do not arrive at the SmartCenter Server are not analyzed. Local logs and logs sent to a customer log module (CLM), for instance, are not checked.

The classes of malicious activity that can trigger successive events alerts include:

- Address spoofing
- Local interface spoofing

- Port scanning

- Successive alerts (an excessive number of alerts generated by policies in the rulebase)

- Successive multiple connections (an excessive number of connections opened to a specific destination IP address and port number from the same source IP address)

Successive Events Detection can look for port scanning; however, newer versions of SmartDefense include a new Port Scanning control and should be used over Successive Events Detection. We are discussing this feature here for backward compatibility.

For each, the administrator can configure the number of events needed in a given period to trigger an action, as well as configure the individual action.

DShield Storm Center

The SmartDefense Storm Center Module enables a two-way information flow between the network's Storm Centers and the organizations requiring network security information. Storm Centers gather logging information about attacks. This information is voluntarily provided by organizations across the globe. Storm Centers then collate and present reports on real-time network security threats in an immediately useful manner.

One of the leading Storm Centers is the SANS Institute's Dshield.org. Check Point SmartDefense integrates with the SANS DShield.org Storm Center in two ways, as discussed in the following sections.

Tools & Traps…

Smart Defense Profiles

Every profile created takes 2 MB of RAM from the user console host on both the Windows and the Motif versions. The more complex and granular you make the profiling, the more resources the firewall requires.

Retrieve and Block Malicious IPs

The DShield.org Storm Center produces a Block List report, which lists address ranges that merit blocking and is regularly updated. The SmartDefense Storm Center Module retrieves and adds this list to the Security Policy in a manner that makes every update instantly effective. SmartDefense enables the system administrator to decide whether to block all the malicious IP addresses received from DShield.org, or whether to block addresses for specific gateways. Additionally, SmartDefense provides the system administrator with the option of being informed using logs, alerts, e-mail messages, and so on when IP addresses from within the IP address ranges in the Block List attempt to contact the network.

Report to DShield

Logs can be sent to the Storm Center to help other organizations combat the threats that SmartDefense and Web Intelligence detected. Administrators can decide which Check Point log type to send to the Storm Center.

The logs submitted to the Storm Center contain the following information:

- Connection parameters, including the source IP address, destination IP address, source port, destination port (i.e., the service), and IP (such as UDP, TCP, or ICMP)

- Rulebase parameters, including time and action

- A detailed description of the log

- The name of the attack and the detected URL pattern, which are sent for HTTP worm patterns detected by Web Intelligence

To protect a client's privacy, SmartDefense can delete information from the destination IP address in the submitted log that could be used for identification. Administrators can configure a mask size that defines how much of an internal address to delete. This ensures the privacy of the organization while allowing the Storm Centers to correlate the attack data.

SmartDefense integrates with the SANS DShield.org Storm Center in the following manner (see Figure 7.1):

1. The DShield.org Storm Center produces a Block List report, which is a frequently updated list of address ranges that are recommended for blocking.

The SmartDefense Storm Center Module retrieves and adds this list to the security policy.

2. The Storm Center sends logs to other organizations to help those organizations combat threats that were directed at the network. To send logs, select the **Security Rules** and **SmartDefense/Web Intelligence** controls for which you want to send logs.

Figure 7.1 How SmartDefense Integrates with the DShield.org Network Storm Center

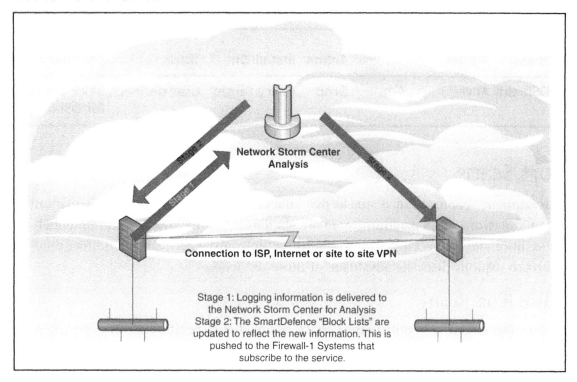

To manually configure the blocking of malicious IPs, follow these steps:

1. In SmartDefense, select **Network Security | DShield Storm Center**.

2. Clear the **Retrieve and Block Malicious IPs** option.

3. Add the **Block List rule** (see Table 7.1) and do the following:

   a. Place the Block List rule as high as possible in the Security rulebase, but below all authentication rules and any other rules for trusted sources that should not be blocked.

b. To retrieve and drop malicious IPs only at particular gateways, specify them in the **Install On** cell of the rule.

c. If you are also submitting logs to DShield and want to report logs generated by blocking malicious IPs, ensure that the **Track** setting is identical to the **Submit Logs of Type** setting in the **SmartDefense DShield Storm Center | Report to DShield** section.

4. Install the Security Policy.

Table 7.1 The Block List Rule for the DShield Storm Center

Source Address	Destination Address	Service	Action	Install On	Track	Comment
CPDShield	Any	Any	Drop	Policy target	User-defined	Block List rule for DShield

Port Scans

Port scans are reconnaissance attacks that attackers implement to learn information about a network in preparation for an attack. This helps the attacker find potential target hosts and the services running on those hosts. Attackers can then direct their efforts to exploits that take advantage of those services.

Host Port Scan

A host port scan is a reconnaissance attack directed at a specific host or network. A scan can determine which services a host offers. For instance, a host port scan could determine that a specified host has TCP ports 23, 25, and 110 open, denoting that it may offer the Telnet, Simple Mail Transfer Protocol (SMTP), and Post Office Protocol 3 (POP3) services.

Sweep Scan

An IP sweep scan looks for a specific open port and determines which hosts are listening in on that port. For example, network worms employ IP sweep scans when they try to find machines they can propagate themselves. For example, the Blaster worm looks for the Remote Procedure Call (RPC) service—searching the complete network looking for that single open service.

Dynamic Ports

A number of application protocols, including the File Transfer Protocol (FTP) and Session Initiation Protocol (SIP), set up connections by opening IP ports dynamically. These ports can sometimes be the same as those employed by a predefined service making use of a well-known port (i.e., lower than 1024). Various attacks take advantage of this fact and attempt to bypass security validation by appearing to be generated by an allowed application that's opening a port dynamically.

SmartDefense allows you to configure which ports are "privileged ports" that will be protected when opening a connection dynamically (e.g., FTP data connections). These ports are a subset of the ports of the TCP and UDP services defined. When an attacker is trying to open a dynamic connection to such a protected port, the connection is dropped. In addition, it is possible to explicitly protect low ports (those lower than 1024).

Application Intelligence

Many of the most serious threats from the Internet come from attacks that attempt to exploit application vulnerabilities. Because application-driven attacks tend to be sophisticated in nature, effective defenses must be equally sophisticated and intelligent. Check Point's Application Intelligence is a set of advanced capabilities which detect and prevent application-level attacks.

Mail

In a mail and recipient content attack, e-mail worms and viruses introduce malicious code that can reach your system and infect other users through harmful attachments. In addition, a number of viruses are transmitted through harmless-looking e-mail messages and can run automatically without the need for user intervention.

Initially defined as a text-based message exchange, e-mail today can be employed to exchange nontext file formats such as audio and video across the Internet. The Multipurpose Internet Mail Extension (MIME), RFCs 2045 and 2046, was created as an extension to the basic e-mail protocols to accommodate these other file types. SmartDefense can recognize MIME attachments and limit their potential to introduce malicious content. By default, SmartDefense does not allow multiple content-type headers. Although the security administrator has the option of allowing multiple content-type headers, the SmartDefense default suggests that such a decision can open the network to malicious behavior and as such recommends a limitation of content-type headers.

SmartDefense strips MIME attachments of the particular type from the message. For example, the message/partial MIME type is stripped to prevent fragmented and reassembled messages. The message/partial MIME type can be employed to bypass most of the security restrictions imposed on e-mail messages (as the messages get divided into smaller segments) so that virus scanners or other content-testing mechanisms cannot detect the malicious messages.

SMTP Content

The SMTP Security Server allows for the stringent validation of SMTP. It protects against malicious mail messages, provides SMTP-centered security, prevents attempts to bypass the rulebase making use of mail relays, and prevents DoS and spam mail attacks.

Usually, the SMTP Security Server is activated by specifying resources in the rulebase. However, selecting **Configuration applies to all connections** will forward all SMTP connections to the SMTP Security Server and will enforce the defined settings on all connections; selecting **Configurations apply only to connections related to rule base defined objects** means that these configurations will apply only to SMTP connections for which a resource is defined in the rulebase.

NOTE

The settings in the Mail and Recipient Content window apply only if an SMTP resource is defined, even if **Configurations apply to all connections** is checked. The SMTP Security Server provides content security that enables an administrator to do the following:

- Provide mail address translation by hiding any outgoing e-mail's "From" address behind a standard generic address that conceals internal network structure and real internal users
- Perform e-mail filtering based on SMTP addresses and IP addresses
- Strip MIME attachments of particular classes from e-mail
- Strip the received information from outgoing e-mail, to conceal the internal network structure
- Drop e-mail messages larger than a given size
- Send many e-mail messages per single connection

- Resolve the domain name system (DNS) address for e-mail recipients and their domain on outgoing connections (MX Resolving)
- Control the load generated by the e-mail dequeue in two different ways: by controlling the number of connections per site, and by controlling the overall connections generated by the e-mail dequeuer
- Provide a rulebase match on the Security Server mail dequeuer which enables an e-mail-user-based policy, better performance of different e-mail content action per recipient of a given e-mail, generation of different e-mail contents on a per-user basis, and application of content security features at the user level
- Perform Content Vectoring Protocol (CVP) checking (e.g., for viruses) with a third-party solution

Mail and Recipient Content

The settings in this section apply only if an SMTP resource is defined, even if all connections in the SMTP Security Server window are checked. The SMTP Security Server does not provide authentication, as there is no person at the system who can be challenged for an authentication. The SMTP Security Server does provide content security that enables the security administrator to supply e-mail address translation by hiding "From" addresses behind a standard generic address that conceals internal network structures and actual internal users, executes e-mail filtering based on SMTP addresses and IP addresses, and strips MIME attachments of particular classes from e-mail.

Here is a summary of the settings on this page:

- **Allow multiple content-type headers** Unchecked by default; if checked, the SMTP server will allow multiple content-type headers.

- **Allow multiple "encoding" headers** Unchecked by default; if checked, the SMTP server will allow multiple "encoding" headers.

- **Allow non-plain "encoding" headers** Unchecked by default; if checked, the SMTP server will allow non-plain "encoding" headers.

- **Allow unknown encoding** Checked by default; if checked, the SMTP server will allow unknown encoding methods.

- **Force recipient to have a domain name** Checked by default; if checked, the SMTP server will force the recipient to have a domain name.

- **Perform aggressive MIME strip** Checked by default:

  - If checked, the complete e-mail body will be scanned for headers such as *Content-Type: text/html; charset=utf-8* and the MIME strip will be performed accordingly.

  - If unchecked, only the e-mail headers section and the headers of each MIME part will be scanned (if a relevant header is located, the MIME strip will consequently be performed).

POP3/IMAP Security

SmartDefense offers options that enable limitations on e-mail messages delivered to the network making use of POP3/IMAP. These options make it possible to recognize and stop malicious behavior. For example, SmartDefense can limit the length of a username and password. An attacker can send a long string of characters when it is not expected and may result in a buffer overflow attack that could crash the machine. Additionally, SmartDefense can verify and restrict binary data enclosed in POP3/IMAP messages.

SmartDefense can test POP3/IMAP usernames and passwords against the user database defined in VPN-1/FireWall-1. Based on this information, administrators can configure SmartDefense to restrict connections when the username and password are identical. SmartDefense ensures that POP3 and IMAP traffic adheres to the established protocols and security best practices. SmartDefense monitors the communication state of connections and can, for example, drop a *LIST* command if the user was not first authenticated as required by the protocol. In addition, SmartDefense can limit the number of *NOOP* commands issued. The *NOOP* command (No Operation) is rarely employed by e-mail clients but is used in selected DoS attacks.

FTP

These sections allow administrators to configure various controls related to FTP.

FTP Bounce

Particularly for FTP when issuing the *PORT* command as part of the FTP control session, the originating host specifies an arbitrary destination address and port for the data connection. However, this behavior also means that an attacker can open a connection to a port of his or her choosing on a host that may not be the originating client.

Making this connection to an arbitrary host for unauthorized purposes is the FTP Bounce attack. SmartDefense protects against FTP Bounce attacks by allowing only

FTP sessions in which the control and data session IP addresses match. Administrators can also configure preferred tracking options.

FTP Security Server

The FTP Security Server provides authentication services and content security based on FTP commands (*PUT/GET*); filename restrictions; and CVP checking (e.g., viruses and other malware). In addition, the FTP Security Server logs FTP *GET* and *PUT* commands, as well as associated filenames.

The FTP Security Server is characteristically enabled by specifying rules in the firewall security policy. If you select the **Configuration applies to all connections** option, the firewall will forward all FTP connections to the FTP Security Server.

Allowed FTP Commands

For security reasons, it is possible to limit the FTP commands allowed to pass through the firewall.

Prevent Known Ports Checking allows you to select whether to allow the FTP Security Server to connect to well-known ports. Thus, it provides a second layer of protection against selected bounce attacks. Even if the attacker manages to bounce a connection, the FTP Security Server will not let the bounce connect to any port running a known service. SmartDefense blocks attempts to issue FTP *PORT* commands to connect to well-known TCP or UDP port numbers (e.g., TCP port 23 for Telnet and TCP 80 for HTTP).

Tools & Traps...

Smart Defense and FTP

By default, SmartDefense is configured to perform known-port checking for FTP connections. By toggling the checkbox to **on**, administrators may disable this enforcement point. In general, disabling this test is recommended only when you need to preserve connectivity for a specific application that cannot act in accordance with the safeguard.

Preventing Port Overflow Checks

To conform to the FTP specifications, the *PORT* command has the originating host specify an arbitrary destination and port for data connection. By using different representations of the same number, attackers can attempt to bypass restrictions and PORT connections. SmartDefense blocks connections that implement multiple representations of the same number in an FTP *PORT* command.

NOTE

By default, SmartDefense is configured to perform PORT overflow checks for FTP connections where toggling the checkbox to **on** disables this enforcement. In general, disabling this test is recommended only when the administrator needs to preserve connectivity for a specific application that cannot act in accordance with the safeguard.

Microsoft Networking

Clicking **Configuration applies to all connections** will enforce settings on all connections.

File and Print Sharing

CIFS, the Common Internet File System (sometimes called SMB for Server Message Block), is a protocol for sharing files and printers in a Microsoft environment. The protocol is widely implemented by Microsoft operating systems. CIFS has many known vulnerabilities, including Null Session exploits and Host Announcement flooding. In addition, many worms that have infected a host exploit CIFS as a means of propagation.

The SANS Institute has acknowledged that unprotected Windows networking shares is one of the top 20 critical threats to Internet security (www.sans.org/top20). This is mainly due to the frequency of exploits that target this vulnerability.

The File and Print Sharing control lets administrators configure worm signatures that can detect and block worm attacks at the Check Point enforcement point. This detection takes place in the kernel and does not require a security server.

Peer-to-Peer Applications

Peer-to-peer applications pose security concerns for organizations as they become increasingly popular and more intelligent in how they interconnect peer nodes. Historically, peer-to-peer applications were simple to block as they employed central servers to coordinate communications. Today, peer-to-peer applications are frequently complex to perceive for numerous reasons, including their capability to exploit proprietary protocols across any accessible port, their ability to masquerade as HTTP traffic across the characteristic TCP port 80 channel, and their inventive mechanisms for making use of reachable peers as a proxy to reach other peers blocked by a firewall. In these ways, peer-to-peer applications have emerged as a potential covert channel for transferring confidential information across the traditional security perimeter.

This control detects and blocks the most widely deployed peer-to-peer applications. Once configured, it can detect peer-to-peer applications running across all 64,535 possible ports. In addition, it inspects HTTP traffic to detect peer-to-peer applications masquerading as HTTP traffic across port 80. This control includes HTTP header value definitions for most common peer-to-peer applications and allows administrators to add additional headers if needed. In addition, the SmartDefense Service allows updates to these headers as they become available.

The **Exclusion Settings** options allow specific ports or hosts to be excluded from peer-to-peer checking. SmartDefense can monitor the following peer-to-peer applications and their variants.

Kazaa

Both iMesh and Grokster are identified in the SmartView Tracker as KaZaA.

Gnutella et al.

Gnutella, Bearshare, Shareaza, and Morpeheus are identified in the SmartView Tracker as Gnutella. The following peer-to-peer applications are also detected.

- eMule
- Skype
- BitTorrent

Yahoo!

SmartDefense recognizes Yahoo! Messenger when used for messaging, voice, video, and file transfer.

ICQ

SmartDefense recognizes ICQ when used for messaging, voice, video, and file transfer and defeats peer-to-peer firewall traversal. Most peer-to-peer applications include firewall traversal features, which look for open ports in the firewall. SmartDefense can detect peer-to-peer applications attempting to traverse any open port.

This also prevents HTTP masquerading. Many peer-to-peer applications can hide by encapsulating their communications in HTTP. SmartDefense can detect and block these connections.

SmartDefense can defeat peer-to-peer proxies as well. In a number of peer-to-peer applications, peer nodes communicate location information in a comparable means as dynamic routing protocols. This information allows an internal peer to commence a connection from inside the network, traversing firewalls that consider any connection initiated from inside the network as safe. SmartDefense blocks these classes of connections.

Instant Messaging

Instant Messaging applications provide communication and collaboration among Internet users using various modes of communication, including the exchange of instant messages, voice and video, application sharing, white boards, file transfer, and remote assistance. The odds are that these applications are already in use within your organization; Check Point adds the ability to monitor and control these applications.

MSN over SIP

MSN Messenger uses SIP for real-time voice, video, and collaboration communication. Just like other network applications, an attacker can exploit MSN Messenger in an attack.

This control provides several security controls for MSN Messenger. SmartDefense can block all MSN Messenger traffic or restrict specific allowable actions, including file transfer, application sharing, white boards, and remote assistant. In addition, SmartDefense will apply the general SIP controls as configured in SmartDashboard.

DNS

DNS is the standard Internet protocol that maps human-readable addresses (e.g., www.syngress.com) to machine-readable IP addresses. To taint a network with malicious content, attackers attempt to change the content of a DNS packet and attempt to make it enter the network undetected. Thus, when clients ask for a name to an IP address resolution from an infected DNS server, they may receive an IP address pointing them to the attacker's site or to a nonexistent host.

SmartDefense is able to distinguish a DNS packet that has been altered. This capability enables SmartDefense to catch potentially harmful packets before they enter the network. DNS queries are generally transmitted over UDP, but in a number of cases they are exchanged over TCP, such as during zone transfers between DNS servers. SmartDefense enables a system administrator to enforce DNS over TCP and UDP. Controls will be applied to all DNS port connections over UDP and TCP to prevent attackers from using DNS for an attack.

Protocol Enforcement

By selecting the **UDP protocol enforcement** option, administrators can configure VPN-1/FireWall-1 to monitor DNS traffic to ensure compliance with DNS RFCs, meaning that the DNS packets are correctly formatted and contain only DNS-related information. DNS RFCs include 1034, 1035, 1996, 2136, 2317, 2535, and 2671. SmartDefense will test several RFC-defined parameters, including lengths, counters, header flags, domain format, and resource record format, among others.

Domain Black Lists

A black list is a group of URL addresses that have been prohibited. SmartDefense contains a black list for the purpose of filtering out undesirable traffic. SmartDefense will not permit a user to access a domain address particular in the black list. You can update the domain black list manually or automatically as part of the SmartDefense Service.

Cache Poisoning

To reduce DNS traffic, name servers maintain cache. Each DNS record includes a TTL value, which tells the DNS server how long the record can be stored in the cache before it should expire. Cache poisoning occurs when DNS caches mapping information that was deliberately altered from a remote name server. The DNS server caches the incorrect information and sends it out as the requested information. As a result, e-mail messages and URL addresses can be redirected and the information sent by a user can be captured and corrupted.

Scrambling

DNS performs limited authentication for DNS transactions, checking only source and destination IP addresses, port numbers, and query IDs. Query IDs are assigned by the host that initiates the DNS query. Attackers exploit a number of techniques to obtain a valid query ID, exploiting weaknesses in random number generators in DNS servers and employing advanced statistical analysis (e.g., the Birthday attack). Given the ID number and source port, an attacker can send a spoofed reply that contains counterfeit information on behalf of the name server to which the request was initially sent. This enables the redirection of the hosts to fake Web sites that can be used to collect private user information.

To guard the corporate DNS server from cache poisoning, SmartDefense has the capability to scramble the source port and query ID number of each DNS request. This control can be applied either to all traffic or to specific servers.

Dropping Inbound Requests

DNS is a distributed protocol whereby information is distributed all over the Internet instead of being hosted in a single site. DNS defines a process that lets clients find the correct DNS server with the information required. Each domain has one or more authoritative domain servers that are responsible for the maintenance and distribution of DNS information for that domain. Consequently, as these are considered the definitive repository of domain information, they are also an attractive target for an attacker. A compromised authoritative DNS server poses an issue for all users on the network trying to connect to an organization's domain (potentially both internally and externally).

SmartDefense minimizes the risk faced by an authoritative domain server from attack. Because the server is authoritative for a predefined set of domains, inbound DNS queries for other domains would not be expected. SmartDefense can restrict inbound requests to a DNS server to only those related to the defined domains. Any inbound requests for domains not defined in SmartDefense are blocked.

Detecting Mismatched Replies

A mismatched reply occurs when a DNS query results in an answer that does not match the requested information. Mismatched replies indicate an attempt to perform DNS cache poisoning. When a large number of mismatched replies occur over a specific period, it can be assumed that the network has been corrupted.

To protect the network from cache poisoning, SmartDefense employs a threshold. The threshold detects mismatched replies when more than a specific number of mismatched replies occur over a specific amount of time. When

Voice over IP (VoIP)

Voice and video traffic, like any other information on the corporate IP network, has to be protected as it enters and leaves the organization. Possible threats to this traffic include:

- Call redirections, where calls intended for the receiver are redirected to someone else

- Stealing calls, where the caller pretends to be someone else

- Unauthorized, free toll calls

- DoS attacks caused by hacking a VoIP device or spoofing a call termination message

- Systems hacking, or making use of ports opened for VoIP connections

Important Capabilities

In addition to the controls and capabilities offered through firewall policies (these include VoIP domains, network address translator [NAT] traversal, and more), SmartDefense provides enhanced security capabilities for VoIP protocols. One of these is dynamic ports, which open firewall ports only when needed. For instance, FireWall-1 opens only the ports that have been negotiated during VoIP call setup, including those transmitted inside the protocol.

Flow enforcement monitors the state of communication between VoIP endpoints and ensures that they follow the flow defined by the individual RFCs. This helps to prevent hijackers from interjecting malicious traffic outside the regular call session process (e.g., sending fake call termination notices in an attempt to deceive a billing system).

H.323 Voice Protocol

H.323 is an International Telecommunication Union (ITU) standard that specifies the components, protocols, and procedures that provide multimedia communication services, as well as real-time audio, video, and data communications over packet networks, including IP-based networks.

SmartDefense supports H.323 Version 2, which includes H.225 Version 2 and H.245 Version 3. It performs the following application layer checks:

- It provides strict validation of the protocol, including the order and direction of H.323 packets.

- If the phone number sent is longer than 24 characters the packet is dropped, preventing buffer overruns in the server.

- Dynamic ports will be opened only if the port is not in use by another service (e.g., if the Connect message sends port 80 for the H.245 it will not be opened, averting well-known ports from being exploited illicitly).

SIP Voice Protocol

SIP is a VoIP protocol transported over UDP. SIP is one of the most widely accepted VoIP protocols with integration in many applications, including Microsoft Windows XP and MSN Messenger. SIP is an application-layer control protocol required for the creation, modification, and termination of sessions with one or more participants. SmartDefense Application Intelligence ensures that packets match the RFC 3261 for SIP over UDP/IP specifications (SIP over TCP is unsupported). It also inspects SIP-based Instant Messaging protocols, and it protects against DoS attacks as well as against penetration attempts such as connection hijacking and connection manipulation.

SmartDefense validates the expected usage of SIP. For example, if an end-of-call message is sent immediately after the start of the call, the call will be denied because this behavior is characteristic of a DoS attack. Application-level checks include:

- Checks for binaries and illegal characters in packets

- Strict RFC validation for header fields

- Header field length restrictions

- Removal of unknown media types

MGCP Voice Protocol

The Media Gateway Control Protocol (MGCP) is a protocol for controlling telephony gateways from external call control devices called *call agents* (also known as Media Gateway Controllers). MGCP is a client/server protocol, which means it assumes limited intelligence at the edge (endpoints) and intelligence at the core (call agent). In this it differs from SIP and H.323, which are peer-to-peer protocols.

SmartDefense provides full network-level security for MGCP. SmartDefense enforces stringent compliance with RFC 2705, RFC 3435 (Version 1.0), and ITU TGCP specification J.171.

Additionally, SmartDefense affords inspection of fragmented packets, anti-spoofing, and security against DoS attacks. SmartDefense restricts handover locations and controls signaling and data connections. NAT on MGCP is not supported. SmartDefense can perform additional content security checks for MGCP connections, thereby providing a greater level of protection. MGCP-specific Application Intelligence security is configured via SmartDefense. Three options are available with this control:

- Define individual MGCP commands to accept or block.
- Verify MGCP header content.
- Allow multicast Real-time Transport Protocol (RTP) connections.

SCCP Voice Protocol

The Skinny Client Control Protocol (SCCP) controls telephony gateways from external call control devices (call agents, or Media Gateway Controllers). SCCP is a VoIP protocol used in many Cisco voice implementations.

SmartDefense provides full connectivity and network-level security for SCCP-based VoIP communication. All SCCP traffic is inspected, and authentic traffic is allowed to pass while attacks are blocked. All SmartDefense capabilities are supported by this control, including anti-spoofing and protection against DoS attacks. SmartDefense restricts handover locations, and controls signaling and data connections. Fragmented packets are examined and secured, making use of kernel-based streaming. NAT on SCCP devices is not supported.

SmartDefense tracks state and verifies that the state is valid for all SCCP messages. For a number of key messages, it also verifies the existence and correctness of the message parameters.

VoIP Enhancements

New SIP features to enhance VoIP include:

- MGCP NAT support
- MGCP on dynamic ports
- SIP NAT support in a Back-to-Back User Agent (B2BUA) configuration

- Static NAT for a SIP proxy in internal networks

- Extended SIP state machine

- Blocked/allowed SIP commands

- Interoperability with Nortel, Broadsoft, Cisco, NEC, Polycom, Sylantro, Avaya, and others

SNMP

SNMP is part of the Internet protocol suite that provides a consistent framework for the management of various network devices. It is frequently implemented for managing network devices. The current version of SNMP is Version 3. In terms of security, SNMP versions 2 and 3 provide enhanced security over Version 1. SNMPv3 contains security features such as authentication, authorization, access control, data integrity, key management, and encryption options not available in previous SNMP versions.

Attackers exploit several issues related to SNMP. SNMP packets can be used to gain information about network devices, which was a particular concern in prior versions of SNMP that did not implement authentication or other security features. Additionally, default community strings are widely known for many vendors. Attackers can exploit this information to monitor or configure devices making use of the default strings.

SmartDefense provides several security features for SNMP. SmartDefense can be configured to permit only the more secure SNMPv3, rejecting SNMP versions 1 and 2. If SNMP versions 1 and 2 are required, SmartDefense can block SNMP packets making use of particular community strings. Several well-known default community strings are preconfigured, but administrators can define their own set of strings to block. This allows continued utilization of insecure SNMP versions 1 and 2 while escalating security through mitigating attacks making use of well-known default community strings.

VPN Protocols

Application Intelligence extends client-to-client communication by defining an Office Mode range of addresses for remote clients, and then including this range of addresses in the virtual private network (VPN) domain of the gateway that acts as the hub. Each remote client directs communication to the remote peer via the gateway; from the remote client's perspective, its peer belongs to the VPN domain of the gateway.

Small IKE Phase II Proposals

Two properties control whether small proposals are used—one for pre-NG with Application Intelligence, and the other for NG with Application Intelligence:

- **phase2_proposal** Determines whether an old client (pre-NG with Application Intelligence) will try small proposals. The default is "false."

- **phase2_proposal_size** Determines whether a new client (for NG with Application Intelligence) will try small proposals. The default is "true." In **Global Properties | Remote Access page| VPN –Advanced subpage | User Encryption Properties**, select **AES-128**. This configures remote users to offer AES-128 as a small proposal.

VPN Attack Prevention

The VPN capabilities of the Application Intelligence feature allow the administrator to validate digital certificates used against the Certificate Revocation List and monitor for preshared secret vulnerability. This provides protection against:

- Internet Key Exchange (IKE) brute force attacks
- Hub-and-spoke topology attacks
- IKE UDP DoS attacks
- Windows 2000 IKE DoS attacks
- VPN IP spoofing attacks
- VPN MITM attacks

Content Protection

VPN-1 provides web content security via its OPSEC partners. This allows URL filtering and network virus protection making use of Check Point best-of-breed partners. VPN-1 also provides a number of integrated Web security capabilities that are configured via the Security rulebase. These include a number of URL-based protections, and the ability to secure XML Web Services (SOAP) on Web servers.

Web Intelligence allows the definition of an error page that can be sent back to the user whose browsing was blocked (see Figure 7.2). This control can be utilized in combination with SmartView Tracker to identify the exact cause of a connection being closed.

Figure 7.2 HTML Error Page Configuration

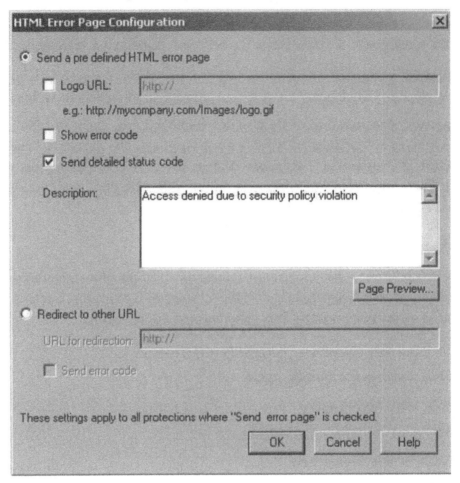

MS-RPC

MS-RPC is a protocol used by many applications in a networked environment. It allows client machines to access (call) a server for selected functions (procedures) as though the server were located on the client machine. Similar to FTP, clients and servers negotiate ports within the MS-RPC session. For firewalls that must open or close ports to provide access control, MS-RPC can pose unique challenges due to the dynamic nature of the protocol. To traverse a firewall, either a wide range of ports must be left open to allow MS-RPC, or the firewall must understand MS-RPC communications. As a consequence of being deployed in the majority of Microsoft applications, MS-RPC is often exploited by attackers in attacks such as the Blaster worm and Spike. These attacks are based on malformed MS-RPC traffic. SmartDefense understands the MS-RPC protocol and routinely applies several security features every time MS-RPC is permitted as part of the firewall security policy. No configuration is required. These controls are based on the understanding of MS-RPC formats, sessions, and defined flow.

Important Capabilities

SmartDefense includes some important capabilities. For example, with strict protocol enforcement, SmartDefense checks and verifies protocol fields. This prevents worms and other attacks from making use of malformed MS-RCP packets for attacks. In addition, with protocol flow enforcement, SmartDefense monitors communication sessions to ensure that the state and flow adhere to the protocol. For example, SmartDefense ensures that new MS-RPC sessions start with a call to the server EndPointMapper (these are commonly called the portmapper or rpcbind) which is defined as part of the MS-RPC protocol. This is done to first establish the ports to be used for the application session.

Dynamic port allocation is used so that SmartDefense only needs to open ports as they are negotiated during the MS-RPC session. This minimizes the number of ports and length of time these ports are open on the firewall. Specific application identification is implemented for each application in an MS-RPC environment. This defines a globally unique identifier (GUID). Applications such as Microsoft Outlook have an assigned GUID. SmartDefense recognizes GUIDs and will restrict MS-RPC calls to only those applications permitted in the firewall policy.

MS-SQL

Application Intelligence provides the capability to block specific MS-SQL attacks. These include:

- SQL resolver buffer overflows
- The SQL Slammer worm

Routing Protocols

Application Intelligence provides additional fortification to IP routing. Dynamic routing protocols, of which the Routing Information Protocol (RIP), Open Shortest Path First (OSPF), and Border Gateway Protocol (BGP) are the most widely deployed, have been increasingly abused by malicious users over the past few years. In the absence of strong authentication validation verifying that routing information comes from the true peer router, a malicious user may spoof or modify valid routing protocol messages and corrupt or change a network's routing tables. This may cause a redirection of network traffic, connectivity problems, excessive bandwidth consumption, and a potential denial of service to the router or, specifically, the routing protocol.

To block routing-protocol-based attacks, Check Point has added a control designed to verify that all traffic is Message Digest 5 (MD5)–authenticated (all protocols) and that all packet headers are valid (RIP, OSPF).

By applying this protection, SmartDefense will enforce the packet header validity advertised by OSPF and RIP, including protocol version, message type, and packet length. This control will also enforce MD5 routing authentication on all protocols and will detect and restrict other authentication mechanisms that are considered insecure (e.g., plain text password authentication).

In addition to protecting dynamic routing protocols, IP controls also stop the following attacks:

- IP record routes
- IP source routes
- Loose source routes
- Strict source routes
- IP spoofing

SUN-RPC

Application Intelligence provides the capability to restrict specific SUN-RPC attacks. These include:

- ToolTalk attacks
- snmpXdmid attacks
- rstat attacks
- mountd attacks
- cmsd attacks
- cachefsd attacks

DHCP

Application Intelligence provides validation of the Dynamic Host Configuration Protocol (DHCP) that offers the following features:

- Performs stringent DHCP option enforcement, allowing only selected and approved DHCP options to be issued to the client

- The capability to drop unauthorized BOOTP clients

- The capability to drop non-Ethernet DHCP clients from the network

SOCKS

Proxy servers use the SOCKS protocol to handle requests from clients and forward these requests across the Internet. The vulnerability impacts applications making use of the protocol by allowing Trojan or backdoor programs to exploit the default SOCKS port (TCP/1080) to bypass firewalls, resulting in remote code execution and data theft.

The SOCKS protocol is increasingly exploited by worms with Trojan capabilities as a communication channel to gain remote control over systems. Some of these worms include:

- The mass-mailing Win32.Mydoom, which opens and listens on TCP port 1080. The worm acts as a SOCKS proxy and can be used to redirect network traffic through the infected system.

- Phatbot/Agobot, which can run a SOCKS proxy on demand and redirect SOCKS traffic.

- Win32/Bagle, which acts as a backdoor Trojan and SOCKS proxy that allows unauthorized access to an affected host.

SOCKS controls may be configured to either drop SOCKS versions other than Version 5 or restrict unauthenticated SOCKS connections altogether. SOCKS versions prior to Version 5 do not deploy authentication. Version 5 may optionally use authentication.

Web Intelligence

Web Intelligence is based on Check Point's Stateful Inspection, Application Intelligence, and Malicious Code Protector technologies, so it is possible to restrict not only specific attacks, but also complete categories of attacks, while allowing genuine traffic to pass. Web Intelligence offers the following features:

- **Malicious Code Protector** This feature blocks attackers from sending malicious code to target Web servers and applications. It can detect malicious executable code within Web communications by identifying not only the existence of executable code in a data stream, but also that code's potential for malicious behavior. Malicious Code Protector is a kernel-based control delivering almost wire-speed performance.

- **Application Intelligence** This is a set of technologies that detect and prevent application-level attacks by integrating a deeper understanding of application behavior into network security defenses.

- **Stateful Inspection** This feature analyzes the information flow into and out of a network so that real-time security decisions are based on communication session information as well as on application information. It accomplishes this by tracking the state and context of all communications traversing the firewall gateway, even when the connection involves complex protocols.

All Web Intelligence defenses can be activated for specific Web servers. If the control is problematic on a particular Web server, it can be turned off for that Web server.

Damage & Defense...

Key Additions to Check Point's NGX R65 Release

Updates to integrated Web filtering enable organizations to keep their employees safe from malicious Web sites such as phishing sites, as well as reduce liability caused by the viewing of inappropriate Web sites. With the rise of client-side attacks, this feature is becoming increasingly critical.

Web Intelligence provides a wide range of security features for Web servers. All Web Intelligence features are implemented in the Kernel Inspection Module, which means that users benefit from very high performance.

Connectivity Implications of Specific Protections

HTTP inspection settings that are too severe can affect connectivity to and from valid Web servers. For example:

- HTTP format size protection restricts URL lengths, header lengths, or the number of headers. This is a good practice, as these elements can be implemented to perform a DoS attack on a Web server. However, these restrictions can also potentially block valid sites. Applying the control for specific Web servers can solve these connectivity problems.

- ASCII-only Request Header protection can obstruct connectivity to Web pages that have non-ASCII characters in URLs. Applying the control for specific Web servers can solve these connectivity problems.

- Some standard and non-standard HTTP methods are unsafe, as they can be implemented to exploit vulnerabilities on a Web server. Microsoft WebDAV methods (used for Outlook Express access to Hotmail), for example, have various security issues, but blocking them can prevent the operation of important applications. Applying the control for specific Web servers can solve the connectivity problems.

Malicious Code

The Malicious Code controls aid in preventing attacks that attempt to run malicious code on Web servers.

Application Layer

The Application Layer class of control prevents attackers from introducing text, tags, commands, or other characters that a Web application will interpret as special instructions. Introducing such objects into forms or URLs can allow an attacker to steal private data, redirect a communication session to a malicious Web site, steal information from a database, gain unauthorized access, or execute restricted commands.

Information Disclosure

Information Disclosure controls thwart an attacker, stopping him or her from gathering information about a system or site. The objective of information disclosure is to obtain information from the Web server that can be implemented to tailor an attack.

HTTP Protocol Inspection

HTTP Protocol Inspection presents stringent validation of HTTP. This ensures that sessions act in accordance with the RFC standards and common security practices.

Monitor-Only Mode

All Web Intelligence controls have a monitor-only mode that enables you to evaluate what impact the control will have on a system's connectivity. It does this by examining logs to review traffic that Web Intelligence has distinguished as possibly being unsafe, while still transmitting uninterrupted traffic flow.

Protection for Specific Servers

It is possible to activate each Web Intelligence defense individually for a specific Web server. If the control is challenging on a particular Web server, it can be disabled (turned off) for that Web server.

Variable Security Levels

Advanced defenses such as Cross-Site Scripting, Command Injection, SQL Injection, and Malicious Code Protectors include changeable security-level settings. If a difficulty with connectivity occurs on a particular Web server, the security level can be reduced individually for that Web server.

Web Intelligence License Enforcement

A gateway or gateway cluster requires a Web Intelligence license if it enforces one or more of the following safeguards:

- Malicious Code Protector
- LDAP Injection
- SQL Injection
- Command Injection
- Directory Listing
- Error Concealment
- ASCII Only Request
- Header Rejection
- HTTP Methods

The licensing requirement depends on the number of Web servers that the gateway or gateway cluster protects. For gateway clusters, a single regular gateway license is essential for any one of the cluster members, and a cluster license is required for each of the other cluster members. Licensing is enforced by counting the number of Web servers that are protected by each gateway.

This quantity is calculated by means of the setting in the **Protected by** field of the Web Server page of the Web Server object in the Firewall policy. If **All** is selected, the number of calculated Web server licenses is augmented for all gateways that implement any Web Intelligence functionality. If the correct license is not installed, it is not possible to install a policy on any gateway.

Summary

SmartDefense not only protects against a variety of recognized attacks that vary from the dissimilar classes of Microsoft networking worms through to DDoS attacks, but it also integrates advanced security technologies that increase a site's protection from complete categories of emerging or unknown attacks.

SmartDefense is founded on Check Point's Stateful Inspection and Application Intelligence technologies, which allow an administrator to drop not only precise attacks, but also complete categories of attacks while still allowing genuine traffic to pass. Application Intelligence is a collection of technologies that detect and prevent application-level attacks by integrating a deeper inspection of application profiles into network security defenses. The core functions of Application Intelligence include:

- Validating compliance to standards and RFCs

- Validating expected usage of protocols

- Blocking malicious data

- Controlling hazardous application operations

SmartDefense blocks attacks at a Check Point enforcement point which may be either a gateway or a single installation of SecureServer on a host. It does this by implementing Check Point's Stateful Inspection and Application Intelligence technologies. A number of SmartDefense facilities are enforced as an incorporated element of the firewall security policy. These are distributed as an element of the enforcement points' security policy. SmartDefense also provides further benefits from the stringent access control to network resources it provides through the deployment of Check Point enforcement points.

Solutions Fast Track

Configuring SmartDefense

- ☑ SmartDefense is completely integrated with other Check Point products.

- ☑ SmartDefense provides object and rule integration across products.

- ☑ Ad hoc or dedicated real-time reports with SmartView Monitor.

- ☑ Historical reports with SmartView Reporter.

Application Intelligence

- ☑ Cross Site Scripting attack blocking
- ☑ Worm pattern matching for CIFS
- ☑ High-performance peer-to-peer support
- ☑ HTTP encoding attack prevention
- ☑ Network Quota and flow shaping for DoS protection
- ☑ System Fingerprint Scrambling
- ☑ VPN Denial of Service Protection

Web Intelligence

- ☑ Interface failover is supported with VPN tunnels.
- ☑ Support for redundant ISP links.
- ☑ Ongoing connections are maintained on link failures.

Frequently Asked Questions

Q: What protocol is most often used to attack the network layer of the OSI stack, and how can Check Point help in stopping these attacks?

A: IP is used for attacks against the network layer. This includes IP fragmentation and DoS attacks. To prevent these attacks, FireWall-1 has an assortment of controls. These include blocking Java code; stripping script, applet, and ActiveX tags; camouflaging default banners; and filtering URLs. With SmartDefense, FireWall-1 is able to proactively determine and prevent possible exploits and DoS attacks.

Q: What does SmartDefense offer that a standard packet inspection firewall can't?

A: A standard packet inspection firewall operates at the network layer, whereas the majority of modern attacks occur at the application level. FireWall-1 works at both OSI levels. Attackers try to exploit application vulnerabilities such as HTTP (TCP port 80) and HTTPS (TCP port 443), as these are open in most networks. Through a process of directly targeting the applications, an attacker can deny service to legitimate users via DoS attacks, gain access to the administrative system and backend information databases, and install Trojan horse software or sniffer software that captures user IDs and passwords. The application layer contains the majority of user data and supports most protocols, and is thus frequently targeted.

Q: What does Application Intelligence provide?

A: Check Point's Application Intelligence feature provides a methodology to both detect and prevent application-level attacks. This is enacted through the following four defense strategies:

- The inspection engine validates compliance to protocol standards such as the RFCs.

- FireWall-1/VPN-1 validates protocols for expected use.

- The engine limits the ability of an application to contain malicious packet data.

- The engine controls application-layer operations by blocking file-sharing operations originating from unauthorized users or systems, restricting connections to particular filenames, and monitoring FTP commands such as *PUT, GET, SITE, REST*, and *MACB*.

Q: What is DoS attack resilience?

A: When the network and systems are experiencing a DoS attack, FireWall-1/VPN-1 gateways will aggressively ensure that legitimate active traffic is not disrupted by malicious traffic. This is achieved through a combination of traffic inspection and rate limiting, and by setting flow limited on selected systems and protocols.

Q: What support does Check Point offer for VoIP?

A: VoIP enhancements have been included with FireWall-1/VPN-1 NGX R65. Enhanced interoperability with Nortel, Broadsoft, Cisco, NEC, Polycom, Sylantro, Avaya, and others has been included to increase security for VoIP applications.

Protocol Summary

The following tables provide a summary of the defenses provided by Check Point's SmartDefense organized by protocol and OSI layer.

Application Layer

Attack Prevention Safeguards	Attacks Blocked
HTTP Client (browser and other client host components)	
Limit maximum response header length.	Code Red worm and mutations
Prohibit binary characters in HTTP response headers.	Nimda worm and mutations HTR Overflow worm and mutations
Validate HTTP response protocol compliance.	MDAC buffer overflow and mutations
Drop user-defined URLs.	Malicious URLs
URL filtering.	User-defined worms and mutations
Restrict download of user-defined files.	Cross-Site Scripting attacks
Restrict peer-to-peer connections.	
Restrict peer-to-peer connections for non-HTTP ports.	
Drop Java code.	
Strip script tags.	
Strip applet tags.	

Continued

Application Layer Continued.

Strip FTP links.

Strip port strings.

Strip ActiveX tags.

HTTP Server

Limit maximum URL length.	Encoding attacks
Limit maximum number of response headers allowed.	User-defined worms and mutations Code Red worm and mutations
Limit maximum request header length.	Nimda worm and mutations
Limit maximum response header length.	HTR Overflow worm and mutations
Specify header length, using regular expressions for header name and value.	Directory traversal attacks MDAC buffer overflow and mutations
Reject HTTP headers that contain specific header names or values.	Malicious URLs Chunked transfer encoding attacks
Prohibit binary characters in HTTP response headers.	Cross-Site Scripting attacks HTTP-based attacks spanning multiple packets
Prohibit binary characters in HTTP requests.	WebDAV attacks
Drop user-defined URLs.	PCT worms and mutations
Restrict non-RFC HTTP methods.	HTTP header spoofing attacks
Enforce HTTP security on nonstandard ports (ports other than 80).	IIS server buffer overflows Santy worm and mutations
Compare transmission to a user-approved SOAP scheme/template.	Spyware and adware attacks LDAP injection attacks
Restrict download of user-defined files.	
ASN.1 buffer overflow.	
Distinguish between different HTTP v1.1 requests over the same connection.	
Restrict unsafe HTTP commands.	
Fingerprint scrambling (spoofing) to hide server information.	

Continued

Application Layer Continued.

SOAP Scheme validation.

SSL overflow attacks.

SSLv3 enforcement.

Restrict header values.

Malicious Code Protector (prohibit malicious executable code against Web servers).

SQL injection.

Command injection.

Restrict binary data in forms.

Restrict HTTP methods.

Drop HTTP traffic featuring negative content-length HTTP headers.

Block Trojans by identifying attempts to receive SCRIPT traffic containing HTML tags.

Drop content disposition in HTTP header.

Define specific network objects as Web servers.

Perform stringent HTTP validation.

Reject HTTP requests that contain illegal SWAT headers.

Strip file extensions in Web traffic.

Drop network access to files with various extensions (to prevent worm infections).

Drop HTML tags from HTTP request headers.

Drop shell commands from HTTP request headers.

Drop HTTP requests containing scripting code using the POST command.

Continued

Application Layer Continued.

Drop non-ASCII characters in
HTTP request/response headers.

LDAP injection protection.

SMTP

Drop multiple "content-type" headers.	SMTP mail flooding
Drop multiple "encoding headers."	SMTP worm and mutations
Camouflage default banners.	Extended Relay attacks
Restrict unsafe SMTP commands.	Message/partial MIME attacks
Header forwarding verification.	SPAM attacks (large number of e-mails)
Restrict unknown encoding.	Command verification attacks
Restrict mail messages not containing sender/recipient domain names.	SMTP Payload worm and mutations Worm encoding
Restrict MIME attachments of a particular type.	Firewall traversal attacks
Strip file attachments with particular names.	SMTP Error DoS attacks
Strict enforcement of RFCs 821 and 822.	Mailbox DoS attacks (excessive e-mail size)
Monitor and enforce restrictions on ESMTP commands.	Address spoofing SMTP buffer overflow attacks
Hide internal mail usernames and addresses.	MyDoom worm and mutations
Perform reverse DNS lookups.	Bagle worm and mutations
Strict enforcement of MAIL and RCPT syntax.	Sober worm and mutations
Restrict mail from a user-defined sender or domain.	Zafi worm and mutations
Restrict mail to user-defined recipients.	Bagz.C worm and mutations
Restrict mail to unknown domains.	
Enforce limits on the number of RCPT commands allowed per transaction.	
Restrict mail relay usage.	
Enforce the ASN.1 standard.	

Continued

Application Layer Continued.

Strip script tags.	
Strip ActiveX tags.	
Drop malicious filenames.	
Drop the X-LINK2STATE SMTP extended verb.	

POP3

Restrict connections with passwords identical to the username.	POP3 buffer overflow attacks
Enforce the maximum number of characters in the username (buffer overflow protection).	
Enforce the maximum password length (buffer overflow protection).	
Restrict binary characters in the username (buffer overflow protection).	
Restrict binary characters in passwords (buffer overflow protection).	
Restrict binary characters in POP3 commands (buffer overflow protection).	
Limit the number of *NOOP* commands, freeing POP3 daemon resources (DoS protection).	

IMAP4

Restrict connections with passwords identical to the username.	IMAP4 buffer overflow attacks
Enforce the maximum number of characters in the username (buffer overflow protection).	
Enforce the maximum password length (buffer overflow protection).	
Restrict binary characters in the username (buffer overflow protection).	
Restrict binary characters in passwords (buffer overflow protection).	

Continued

Application Layer Continued.

Restrict binary characters in POP3 commands (buffer overflow protection).

Limit the number of *NOOP* commands, freeing POP3 daemon resources (DOS protection).

RSH

Auxiliary port monitoring.

Restrict reverse injection.

RTSP

Auxiliary port monitoring

IIOP

Auxiliary port monitoring

FTP

Analyze and restrict hazardous FTP commands.	FTP bounce attacks
Drop custom file types.	Passive FTP attacks
Camouflage default banners.	Client and server bounce attacks
Strip FTP references.	FTP port injection attacks
	Directory traversal attacks
	Firewall traversal attacks
	TCP segmentation attacks

DNS

Restrict DNS zone transfers. attacks.	Protect against DNS cache poisoning
Restrict usage of the DNS server as a public server.	DNS query malformed packet attacks DNS answer malformed packet attacks
Provide a separate DNS service for private versus public domains.	DNS query-length buffer overflow DNS query buffer overflow— Unknown request/response

Continued

Application Layer Continued.

Enforce DNS over TCP.	MITM attacks
Restrict domains on the "not allowed" list.	
Provide cache protection.	
Restrict inbound requests.	
Restrict mismatched replies.	
Enforce the DNS query format.	
Enforce the DNS response format.	

Microsoft Networking

CIFS filename filtering (protect against worms utilizing the CIFS protocol).	Bugbear worm Nimda worm
Restrict remote access to the Registry.	Liotan worm
Restrict remote null sessions.	Sasser worm
Restrict pop-up messages.	Opaserv worm
Enforce the ASN.1 standard.	MS05-003 Indexing Service
	MS05-010 License Logging Service

SSH

Enforce the SSH v2 protocol.	SSH v1 buffer overflow attack

SNMP

Restrict SNMP *GET/PUT* commands.	SNMP flooding attacks
Restrict known dangerous communities.	Default community attacks
Enforce or require the SNMPv3 protocol.	Brute force attacks
	SNMP Put attacks

MS SQL

Drop remote command execution.	SQL resolver buffer overflow
Restrict potentially dangerous commands (information leakage).	SQL Slammer worm Buffer overflow (various attack variations)

Continued

Application Layer Continued.

Restrict usage of the default system administrator password.	MS SQL networking DoS (various DoS attack variations) Heap overflow attacks

Oracle SQL

Verify dynamic port allocation and initiation.	SQLNet v2 MITM attacks

SSL

Enforce the SSL v3 protocol	SSL v2 buffer overflow

H.323

Verify protocol fields and values.	Buffer overflow attacks
Identify and restrict the *PORT* command.	MITM attacks
Enforce the existence of mandatory fields.	
Enforce user registration.	
Prevent VoIP firewall holes.	
Disable H.323 audio and video transmissions.	
Enforce H.323 call duration limits.	
For H.323, allow only traffic associated with a specific call.	
For H.323, restrict blank source in calls.	

MGCP

Verify protocol fields and values.	Buffer overflow attacks
Identify and restrict the *PORT* command.	MITM attacks
Enforce the existence of mandatory fields.	
Enforce user registration.	
Prevent VoIP firewall holes.	

Continued

Application Layer Continued.

Enforce MGCP.	
Verify the state of MGCP commands.	
Restrict unknown and unsafe MGCP commands.	

SCCP (Cisco VoIP)

Enforce SCCP.	Buffer overflow attacks
Secure SCCP dynamic ports.	MITM attacks
Verify the state of SCCP commands.	
Verify protocol fields and values.	
Identify and restrict the *PORT* command.	
Enforce the existence of mandatory fields.	
Enforce user registration.	
Prevent VoIP firewall holes.	

SIP

Limit the number of invite commands (DoS protection).	Buffer overflow attacks MITM attacks
Restrict SIP-based instant messaging.	
Verify protocol fields and values.	
Identify and restrict the *PORT* command.	
Enforce the existence of mandatory fields.	
Enforce user registration.	
Prevent VoIP firewall holes.	
Restrict MSN Messenger file transfers.	
Restrict MSN Messenger application sharing.	
Restrict MSN Messenger white board sharing.	

Continued

Application Layer Continued.

Restrict MSN Messenger remote assistance.

X11

Restrict reverse injection.

Drop special clients.

DHCP

Perform stringent DHCP option enforcement.

Drop BOOTP clients.

Drop non-Ethernet DHCP clients.

Peer-to-Peer

Drop the IRC protocol on all TCP high ports.

Restrict P2P connections.

Restrict P2P connections on non-HTTP ports.

SOCKS

Drop SOCKS versions other than Version 5.

Drop unauthenticated SOCKS connections.

Routing Protocols

Enforce MD5 routing authentication on various routing protocols (e.g., OSPF, BGP, and RIP).

Enforce the validity of IGMP packets.

Content Protection

Drop malformed JPEGs.

Continued

Application Layer Continued.

Drop malformed ANI files.

Drop malformed GIFs.

Instant Messengers

Drop invalid MSN Messenger over MSNMS patterns (prevent worm infection).	Bropia.E worm Kelvir.B worm
Drop file transfer in instant messages via MSN/Windows Messenger.	
Drop the MSN_Messenger group.	

Remote Control Applications

Drop VNC connections on the VNC port and on other ports.

Drop Remote Administrator connection attempts made both on the Remote Administrator well-known port and on other ports.

Enforce authentication scheme on Radmin connections.

Session Layer

Attack Prevention Safeguards	Attacks Blocked
RPC	
Drop RPC portmapper exploits.	ToolTalk attacks snmpXdmid attacks rstat attacks mountd attacks cmsd attacks cachefsd attacks

Continued

Session Layer Continued.

DEC-RPC

Drop DCE-RPC portmapper exploits.	Blaster worm
Allow endpoint mapper communications via the EPM port only.	Sasser worm
Allow only authenticated DCOM.	

SUN-RPC

Drop SUN-RPC interface scanning.

Enforce RPC through inspection of packet lengths.

HTTP Proxy

HTTP Proxy enforcement: Enforce HTTP session logic in proxy mode.

VPN

Validate digital certificates used against Certificate Revocation List.	IKE brute force attacks Hub-and-spoke topology attacks
Monitor for preshared secret vulnerability.	IKE UDP DoS attacks Windows 2000 IKE DoS attacks
	VPN IP spoofing attacks
	VPN MITM attacks
	IKE aggressive mode attacks

SSL

Protect against SSL null pointer attacks.	Microsoft PCT worm

Transport Layer

Attack Prevention Safeguards	Attacks Blocked
TCP	
Enforce correct usage of TCP flags.	ACK DoS attacks

Continued

Transport Layer Continued.

Limit per-source sessions.	SYN attacks
Enforce the minimum TCP header length.	Land attacks
Drop unknown protocols.	Teardrop attacks
Restrict FIN packets with no ACK.	Session hijacking attacks
Enforce that TCP header length as indicated in header is not longer than packet size indicated by header.	Jolt attacks Bloop attacks
Drop out-of-state packets.	Cpd attacks
Verify that first connection packet is SYN.	Targa attacks
Enforce three-way handshake: Between SYN and SYN-ACK, client can send only RST or SYN.	Twinge attacks Small PMTU attacks
Enforce three-way handshake enforcement: Between SYN and connection establishment, server can send only SYN-ACK or RST.	Session hijacking attacks (TCP sequence number manipulation) TCP-based attacks spanning multiple packets
Drop SYN on established connection before FIN or RST packet is encountered.	XMAS attacks
Restrict server-to-client packets belonging to old connections.	Port scans Witty worm
Drop server-to-client packets belonging to old connections if packets contain SYN or RST.	Cisco IOS DoS
Enforce minimum TCP header length.	
Drop TCP fragments.	
Drop SYN fragments.	
Scramble the OS fingerprint.	
Verify the TCP packet sequence number for packets belonging to an existing session.	

Continued

Transport Layer Continued.

Enforce TCP session sequence verification (protect persistent unauthenticated network sessions).

Network Quota: enforcing a limit upon the number of connections that are allowed from the same source IP, to protect against DoS attacks.

Anomaly detection; used ports.

Drop ICMP error packets that belong to established TCP connections.

UDP

Verify the UDP length field.	Port scans
Match UDP requests and responses.	
Non-TCP flooding; limit percentage of non-TCP connections to prevent DoS.	

Network Layer

Attack Prevention Safeguards	Attacks Blocked
IP	
Enforce minimum header length.	IP address sweep scans
Restrict IP-UDP fragmentation.	IP timestamp attacks
Enforce that header length indicated in IP header is not longer than packet size indicated by header.	IP record route attacks IP source route attacks
Enforce that packet size indicated in IP header is not longer than actual packet size.	IP fragment DoS attacks Loose source route attacks
Scramble OS fingerprint.	Strict source route attacks
Control IP options.	IP spoofing attacks
ICMP	
Drop large ICMP packets.	Ping-of-Death attacks
Restrict ICMP fragments.	ICMP floods
Match ICMP requests and responses.	

Chapter 8

High Availability and Clustering

Solutions in this chapter:

- ClusterXL Overview
- Configuring ClusterXL
- Third-Party Solutions
- ISP Redundancy

- ☑ Solutions Fast Track
- ☑ Frequently Asked Questions

Introduction

Check Point has an extensive set of clustering options which have evolved throughout the years. In the early days, only high availability was available, and full load balancing required the use of third-party software such as StoneBeat FullCluster or RainWall. Today, Check Point offers a clustering feature set called ClusterXL, which has both high availability and load-sharing capabilities. ClusterXL also handles state synchronization to maintain connections in case of a failover.

In addition to Check Point's ClusterXL, several OPSEC-compliant third-party clustering solutions are available. This chapter details the ClusterXL feature set and introduces some of these third-party clustering solutions. Whether you have a large or a small network, the fact that you rely on uptime to allow your customers access to your protected applications is critical. In fact, any sort of network downtime is almost unacceptable today. Fortunately, as demand for high availability increases, it is becoming easier to set up this capability and ensure optimal network performance for your customers.

ClusterXL Overview

ClusterXL is a software-based solution for Check Point gateways that offers both active/passive and active/active high availability. It operates in two different modes. In *High Availability mode*, one gateway is active while the other is passive. In this sense, *active* means the gateway is processing traffic, and *passive* means the gateway is only in a backup state and is not processing packets. In *Load Sharing mode*, both firewalls are active in the sense that they are both processing traffic at the same time. Figure 8.1 shows the different capabilities of each mode.

Figure 8.1 ClusterXL Options

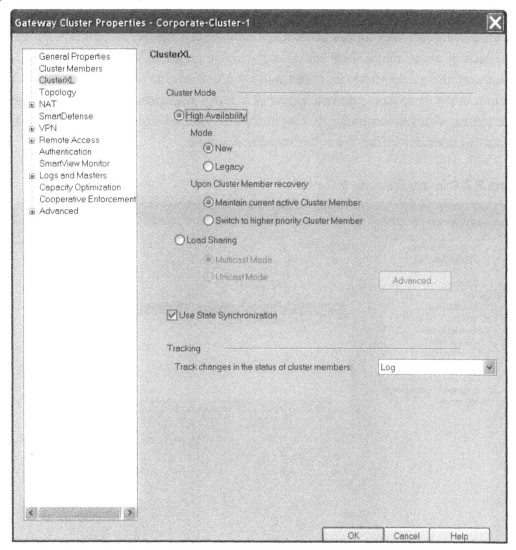

To set up ClusterXL, you must first determine which mode you want to use on your network, and you need to make sure you meet the prerequisites for ClusterXL. The prerequisites include a distributed installation, the same operating system, the same Check Point versions, and a proper license to activate ClusterXL. The use of the same NTP server for each cluster member is highly recommended, because it's all about timing. If a member goes down, you want to ensure that the backup gateway has the correct time so that it doesn't drop any connections by thinking that the connection is too old.

When running in High Availability mode, you have two different recovery methods, whether you are using Legacy High Availability or New Mode High Availability (both which we will cover later in this chapter). Whenever failover occurs, traffic is processed to the backup node, which then becomes the active member. When the faulty original active member recovers from its failed state, you can decide whether you want it to resume as active or to stay as passive. Figure 8.2 shows this decisive configuration option. In the figure, whichever member is first in the list receives a primary status by default. The second member in the list is the standby machine.

Figure 8.2 Primary/Standby Priority

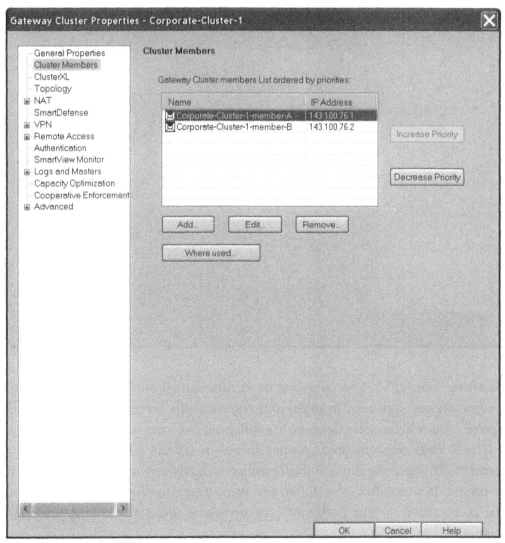

In Figure 8.2, Corporate-Cluster-1-member-A is listed first, and therefore it has primary status; Corporate-Cluster-1-member-B has standby status. You can change the order of these members by selecting the gateway in question and then selecting **Increase Priority** or **Decrease Priority**. You may decide to give a certain member priority over another simply because one machine has a quicker CPU and more RAM, or because you simply prefer one over the other.

The Cluster Control Protocol

The Cluster Control Protocol (CCP) is a proprietary protocol that Check Point developed for ClusterXL. It is used to transfer the stateful information from each firewall so that they can be synchronized in case of failure. CCP uses User Datagram Protocol (UDP) port 8116; if you have any issues with state synchronization, verify that your firewall rules permit this traffic even though it should be allowed through the implied rules. CCP is also used to send members' state information regarding link failures and overall status. It is important for each member to be aware of the other to ensure a smooth transition in case of failure.

CCP is passed along the sync network. The sync network should be a dedicated network and shouldn't have any other traffic passing along it. Heavy amounts of traffic will be passed on this network, and other types of traffic shouldn't be able to interfere with it.

Legacy High Availability Mode

Legacy High Availability mode used to be the default mode for Check Point, but it isn't really used anymore. Instead, Check Point offers the New Mode High Availability mode, starting with NG FP3 (Version 5.3), and today this mode is highly recommended for new installs. However, if you are still working with Legacy High Availability mode (and we hope few people are), you should be aware that the gateways will share the same Internet Protocol (IP) addresses and Media Access Control (MAC) addresses with each other. Also note that there are some switch (Layer 2 forwarding) considerations that you need to be aware of prior to configuration. Historically, most switches have had difficulties with multicast packets, so you'll need to ensure that your switch is capable.

New Mode High Availability Mode

New Mode High Availability mode is different from Legacy High Availability mode and is the setup of choice for most administrators. New Mode is easier to set up and doesn't require any complicated devices. In New Mode, each gateway has a unique IP address and uses the Virtual Internet Protocol (VIP). To visualize the notion of a VIP, picture that .1 is gateway A and .2 is gateway B. The VIP will be .3 and will be shared between .1 and .2 depending on who is the active member. The active member will respond to all Address Resolution Protocol (ARP) requests for the VIP with its own MAC address. The VIP will most often be the default gateway for all your devices internally. When using the VIP as the default gateway for your devices, they will never know who is actually processing traffic. When the active member fails, the VIP will be moved to the passive gateway which will now take the role of the active member. New Mode High Availability uses Unicast in its communication process through broadcast messages, and sometimes uses gratuitous ARP to advertise who will be responding to the VIP.

When working with New Mode High Availability, you can see who is responding to the VIP by connecting to the switch it faces and looking at the ARP entries. We suggest that you try this to test for failover. When a failover occurs and you verify the ARPs once again, the ARP for the VIP should be given the MAC address of the new active member.

Tools & Traps…

Switch Considerations

If you are using New Mode High Availability mode, ensure that your switch supports Unicast. Likewise, if you are using Legacy High Availability mode, ensure that your switch supports Multicast. Most switches support both Unicast and Multicast; however, double-check with your switch manufacturer to be sure that your switch supports the proper method of message transmittal.

Load-Sharing Multicast

Load sharing is the ultimate challenge, and once this capability is properly configured it is the quickest solution around whether you are using Multicast or Unicast. With Multicast, regardless of who has requested the VIP address, the request will be sent to all members of the cluster. Once the Multicast packet hits the cluster members, the members will decide who will process the packet. This decision factor is the core of ClusterXL and is proprietary to Check Point.

In Multicast mode, when a packet arrives through gateway-a and then returns through gateway-b, the Check Point state information will permit the traffic to go through because it is in the state table.

Load-Sharing Unicast

The difference between Unicast mode and Multicast mode is that in Unicast mode, a single cluster member processes all initial packets. Check Point identifies this member as being the Pivot machine. The Pivot machine accepts all initial traffic and decides which member should process it. The Pivot machine takes a slightly heavier load than the remaining members because it handles all initial requests. The Pivot machine decides who should process the packets by using a proprietary decision algorithm.

The Pivot machine is an active member in the sense that it is participating in the processing of packets inbound and outbound. It doesn't sit idle; however, it can assign itself fewer connections to process.

Configuring ClusterXL

Configuring ClusterXL requires some planning prior to implementation. Figure 8.3 represents the basic four-network topology we will use in the rest of this chapter. Figure 8.3 shows an external network, an internal network, a DMZ, and a sync network. The three-line connector for each network except for the sync network consists of member-A, member-B, and the VIP for the network in question. The sync network does not have a VIP because it communicates directly to each other and nobody else.

Figure 8.3 Cluster Architecture

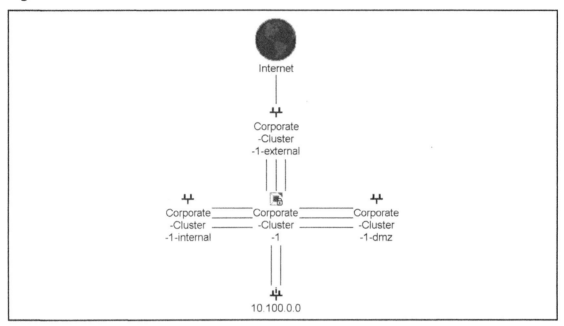

Once you have decided on the type of clustering method you want to use, you must activate ClusterXL. You can configure ClusterXL when you're installing the gateway. During gateway installation, ClusterXL will ask whether the gateway will participate in a cluster. If you answer no to that question, you don't have to reinstall the software. If you don't want to configure ClusterXL when you're installing the gateway, you can activate it at a later time by using the command *cpconfig*. One of your choices with *cpconfig* is to enable cluster membership, as shown in the following code snippet:

```
[member-A]# cpconfig
This program will let you re-configure
your Check Point products configuration.
Configuration Options:
----------------------
(1) Licenses
(2) SNMP Extension
(3) PKCS#11 Token
(4) Random Pool
(5) Secure Internal Communication
(6) Enable cluster membership for this gateway
(7) Automatic start of Check Point Products
(8) Exit
```

Enter your choice by typing the number that corresponds to the option you want to configure.

Note that enabling cluster membership at this point will require a reboot, which you must do on all members that will participate in the cluster. Prior to configuring the remaining options (which you will do with the Dashboard), you should double-check your member interfaces to ensure that the netmask and the default gateway are identical. If they are not, this will cause some topology errors later when you create the Check Point cluster object within the Dashboard.

Once you have configured each gateway member at the operating system level, it's time to define the objects within the Dashboard. You have the option to either create the cluster object by first creating two separate gateways and then adding them to the cluster object, or creating the cluster object and then defining the two gateways. Figure 8.4 displays the creation of the cluster and then adding the gateway members to the cluster by selecting **Manage | Network Objects | New | Check Point | VPN-1/UTM Cluster | Simple Mode**.

Figure 8.4 Cluster Object Creation

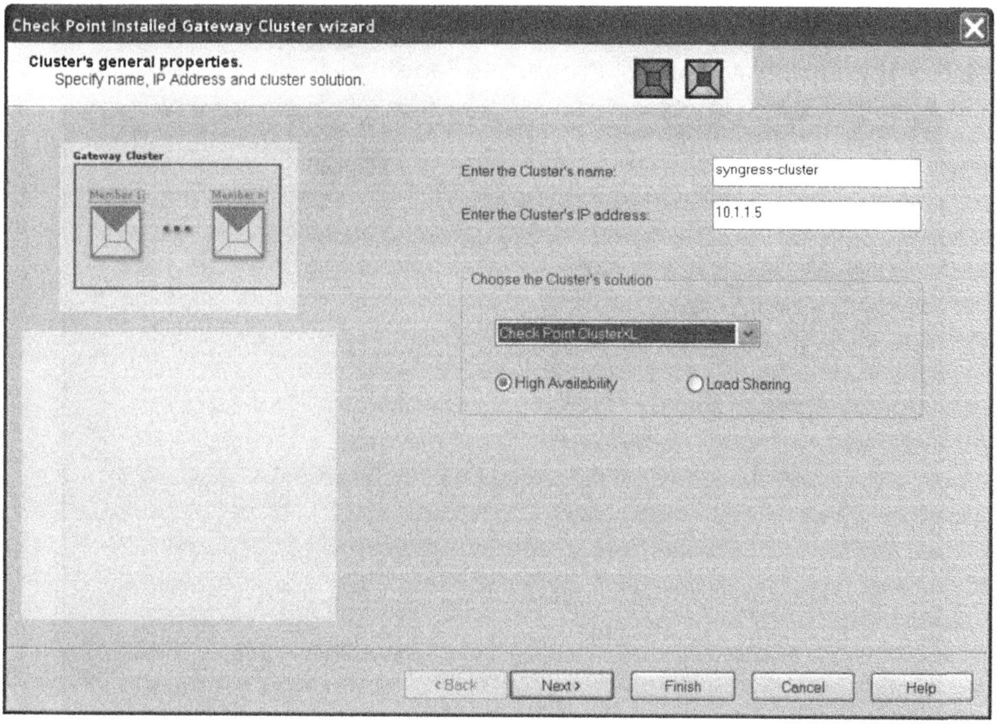

Notice in Figure 8.4 the information you are asked to provide. The first field you must fill in asks for the cluster name, which in this example is *syngress-cluster*. Keep in mind that the cluster name should be relevant to your environment or location; if several Check Point objects are defined in your SCS, having logical names will help you to know where the Check Point is physically located. Some international examples for naming conventions that seem to work well are airport codes. Airport codes are already defined, and most cities, even small ones, have an airport close by.

The second field that you must fill in asks for the main cluster's IP address. The cluster's IP address should be the external routable address, wherever the default gateway points to. You can create Check Point objects with the external routable IP address for virtual private network (VPN) certificate exchanges and secure internal communication (SIC) activation keys.

The third field you must fill in asks for the type of clustering method being used. The default method is via ClusterXL; however, you can use other solutions, including Nokia VRRP, Nokia IP Clustering, and OPSEC. OPSEC covers a wide range of third-party solutions. Visit www.opsec.com for a complete list of Check Point's OPSEC-certified partners.

Once you have filled in these fields, click **Next**; this will bring you to the **Cluster members' properties** page, as shown in Figure 8.5.

Figure 8.5 The Cluster Members' Properties Page

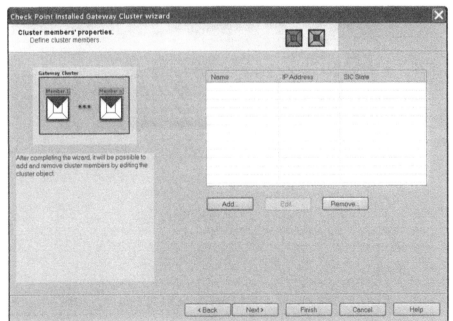

The **Cluster members' properties** page is where you have the option to add gateway members. Clicking **Add** brings you to two options: **New Cluster Member** and **Add Gateway to Cluster**. If you haven't already defined your gateway objects within the Dashboard, select **New Cluster Member** and enter the IP address and the SIC activation key. If your gateway already exists on the SCS, when you add the gateway to the cluster, the cluster will inform you that the gateway will inherit new properties from the cluster. This is more of an information message than a warning. Whichever way you feel comfortable adding members to the cluster, keep in mind that you can always add or remove them later on.

At this point, you should have a cluster object with a minimum of two gateways participating in the cluster. The next step is to configure the topology information for the cluster. The topology definition for the cluster is essential with ClusterXL. To configure the cluster topology options, you must select your cluster object through the Dashboard and then select **Topology | Edit Topology**. Figure 8.6 shows the cluster topology information for our cluster object, Corporate-Cluster-1.

Figure 8.6 Cluster Object: Edit Topology

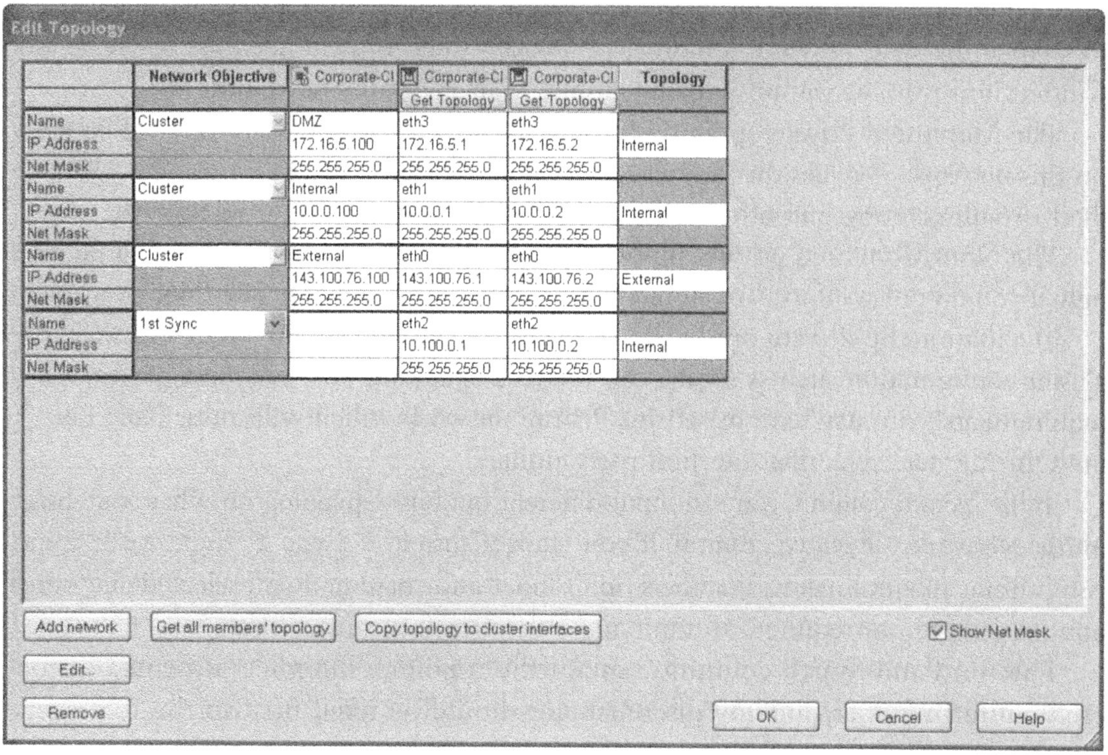

To receive information similar to that shown in Figure 8.6, select **Get all members' topology**. Within the **Edit Topology** section of the cluster object are five columns that you can modify.

The first column, labeled "Network Objective," is where you set the objective of the defined network interface. You can choose from the following: Cluster, Cluster 1st Sync, Cluster 2nd Sync, Cluster 3rd Sync, 1st Sync, 2nd Sync, 3rd Sync, Monitored Private, and Non Monitored Private.

The Cluster option is the most common option because it will represent the cluster's VIP. This Cluster IP is the IP address that will be shared among the cluster members. The Cluster IP has to be different from any other gateway member interface.

The 1st Sync, 2nd Sync, and 3rd Sync options are the synchronization network definitions that the two gateways will use to pass traffic to each other regarding state information and cluster member status. The synchronization network has all the state information and is extremely important for the functionality of your cluster. As noted earlier, the sync network should be on a dedicated network and should not have any other traffic passing on it. The 2nd Sync and 3rd Sync options give you the option of using a second or third network for synchronization.

The Cluster 1st Sync, Cluster 2nd Sync, and Cluster 3rd Sync options aren't recommended because they leave an unsecured option for using an internal cluster interface to serve as the sync network. You don't necessarily want to use a network for Sync and Cluster; however, the option remains should your environment require it.

The Monitored Private option is not related to ClusterXL and no VIP will be used on this network. Devices that are placed on this network will not be using a VIP as their default gateway, but rather the actual IP address of the cluster member(s).

The Non-Monitored private option also isn't related to ClusterXL and will be used only if you do not want to have an interface/network monitored or offer high availability.

In addition, the Private option is not related to ClusterXL; however, a third-party cluster configuration such as Nokia can use it. Depending on your third-party requirements, you may have to set this Private network which will most likely be used for the state sync that the third party utilizes.

In the second column, you can input different options depending on what you chose in the Network Objective column. If you chose Cluster, 1st Sync, 2nd Sync, or 3rd Sync, you can use a logical name, IP address, and subnet information. If you selected any other option, you are not required to input any information in this column.

The third and fourth columns contain the topology interface information for each cluster member, and any discrepancies should be fixed first on the OS layer.

At that point, you can try to redo a **Get all members topology information** so that it corrects itself.

The fifth column, which is labeled "Topology," will populate itself based on calculated topology request information from the cluster.

Once you have created the cluster object, you are ready to configure the security rules. The security rules won't require any special modifications, unless you notice that the CCP is being blocked, in which case you may have to enable a specific rule to allow the traffic to go through. The security rules will work in conjunction with your network address translator (NAT) rules, where you'll want to use Hide NAT for your internal networks and the cluster external IP as the hidden address.

Monitoring the Cluster

Having the ability and the knowledge to monitor the cluster is crucial. You should be informed when the cluster has switched from a high-availability state, or simply whether a member is down. Figure 8.7 displays the ClusterXL SmartView Monitor, which provides the overall status for Corporate-Cluster-1-member-A. The green checkmarks in the ClusterXL section of the figure indicate that everything is of. This section also provides basic information such as the cluster's working mode and member state; click **More**, and you'll receive the member ID with the number of connections and interfaces.

Figure 8.7 Cluster SmartView Monitor

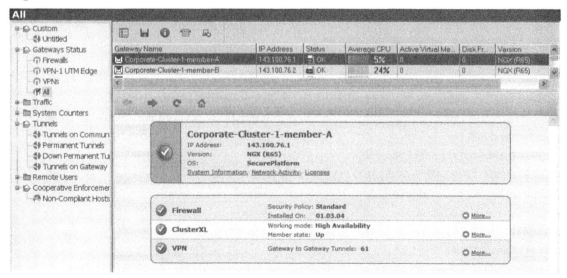

Using the limited free features of SmartView Monitor will give you a graphical representation of the current cluster status for all members individually. To verify the status of the cluster members use the *cphaprob stat* command. You must run this command separately on each cluster member. If you run it without any parameters, you will receive a help menu, as shown in the following example:

```
[Expert@member1]# cphaprob
Usage:
cphaprob state
cphaprob [-a] if
The following commands are NOT applicable for 3rd party:
cphaprob -d <device> -t <timeout(sec)> -s <ok|init|problem> [-p] register
cphaprob -f <file> register
cphaprob -d <device> [-p] unregister
cphaprob -a unregister
cphaprob -d <device> -s <ok|init|problem> report
cphaprob [-i[a]] [-e] list
cphaprob igmp ................ IGMP membership status
cphaprob [-reset] ldstat ....... Sync serialization statistics
cphaprob [-reset] syncstat ..... Sync transport layer statistics
cphaprob fcustat ............. Full connectivity upgrade statistics
cphaprob tablestat ............ Cluster tables
[Expert@member1]#
```

The most common command for viewing the status of your cluster member is cphaprob state. The following will result in the command from each active cluster member:

```
[Expert@member1]# cphaprob state
Cluster Mode: New High Availability (Primary Up)
Number      Unique Address    Assigned Load    State
1 (local)   10.100.0.1        100%             Active
2           10.100.0.2        0%               Standby
[Expert@member1]#
[Expert@member2]# cphaprob state
Cluster Mode: New High Availability (Primary Up)
Number      Unique Address    Assigned Load    State
1           10.100.0.1        100%             Active
2 (local)   10.100.0.2        0%               Standby
[Expert@member2]#
```

The *cphaprob state* command shows you who is active (depending of the cluster mode) and who is on standby. If the cluster was using load sharing, it would indicate as such in the Cluster Mode section.

NOTE

Running *cphaprob state* should issue the IP address that is facing the state synchronization network.

Third-Party Solutions

A major advantage that Check Point gateways have over those of other manufacturers is that Check Point has always offered administrators the ability to work with other specialized manufacturers through the OPSEC Alliance. Check Point's core business is stateful inspection, with its VPN-1/FireWall-1 product line. Since its formation in 1997, Check Point has partnered with several manufacturers specializing in clustering technologies, including Rainfinity (RainWall), Stonesoft (StoneBeat FullCluster), and Nokia (VRRP).

Over time, partners offering third-party clustering solutions have come and gone; however, Check Point has continued to develop its own technologies, and although its NGX R65 product lacks some of the features of past legends, such as the RainWall product suite, it is simple to set up. Nevertheless, the loss of partners such as Rainfinity has enabled other manufacturers to enter the market and test themselves. Two of these manufacturers, Resilience and Crossbeam, offer another approach to clustering solutions that includes specialized hardware and software mechanisms. We discuss each of these solutions in the following sections.

Resilience

The Resilience solution for VPN-1/FireWall-1 is an appliance and software-based solution. The appliance offers a combination of Check Point VPN-1/FireWall-1 and Resilience hardware and software, designed to provide *integrated High Availability* (iHA).

Each gateway appliance module is a self-contained computer comprising a motherboard, interface cards, a power supply, and a disk drive. It's basically an Intel system with preconfigured sync networks. Different Resilience solutions provide one or two different synchronization networks depending on the size of your enterprise.

Third-party solutions almost always use a modified hardened flavor of the Linux operating system, and this is true with the Resilience product. You may view this as a good thing because you can modify several parameters; however, not always supported by them. The Check Point software is preloaded on the appliances and only needs to be activated according to the type of high availability you will be performing. Resilience offers two different high-availability systems: iHA Hot Standby and iHA with ClusterXL.

The iHA Hot Standby system combines two appliances and Resilience iHA to provide a hot standby solution with the ability to simply fail over either manually or automatically. The nice thing about this is that it requires only one Check Point VPN-1 license because the SCS sees the Resilience appliances as a single system.

The iHA with ClusterXL system provides full high availability because both members are active. It combines the Resilience infrastructure with Check Point's ClusterXL to provide full state synchronization and automatic failover with no sessions lost.

Nokia IPSO Clustering

The Check Point/Nokia alliance has existed for a long time. For those of you still using the uber-popular IP330 or IP440 appliance, it's definitely time to change! For starters, those classic but super-old machines are slow; furthermore, the IP440 doesn't support IPSO 4.2.

IPSO is the Intel-based operating system used in Nokia appliances. IPSO is derived from FreeBSD and was created by Ipsilon Networks, which Nokia acquired in the late 1990s. The names of the Nokia appliances start with the letters *IP*, followed by numbers; the higher the number, the faster the appliance. The Nokia version of clustering uses the Virtual Router Redundancy Protocol (VRRP). VRRP is not a proprietary protocol in that any system that is running Linux can use it. Nokia provides an easy-to-use interface in the creation of virtual routers which the Check Point cluster will recognize as VIPs. Figure 8.8 shows the creation of the VRRP, which you can access by connecting to the Nokia appliance through HTTP(S).

Figure 8.8 Nokia VRRP

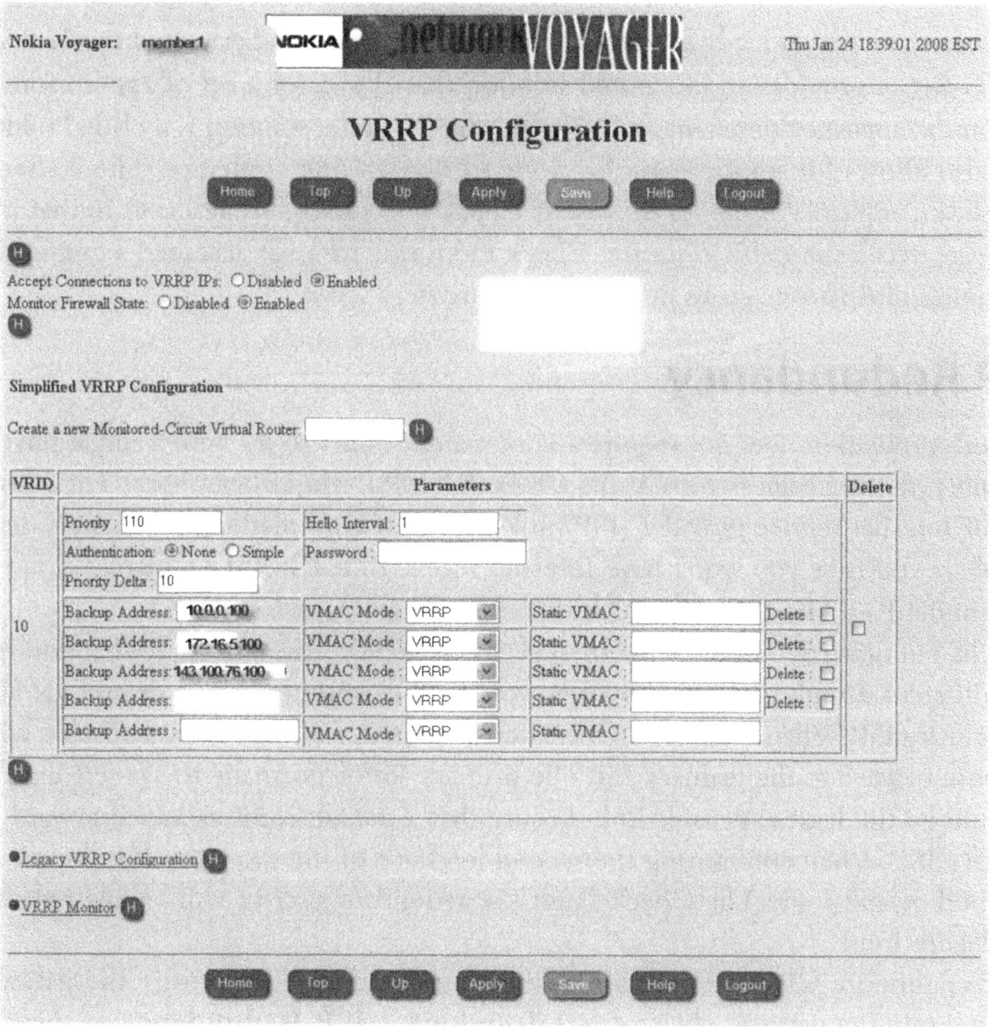

NOTE

The definitions on this page will be used to identify which VIP address is being used and which member has priority.

Crossbeam

Crossbeam offers two hardware appliance product lines: the C-Series and the X-Series. The C-Series provides an integrated solution that allows for a set of applications to run on the appliance simultaneously. The flagship X-Series solution is a bladed solution that also allows for multiple applications to run on one appliance. The X-Series Crossbeam appliance is one of the fastest Check Point solutions available, in that it can hardware-accelerate traffic once the Check Point rule base has accepted a connection. For more information, go to http://crossbeamsystems.com/.

ISP Redundancy

If your corporation does not require a cluster and decides to go with a single physical machine, you may want to look at the ClusterXL ISP Redundancy option. For example, if your Internet service provider (ISP) link goes down, no matter how many gateway members you have you won't have Internet access. To use ISP Redundancy you must be running Red Hat Linux 7.2 or later, SecurePlatform, and/or IPSO.

The configuration options for the ISP Redundancy feature require that you have two different default gateways; however, you need to enter only one default gateway, the primary ISP. When configuring the external interfaces of your gateway, decide which one will be used as the primary ISP. The primary ISP is normally the fastest link, but it could be the least expensive link. Ensure that a default route is added toward the primary ISP. When configuring the second interface of the gateway's ISP, do not add a second default route. The Check Point ISP redundancy script will handle switching the default route.

To configure Check Point ISP Redundancy you have to modify the gateway object. From the gateway object, select **Topology | ISP Redundancy**, as shown in Figure 8.9.

Figure 8.9 ISP Redundancy

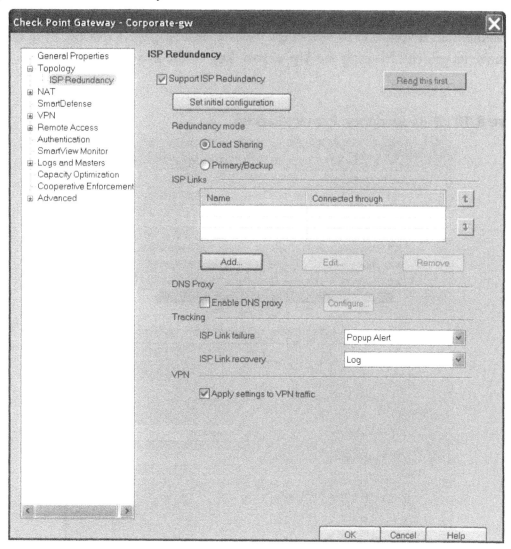

Within the ISP Redundancy configuration page you have two different modes that you can configure: Load Sharing and Primary/Backup. In a load-sharing environment, both ISPs will be used, whereas in a primary/backup environment, you must define a primary ISP where all traffic will default to and a backup ISP in case the primary link goes down. When you select Primary/Backup, the order of priority is determined by whichever link will be displayed first.

Figure 8.10 displays the configuration options in Primary/Backup mode. Note that we have given the name ISP1_10MB for the primary link and ISP2_ADSL for the backup link. If you want to switch the order of priority, select the link in question and move its priority by using the **Up-arrow key** or the **Down-arrow key**.

Figure 8.10 ISP Redundancy: Primary/Backup

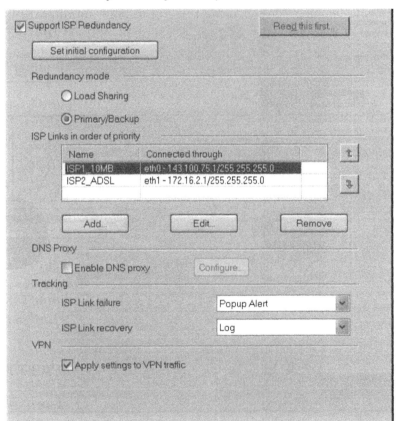

The Check Point redundancy script can monitor devices by sending Internet Control Message Protocol (ICMP) packets from each link. You can configure this by selecting the link in question and then selecting **Edit** | **Advanced tab**, as shown in Figure 8.11.

Figure 8.11 ISP Monitored Hosts

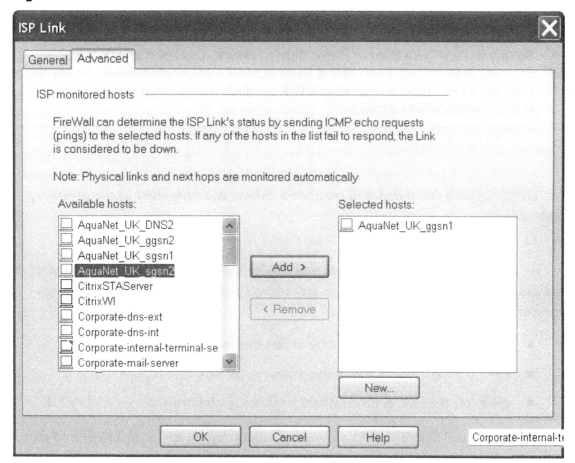

Within the ISP link's Advanced tab, you can specify which hosts you want to monitor. If these hosts stop responding to ICMP echo requests sent from the gateway, the link in question will be considered down and the gateway will switch to ISP2 for all traffic. When the gateway decides to switch gateways, the ISP redundancy script will issue a new default route automatically. You can find the default route on the General tab of the ISP Link properties window. The General tab is where you can set the next hop IP address, which is the new default gateway should you have a change in ISPs.

You also can enable or modify a few different settings for tracking options. For instance, you can track the ISP link failure and ISP link recovery. The options are the same general settings which Check Point comes bundled with.

> **NOTE**
>
> Once you configure the ISP Redundancy feature, you must check that it's working properly. You can test it by removing a physical interface or via the command line. The command line will simulate a link failure, thus forcing traffic through the second link.

The *fw isp_link* command will simulate a failure, as exemplified in the following code snippet:

```
fw isp_link Corporate-gw ISP1_10MB down
```

By itself, the *fw isp_link* command will display the proper usage in case you forget the proper arguments. In terms of the preceding example, keep the following arguments in mind:

- *Corporate-gw* is the object name of the gateway.
- *ISP1_10MB* is the name of the primary ISP link that is active.
- *down* sets the link status to down so that it switches to the secondary ISP.

Testing the ISP failure should produce excellent results, and you should find that you're not losing any packets. A good test is to start a File Transfer Protocol (FTP) transfer with the hash marks on before conducting the simulated failure. When the transfer begins, the hash marks will be displayed, thus showing the progress of the transfer. When switching, the hash marks should pause for about a second and then continue the transfer. Whether you are in a VPN or not, the failover should happen smoothly.

A complete ISP redundancy solution will require that you maintain your domain name system (DNS) Start of Authority (SOA). When clients make inbound connections toward your Web server, for example, it will first do a DNS query to see what IP it belongs to. If you are not managing your DNS server, the responsible must be aware of the new ISP link and netblock. Even if the DNS server is hosted elsewhere, to what

IP will they be redirecting clients? ISP1 or ISP2? How will they know which link is up or down? Check Point resolves this important point by providing a built-in mini DNS server, as shown in Figure 8.12. To configure the built-in DNS server to respond to public DNS requests, select **Enable DNS proxy | Configure**.

Figure 8.12 DNS ISP Redundancy

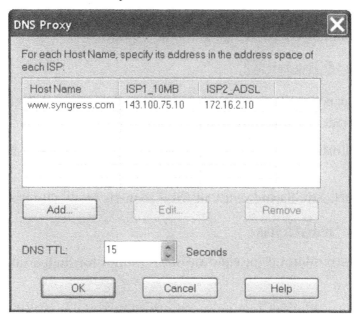

Figure 8.12 lists the DNS entry for the Web page. Notice that we must enter the full host name and the public routable IP from each ISP. Using the preceding example, if we were in a Primary/Backup configuration and ISP1 was active, anybody querying for www.syngress.com would be directed to 143.100.75.10. Should ISP1 fail, all DNS requests would receive 172.16.2.10, assuming that this was a routable IP address. For this reason, it is important to advise your ISP DNS administrators to change the DNS SOA for your domain to each physical IP address of the gateway. When you do so, all DNS requests will go to the gateway and a security rule must be enabled to allow the query through. In addition, all security rules and, more important, NAT rules must be created for each ISP segment to allow inbound traffic to each destination.

Solutions Fast Track

ClusterXL Overview

☑ High Availability mode enables one active member at a time.

☑ When the active member fails, traffic is taken over by the secondary member.

☑ If the primary member resumes from a failover, you have the option to allow it to regain control or to stay in standby mode.

Configuring ClusterXL

☑ Load Sharing mode must be properly thought out for and symmetric routing must be taken into consideration.

☑ Unicast Load Sharing uses a Pivot cluster member through which all traffic is routed.

☑ Multicast Load Sharing sends all ARP requests to all cluster members.

Third–Party Solutions

☑ Third-party solutions provide various solutions for high availability and load sharing.

☑ The Nokia solutions require specific hardware and use VRRP.

☑ You configure Nokia clusters through Nokia Web Voyager access.

ISP Redundancy

☑ ISP redundancy is built into ClusterXL via SecurePlatform.

☑ All ISP redundancy configuration options are made through the gateway object defined through the Dashboard.

☑ Primary/Backup is the simplest ISP redundancy solution and is easily configurable and reliable.

☑ Check Point provides a built-in mini DNS server to respond to inbound DNS requests to ensure full inbound ISP redundancy.

Frequently Asked Questions

Q: ADSL connections with PPPoE are inexpensive, and we may use them for our backup ISP link. Does Check Point require any special configuration options to support ADSL/PPPoE?

A: As long as your OS supports PPPoE, you shouldn't have a problem. Check Point SecurePlatform supports PPPoE and is recognized as a regular IP address through the Topology tab. The configuration options are identical regardless of IP connection type. SPLAT supports; secondary IP, VLAN, PPPoE, PPTP, ISDN and DHCP.

Q: I created my cluster, and when I installed the policy, I lost all SmartConsole connectivity from the SmartCenter Server. What happened?

A: Usually this happens if you have defined the gateway members' IPs with an external interface. The SCS is using the VIP as a default gateway, and therefore, two manual routes should be added on the SCS to identify each internal gateway IP as the default route for the external IP address of the gateway. If the routes are not added, the SCS will use the VIP, which will usually fail.

Q: I cannot add an already created gateway to the cluster object. It says that the cluster object is being used in places that clusters are not allowed. How do I add the gateway?

A: This is common, because your Gateway is already used in several places where it must be removed from before. Places such as; Install On, manual NAT rules, VPN communities and QoS are the most common place where the gateway must be removed first.

Q: I tested my high-availability capability with SecurePlatform, but it's not failing to the second gateway. What should I do?

A: Ensure that all gateway members can ping each other with a removed security policy, especially the sync network, and then ensure that the second member has the same default route as the primary member. Finally, verify the logs and look for any drops or reject and allow CCP for sync purposes.

Q: Can I easily switch from the older Legacy mode to the New Mode High Availability configuration?

A: Sure thing. You can make the configuration on the cluster object itself. Also, you should change the IP address on the secondary node at the OS level.

Q: Does ClusterXL require a special license?

A: Yes. Secondary gateways for high availability and load sharing are available at approximately 80% of the list price of the primary gateway. You need the ClusterXL license for load-sharing capabilities and the SKU is CPMP-CXLS.

Q: How do I remove the SmartCenter server from the gateway so that I can have a distributed installation and, eventually, a cluster configuration?

A: You can remove the SmartCenter server from the current stand-alone configuration in several ways. But basically, you must remove all packages from the gateway and leave only the gateway packages. Prior to package removal, you may want to back up your SCS configuration with the built-in Backup/Restore utility on SPLAT.

Chapter 9

SecurePlatform

Solutions in this chapter:

- Installation
- Configuration
- SecurePlatform Shell
- Secure Shell
- SecurePlatform Pro
- Hot Fix Accumulators

☑ Summary

☑ Solutions Fast Track

☑ Frequently Asked Questions

Introduction

The Check Point software suite runs a variety of operating systems including Windows Server, Nokia IPSO, Sun Solaris, and Red Hat Linux. In version 4.x of FireWall-1, Check Point began custom development of Red Hat Linux as a firewall platform. SecurePlatform (or SPLAT) is the current evolution of that work.

This chapter covers the benefits gained from using Check Point's own custom operating system as well as the installation, configuration, and maintenance of the platform.

Installation

The installation of SecurePlatform is not particularly complicated. If you have three PCs, you can bring a cluster and a management station online in about 30 minutes. This section covers the installation process utilizing both the web user interface (WUI) as well as the command line interface (CLI).

Installation Using the NGX R65 CD

To begin installation of SecurePlatform, insert the NGX R65 CD into a CD-ROM drive and either restart or boot the system. Be sure the BIOS is set to boot from the CD-ROM drive. The SecurePlatform CD will automatically start and you will be greeted with a welcome screen. You have 90 seconds to press **Enter** and begin the installation process. If you do not press **Enter**, the installation will terminate. This is a failsafe, in case the CD has been accidentally inserted or left in a drive.

After the server boots the first screen identifies whether the hardware is suitable for installation of SecurePlatform. If device drivers are needed for network cards or hard disk controllers, selecting **Add Driver** will allow you do this. If there are no drivers to add and the installation screen indicates the hardware is *Suitable for installing SecurePlatform*, select **OK**.

The next installation screen asks for the version of SecurePlatform to install. Select SecurePlatform unless you intend using the advanced routing capabilities included with SecurePlatform Pro. You will also need the appropriate licenses to run SecurePlatform Pro. After highlighting the appropriate system, press **Tab**, then **OK**.

You will now be prompted to identify the keyboard type attached to the system. Select the corresponding keyboard and select **OK**. You will then be asked to configure a network interface, subnet mask, and default gateway. The IP address you enter will be the IP address you will use to connect to the WUI once the initial installation is complete. Once the network information is entered, select **OK**. The next screen enables you to define the port the WUI will listen on. By default the webserver listens on TCP port 443. The listening port can be changed now or in the future. If you do not want to utilize the WUI for SecurePlatform simply highlight *Enable web based configuration*, and press the spacebar. (Note: Most people leave this enabled as an alternate means of administering this device. Select **OK** to proceed to the next screen.)

The hard drives will now be formatted and the Check Point software will load onto your server. Completion time for this process varies depending on your hardware. When this is complete you will be asked to reboot. Be sure the installation disk has been removed from the drive.

Tools & Traps...

Hardware Compatibility

If you are considering which system to install SecurePlatform on you should reference Check Point's Hardware compatibility list. It would be nearly impossible for Check Point to support every possible configuration, so they have a list of tested and supported systems for you to consult. Buying a server from this list greatly reduces the time it takes to get traction if you need to contact Check Point support.

The list is located at www.checkpoint.com/services/techsupport/hcl/index.html.

Bootable Floppy and Network Installation

Instead of booting from the CD there is an alternative way to configure the security appliance. This is accomplished by utilizing a bootable floppy and network installation.

To begin the installation you must create a bootable floppy, which requires a blank, formatted floppy disk and a Windows PC. Insert the floppy into the drive. Next insert the CD into the CD-ROM drive. Open the CD by using Windows Explorer and browse to the SecurePlatform/images directory. Drag the boot.img over the cprawrite.exe icon. The next steps will guide you through the process of creating the bootable floppy.

Confirm the firewall system's BIOS is configured to boot from the floppy drive. Insert the newly created floppy and power up the system. After the system has finished booting you will be prompted to add network information.

You will also need to define where the SecurePlatform installation files are located. The SecurePlatform files can either be located on a CD or by copying the contents of the CD to a hard disk and making them available via FTP, NFS, or HTTP. Once a method is selected the rest of the installation is the same as the CD-ROM-based installation.

If your machine does not have a floppy drive or a CD-ROM drive you can still install SecurePlatform. To do this read "Installation on Computers without Floppy or CD-ROM Drives" in Appendix A of the *Checkpoint_R65_SecurePlatform_SecurePlatform Pro_AdminGuide*.

Configuration

The initial configuration is accomplished by using either the Web User Interface (WUI) or the Command Line Interface (CLI). We will cover both configuration utilities in this section. Since there are many tools that can be utilized in the CLI, it is excellent practice to configure the system via the command line.

Web User Interface

The WUI is the easiest way to configure SecurePlatform because it is browser based and most configuration options can be displayed on a single screen. If you did not change the port the webserver listens on, open a browser and type **https://<IP address you supplied during the installation>** and then press **Enter**.

Tools & Traps...

Connectivity Problems

If you cannot initially connect to the WUI make sure your network interface card (NIC) is on the same network as the NIC of the SecurePlatform device.

If you changed the default listening port, you need to append the IP address with the port number. For example, if you decided to use port 4433

Continued

---

instead of port 443, the WUI address will be **https://<IP address you supplied during the installation>:4433**.

It is also a good idea to add the IP address of the WUI to the exceptions list of any pop-up blocker you may be running.

Once connectivity is established you will be presented with a standard SSL certificate, which you should accept in order to continue. The next screen displays the license agreement. Be sure to memorize every word of it, just as you do for all other license agreements. Once you accept this agreement you are ready to log into the WUI.

The required login credentials to the SecurePlatform WUI the first time are (username) admin, (password) admin, as shown in Figure 9.1.

Figure 9.1 SecurePlatform Login Screen

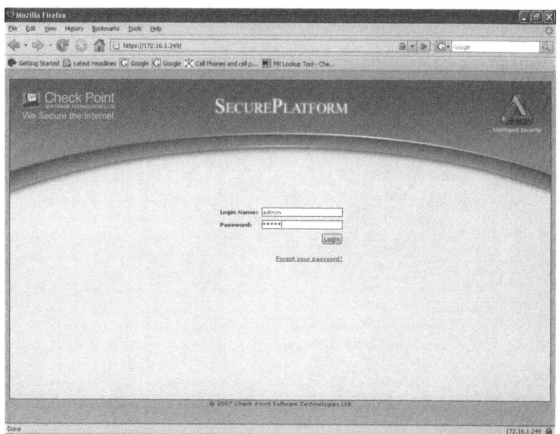

You will need to change your password during the initial configuration (see Figure 9.2). Your new password must be 6 to 32 characters and must be a combination of letters or symbols that do not appear in a dictionary. If your selected password is too short (or long), does not match the stored password, or appears in a dictionary, you will get an error message and will need to supply a different password.

SPLAT also offers a downloadable password recovery token. To receive this token click **Download**. You will be prompted to supply a challenge question and a response. The response must be at least six characters long. The token will help you log in if you forget your password. You should save the downloaded password in a secure location. Once you have changed your password and download the token, click **Save and Login**.

Figure 9.2 Changing a Password

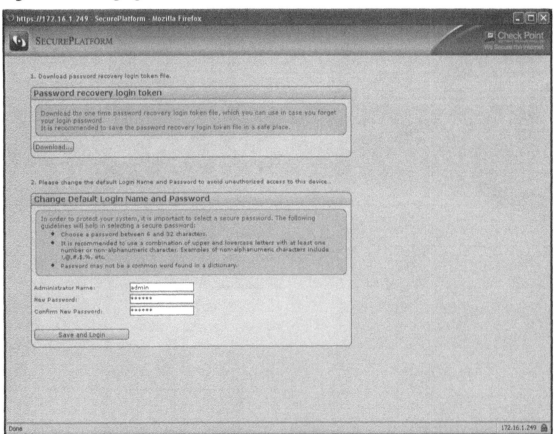

Figure 9.3 welcomes you to the initial configuration wizard. Click **Next** at the top of the screen to commence.

Figure 9.3 First Time Configuration Wizard

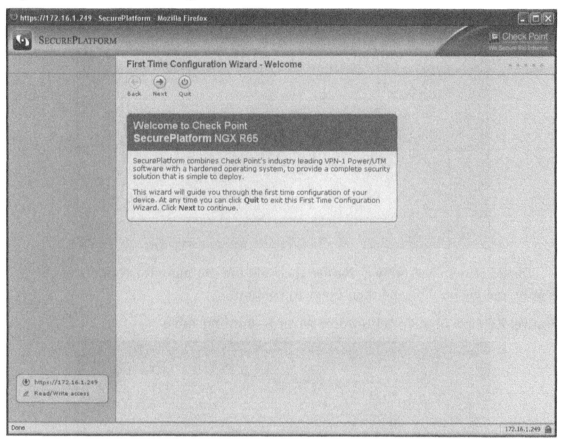

Figure 9.4 lists the network interfaces currently active on your system. To configure or reconfigure your network connections click the interface name. You can now modify properties of the interface, such as IP address, netmask, link speed, and duplex. Once you have defined all interfaces click **Next**.

Figure 9.4 First Time Configuration Wizard—Network Connections

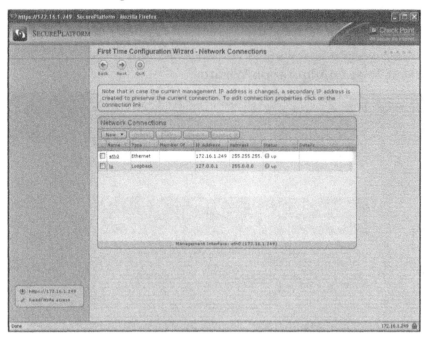

To add routes click **New | Route** then add the routing information and click **Apply** (see Figure 9.5), and then **Next** to continue.

Figure 9.5 First Time Configuration Wizard—Routing Table

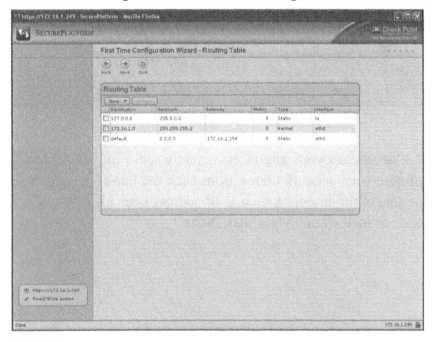

Up to three DNS servers can be added on this screen (see Figure 9.6). Be sure these DNS servers are trusted. Using trusted servers mitigates the risk of attacks such as DNS cache poisoning. Click **Next** to continue.

Figure 9.6 First Time Configuration Wizard—DNS Servers

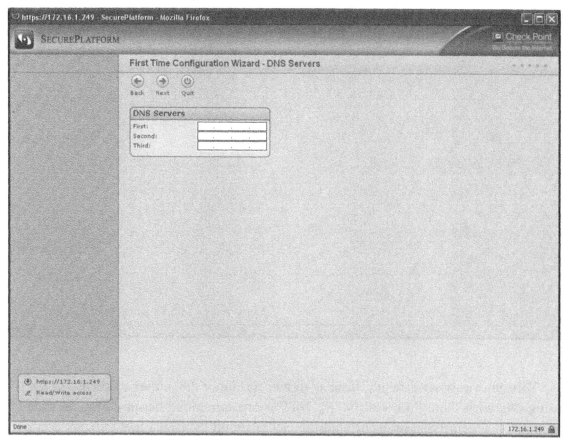

This screen is critical if this server is going to be a management station (see Figure 9.7) because the Internal Certificate Authority (ICA) is based on the host name. If the host name is not set correctly you will experience problems with connectivity and will need to reset the ICA. This is nontrivial, especially if you have enforcement modules deployed. You also set the domain name and the primary management interface on this screen.

Figure 9.7 First Time Configuration Wizard—Host and Domain Name

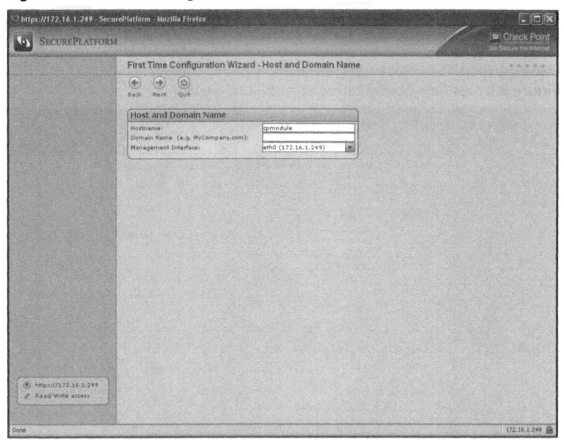

You must now set date and time as shown in Figure 9.8, either manually or by using Network Time Protocol (NTP). NTP is recommended because logs are time stamped. If a security event occurs and the clocks are off by even a few minutes, accurate analysis is much more difficult. Also if you plan to use VPNs in your configuration, time is important, particularly with regard to key renegotiation. There are many good public time servers available. The best are in the same time zone as the security appliance.

Figure 9.8 First Time Configuration Wizard—Device Date and Time Setup

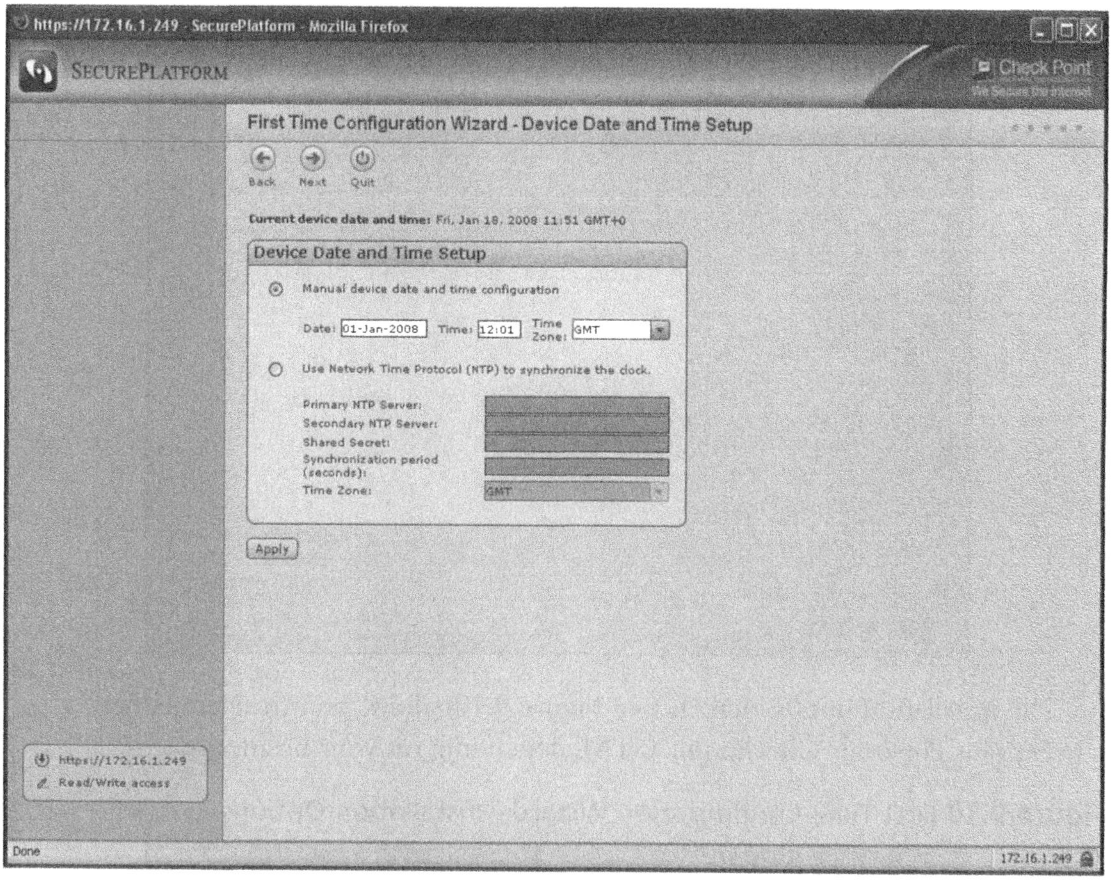

Figure 9.9 assists in defining IP addresses that can access this device. By default *any* is enabled. To add an IP address click the **Hostname/IP address** radio button and type the hostname or IP address. Alternatively you can allow a network to access the device by clicking the **Network** radio button and defining the IP address and Netmask. Once you have defined a host or network, click **Apply**. Now is a good idea to remove the *any* group. Click **Next** to continue.

Figure 9.9 First Time Configuration Wizard—Web/SSH Client

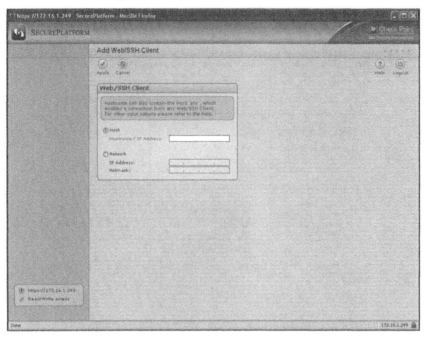

The installation options screen (see Figure 9.10) allows you to select either Checkpoint Power or Checkpoint UTM, depending on your business needs.

Figure 9.10 First Time Configuration Wizard—Installation Options

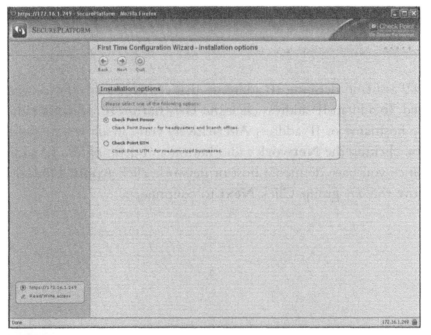

Figure 9.11 is also important because it defines your SecurePlatform installation as a firewall, a management station, or both. If you want firewall only, select *VPN-1* under *Gateway*. If you want management server, select *SmartCenter* under *Management Server*. And, if you want to have a standalone (both firewall and management server on the same system) select *VPN-1* and *SmartCenter*. If you are unsure what products come with each distribution, simply mouse over the product to display a brief description. Once you have selected your products, click **Next** to continue.

Figure 9.11 First Time Configuration Wizard—Products

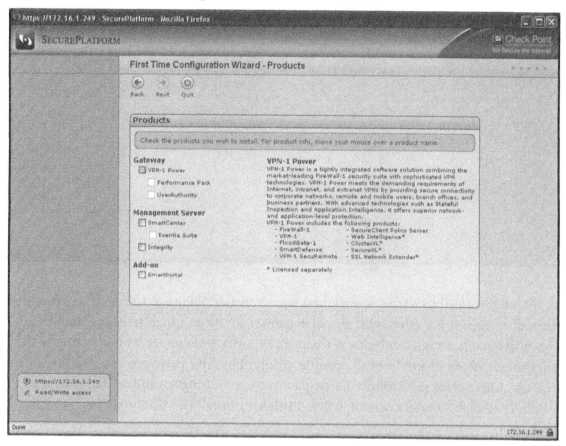

If you selected Gateway the next screen asks if you want to define gateway type (see Figure 9.12). This screen is useful only if the gateway will have a dynamic address, or will be part of a cluster. If either of these parameters is required, click the **Define the gateway type** checkbox and select the appropriate option. Click **Next** to continue.

Figure 9.12 First Time Configuration Wizard—Gateway Type

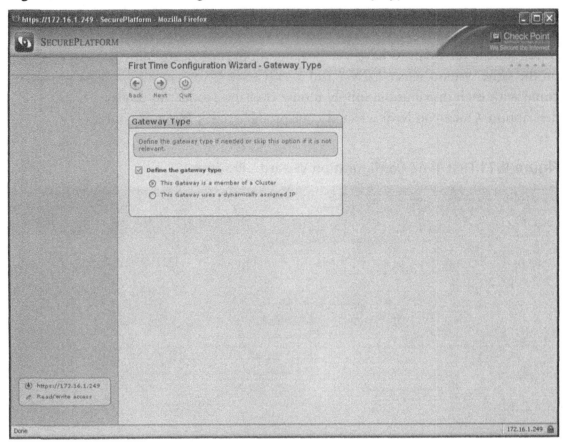

Next you need to define a one-time password (see Figure 9.13), which allows the firewall to establish a trust with the management station. Once trust is established you will be able to receive logs, create/push security policies, as well as monitor the physical elements of the firewall module. (Note: The SIC password is good for only one use. Once trust is established, that password is no longer valid.) Click **Next** to continue to the summary screen. Click **Finish** to install the Gateway.

Figure 9.13 First Time Configuration Wizard—Secure Internal Communication (SIC) Setup

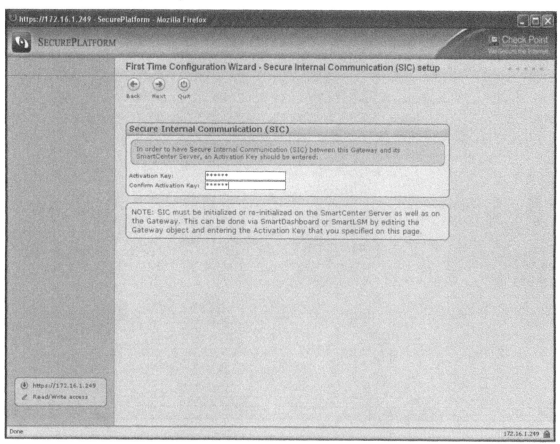

If you have configured this installation to be a SmartCenter server (see Figure 9.11), Figure 9.14 defines server type. If this is a new installation select **Primary Smartcenter**. If this is a secondary SmartCenter, or log server, select the corresponding product. Click **Next** to continue.

Figure 9.14 First Time Configuration Wizard—Smart Center

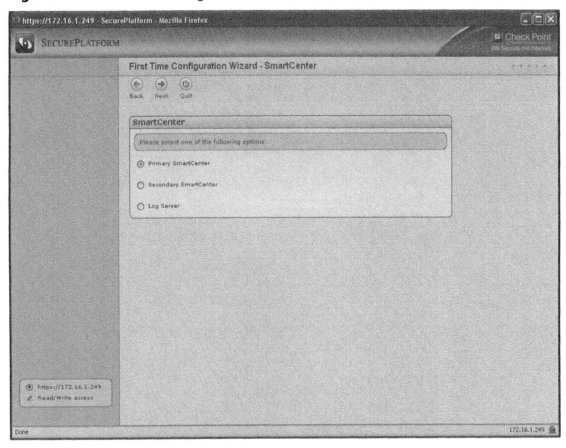

This is a new feature in R65. If you plan using Connectra, a clientless SSL VPN solution, this plug-in enables centralized device or cluster management (see Figure 9.15). This is checked by default. Click **Next** to continue.

Figure 9.15 First Time Configuration Wizard—Connectra Plug-In

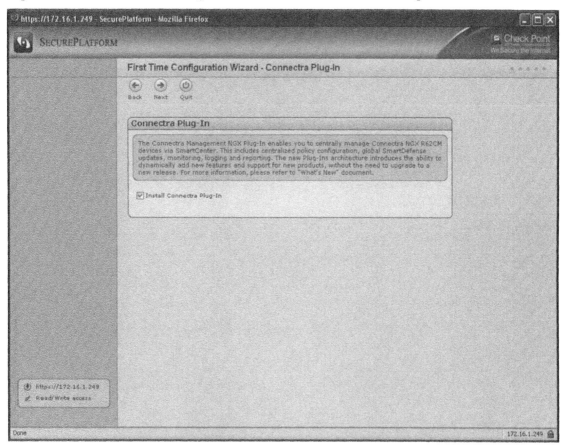

A GUI client is a host able to log onto the SmartCenter to view or manage security polices using a SMART client (see Figure 9.16). GUI clients are defined in several ways—individual hosts, networks, or *any*. You should not allow *any* IP address to access to your SmartCenter. Click **Add** then enter the IP address or network. If you want to allow any host to connect to the Smartcenter using the SMART clients type *any* as the host. After defining the hosts or networks, click **Apply**. Once you have your GUI Clients defined Click **Next** to continue.

Figure 9.16 First Time Configuration Wizard—SmartCenter GUI Clients

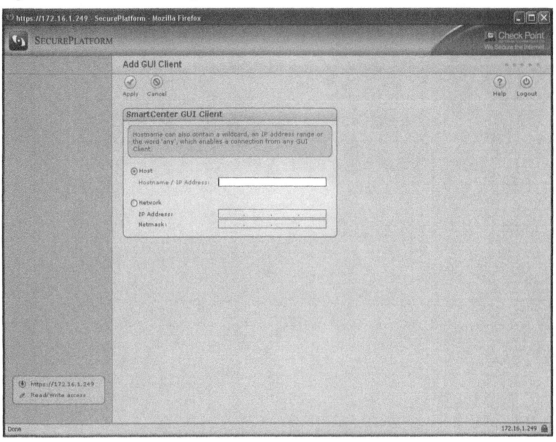

On this screen you must define administrators for the SmartCenter (see Figure 9.17). This administrator account is different from the administrator account that is set up for SecurePlatform. A SmartCenter administrator is allowed to log into the management station using one of the SMART clients, and has Read/Write access to the policy.

To add an administrator click **Add**, then type the administrator's name and the password (4–10 characters). You will be able to define only one administrator here. If you need to define others you will need to use the Smart Dashboard. Once you have defined your administrators click **Next** to proceed to the Summary page. The products field will summarize the products you are about to install. Click **Finish** to complete the installation.

Figure 9.17 First Time Configuration Wizard—SmartCenter Administrators

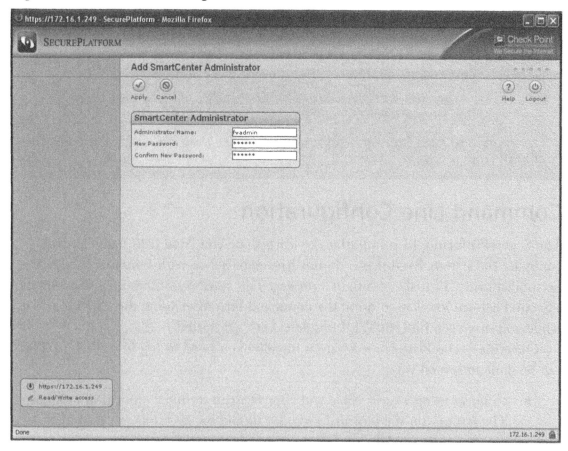

Tools & Traps…

Resetting both the GUI Clients and Administrators

Deleting GUI clients and the Administrators can be done via cpconfig. However, if you have many GUI clients and administrators defined and need to create a fresh list this can be quite lengthy because you are required to delete entries one at a time. There is an easier way. The two relevant files are *gui-clients* and *fwmusers* and are both located in the *$FWDIR/conf* directory on the SmartCenter. Deleting, renaming, or moving these files will allow you to start a fresh list.

Continued

> You need to be in expert mode to do this (expert mode is covered later in this chapter):
>
> 1. Change directory to *$FWDIR/conf*.
> 2. Delete, move, or rename the *gui-clients* and/or *fwmusers* file.
> 3. Type **cpconfig** and select the corresponding option to redefine the GUI Clients and/or Administrators.
>
> Be sure to run **cpconfig** right after you delete these files or no one will be able to connect to the SmartCenter.

Command Line Configuration

The SecurePlatform CLI is important to learn since you need it to maintain and configure the system. Even if you do not have experience with Linux or UNIX, the SecurePlatform CLI makes configuration easy. This section outlines how to configure a SecurePlatform installation using the command line. After using the CLI for a while you may even find the WUI obsolete. Let's get started.

Once the SecurePlatform software is installed you need to log into the CLI. This can be done in several ways:

- Connect using a serial cable and your favorite terminal emulation program. The settings on the terminal program should be 9600 bits per second, 8 data bits, No parity, and 1 stop bit.

- Connect using a monitor and keyboard. This is the easiest way but it not always available.

- Connect using Secure Shell (ssh). SSH is covered later on in this chapter.

When you login for the first time use these credentials—username: admin; password: admin. You will be prompted to change the default password. The new password must be 6 to 32 characters and cannot be based on a dictionary word.

You must change the default password:

```
Enter new password:
```

Once your new password has been set you have the option to change the administrator's name from *admin*. Pressing **Enter** will keep the administrator's name *admin*.

```
You may choose a different user name.
Enter new user name:
```

```
User name was not changed.

? for list of commands
sysconfig for system and products configuration

[cpmodule]#
```

Sysconfig

The *sysconfig* command is one of the most powerful utilities included with SecurePlatform. It is a text-based menu-driven utility and it is used to configure SecurePlatform and its components. Since we have the software installed we are now ready to configure our system using this utility. Type **sysconfig** and press **Enter** to begin configuration. You will see a welcome screen:

```
Welcome to Check Point SecurePlatform NGX (R65)

This wizard will guide you through the initial
configuration of your SecurePlatform device.

At any time you can choose Quit (q) to exit this Wizard.
Choose Next (n) to continue.

---------------------------------
Press "q" for Quit, "n" for Next
---------------------------------

Your choice:
```

Press **n** to proceed or **q** to quit the configuration, then press **Enter**. The next screen enable setting of parameters such as Host Name, Domain Name, DNS, Network Connections, and Routing. To choose a field select the number that corresponds to the parameter and press **Enter**.

```
Network Configuration

-------------------------------------------------------
1) Host Name
2) Domain Name
3) Domain Name Servers
4) Network Connections
5) Routing

-------------------------------------------------------
Press "q" for Quit, "p" for Previous, "n" for Next
-------------------------------------------------------
Your choice:
```

Setting the Host Name

Select option 1 to set the host name. When setting the host name you will need to join the host name with an IP address. It is a good idea to tie the host name to the external IP address. VPNs can have a problem if the main IP address corresponds to the internal interface.

To set the host name select choice **1) Host Name**:

```
Choose an action ('e' to exit):

----------------------------------------------------------------

1) Set host name
2) Show host name

----------------------------------------------------------------

Your choice: 1
Enter host name: SplatR65
Enter IP of the interface to be associated with
this host name (leave empty for automatic assignment): 172.16.1.1

The host name is set.

Press Enter to continue...
```

Press **Enter** to return to the host name menu and then press **e** to return to the main menu

Setting the Domain Name

Here you will set the domain name. In this case we will use *example.com*:

```
Choose an action ('e' to exit):
----------------------------------------------------------------

1) Set domain name
2) Show domain name

----------------------------------------------------------------

Your choice: 1
Enter domain name: example.com

The domain name is set.

Press Enter to continue...
```

Setting the DNS Servers

Now we'll configure the DNS servers.

```
Choose a DNS configuration item ('e' to exit):
```

```
-------------------------------------------------------------------
1) Add new domain name server
2) Remove domain name server
3) Show configured domain name servers
-------------------------------------------------------------------
Your choice: 1
Enter IP address of the domain name server to add: 172.16.1.53
```

Configuring the Network Connections

This screen allows you to add, remove, configure, and show the interface summary. This menu also permits you to assign or reassign the management interface. If there are installed interfaces that do not appear, confirm the cards are supported, seated properly, and appear in the /etc/modules.conf file. (Expert access is needed to view the modules.conf file). In this section we will configure a network interface.

```
Choose a network connections configuration item ('e' to exit):
-----------------------------------------------------------------------------------
1) Add new connection   3) Remove connection      5) Show connection configuration
2) Configure connection 4) Select management connection
-----------------------------------------------------------------------------------
Your choice: 2

Select the interface to configure:

Choose a connection to configure ('e' to exit):
-----------------------------------------------------------------
eth0
eth1
eth2
eth3
-----------------------------------------------------------------
Your choice: 1
```

In this example we will configure interface eth0. The next screen displays the variable parameters for the interface. We will set the IP address.

```
Choose eth0 item to configure ('e' to exit):
-----------------------------------------------------------------
1) Change IP settings
2) Change MTU settings
3) Remove IP from interface
4) Change from static to dynamic IP
-----------------------------------------------------------------
```

```
Your choice: 1
Enter IP address for eth0 (press 'c' to cancel): 172.16.1.248

Enter network mask of the interface eth0 (press 'c' to cancel): 255.255.255.0
Enter broadcast address of the interface eth0 (leave empty for default):

The interface is configured.
Current interface configuration is:

eth0 ip: 172.16.1.248, broadcast: 172.16.1.255, netmask: 255.255.255.0

Press Enter to continue…
```

Press **Enter** to continue, then press **e | Enter** twice to return to the main menu. At the main menu select option 5 *routing* and press **Enter**. This menu will allow you to set the default route. Once this is done return to the main menu and press **n** to continue configuration.

```
Enter default gateway IP address (press 'c' to cancel): 172.16.1.254
Enter metric for this route (press 'c' to cancel or leave empty for default):
```

Setting Time and Date

There are several parameters to consider. First you need to set local time zone. For this example we will set it to Eastern Standard Time. First select a time zone:

```
Choose a time and date configuration item:
-----------------------------------------------------------------
1) Set time zone
2) Set date
3) Set local time
4) Show date and time settings
-----------------------------------------------------------------
Press "q" for Quit, "p" for Previous, "n" for Next
-----------------------------------------------------------------
Your choice: 1
Identify a location so that time zone rules can be set correctly.
Select a continent or ocean.

1) Africa              7) Australia

2) Americas            8) Europe

3) Antarctica          9) Indian Ocean

4) Arctic Ocean        10) Pacific Ocean

5) Asia                11) none - I want to specify the time zone using GMT<+|->N
                           format.

6) Atlantic Ocean      12) cancel - I want to quit without changing the time zone.
#? 2
```

Select a country.

1) Anguilla	18) Ecuador	35) Paraguay
2) Antigua & Barbuda	19) El Salvador	36) Peru
3) Argentina	20) French Guiana	37) Puerto Rico
4) Aruba	21) Greenland	38) St Kitts & Nevis
5) Bahamas	22) Grenada	39) St Lucia
6) Barbados	23) Guadeloupe	40) St Pierre & Miquelon
7) Belize	24) Guatemala	41) St Vincent
8) Bolivia	25) Guyana	42) Suriname
9) Brazil	26) Haiti	43) Trinidad & Tobago
10) Canada	27) Honduras	44) Turks & Caicos Is
11) Cayman Islands	28) Jamaica	45) United States
12) Chile	29) Martinique	46) Uruguay
13) Colombia	30) Mexico	47) Venezuela
14) Costa Rica	31) Montserrat	48) Virgin Islands (UK)
15) Cuba	32) Netherlands Antilles	49) Virgin Islands (US)
16) Dominica	33) Nicaragua	50) cancel
17) Dominican Republic	34) Panama	

#? 45

Select one of the following time zone regions.

1) Eastern Time
2) Eastern Time - Michigan - most locations
3) Eastern Time - Kentucky - Louisville area
4) Eastern Time - Kentucky - Wayne County
5) Eastern Time - Indiana - most locations
6) Eastern Time - Indiana - Crawford County
7) Eastern Time - Indiana - Starke County
8) Eastern Time - Indiana - Switzerland County
9) Central Time
10) Central Time - Indiana - Daviess, Dubois, Knox, Martin, Perry & Pulaski
12) Central Time - Michigan - Dickinson, Gogebic, Iron & Menominee Counties
13) Central Time - North Dakota - Oliver County
14) Mountain Time
15) Mountain Time - south Idaho & east Oregon
16) Mountain Time - Navajo
17) Mountain Standard Time - Arizona
18) Pacific Time
19) Alaska Time
20) Alaska Time - Alaska panhandle
21) Alaska Time - Alaska panhandle neck

```
22) Alaska Time - west Alaska
24) Hawaii
25) cancel
```

#? 1

```
The following information has been given:

    United States
    Eastern Time

Therefore TZ='America/New_York' will be used.
Is the above information OK?
1) Yes
2) No
3) Cancel
#? 1
```

Once time zone is configured the next step is to set date. To do this select option **2**:

```
Choose a time and date configuration item:
--------------------------------------------------------
1) Set time zone        3) Set local time
2) Set date             4) Show date and time settings
--------------------------------------------------------
Press "q" for Quit, "p" for Previous, "n" for Next
--------------------------------------------------------
Your choice: 2
Enter date in format MM-DD-YYYY: 01-01-2008
```

Once you apply this change you will see: *Date is set*. Finally, set local time. Select option 3 to do this:

```
Choose a time and date configuration item:
--------------------------------------------------------
1) Set time zone        3) Set local time
2) Set date             4) Show date and time settings
--------------------------------------------------------
Press "q" for Quit, "p" for Previous, "n" for Next
--------------------------------------------------------
Your choice: 3
Enter time in format HH:MM: 13:51
```

You should now proceed to the next screen, where you will be asked if you want to import a configuration from a tftp server. If you have a tftp server set up enter the information and your configuration will be imported into SecurePlatform. If you do not have a configuration press **n** then **Enter** to complete this portion of the configuration.

Setting up the Check Point Product Suite

Once the basic system is configured you need to configure the Check Point products. The first screen is a Welcome Screen. Press **n** to start configuring the Checkpoint Product Suite.

```
Welcome to Check Point Suite!      NGX R65

Thank you for choosing Check Point Software Technologies, the worldwide
leader in Internet security.

Please make sure you have obtained a license before continuing.
If you do not have a license, see your reseller
or visit the Check Point User Center
We recommend that you close all other applications before running
this installation program.
```

The next screen displays the license agreement. To proceed press **y**. You will now be asked if you want to install Checkpoint Power or Checkpoint UTM. Select the appropriate system. To select between Power and UTM simply press **1** or **2** depending on which software you want to install. Then press **Enter**.

```
Check Point Power - for headquarters and branch offices
Check Point UTM - for medium-sized businesses

1 (*) Check Point Power
2 ( ) Check Point UTM
```

Once you have selected the appropriate system press **n** to proceed to the next screen where you can generate a fresh configuration or import a configuration from a saved file. Here we will set up a new configuration.

```
Please select one of the following options

1 (*) New Installation
2 ( ) Installation Using Imported Configuration
```

The next screen is important because it defines whether this installation is an enforcement module, SmartCenter, or both.

Installing a Firewall Module

Select **VPN-1 Power** for an enforcement module. Press **1** and the *VPN-1 Power* parameter will be selected. If you select a product by mistake press the corresponding number again. Once you have selected you products, press **n**. The next screen summarizes the product you are installing. Press **n** again.

```
The following products are available in this version
Please select product(s)

1 [*] VPN-1 Power
2 [ ] UserAuthority
3 [ ] SmartCenter
4 [ ] Eventia Suite
5 [ ] Integrity
6 [ ] Performance Pack
7 [ ] SmartPortal

You are now installing a firewall module:

     Starting installation procedure
Installing VPN-1 Power ...
```

This process will take some time depending on your hardware. There will be some questions to answer along the way, so don't walk away quite yet.

We are not using a Dynamically Assigned IP address; we will select **n**. Since **n** is selected by default simply pressing **Enter** will bring you to the next screen. The next screen asks if you want to utilize the clustering protocols.

(Note: If you plan on deploying two or more firewall enforcement modules acting as a single redundant entity, or cluster, select **y**.)

```
Welcome to Check Point Configuration Program
=================================================
Is this a Dynamically Assigned IP Address gateway installation ? (y/n) [n] ?
Would you like to install a Check Point clustering product (CPHA, CPLS or State
Synchronization)? (y/n) [n] ? y
IP forwarding disabled
Hardening OS Security: IP forwarding will be disabled during boot.
Generating default filter
Default Filter installed
Hardening OS Security: Default Filter will be applied during boot.
This program will guide you through several steps where you
will define your Check Point products configuration.
```

```
At any later time, you can reconfigure these parameters by
running cpconfig
```

As just shown, certain security measures are implemented to include a default filter. This is simply the first rulebase. Don't worry: your system is not vulnerable, and you will be able to log in. The next step is to add licenses. You do not have to add licenses immediately because a 15-day eval license is included with the initial installation.

```
Configuring Licenses...
=========================
Host Expiration Signature Features

Note: The recommended way of managing licenses is using SmartUpdate.
cpconfig can be used to manage local licenses only on this machine.

Do you want to add licenses (y/n) [y] ?

The next stage of the installation is automatic:

Configuring Random Pool...
============================
Automatically collecting random data to be used in
various cryptographic operations.
        [.................]
Automatic collection of random data is done.
```

Since we have configured a firewall enforcement module, a Secure Internal Communication (SIC) key needs to be set up. It enables trust between this firewall module and a management station that holds the same SIC key. Type a pass phrase and press **Enter**.

```
Configuring Secure Internal Communication...
=========
The Secure Internal Communication is used for authentication between
Check Point components

Trust State: Uninitialized
Enter Activation Key:

The only step left is to reboot. Press Enter and type reboot | Enter on
the command line. Confirm by pressing y then Enter.

IMPORTANT: Don't forget to reboot in order to complete the installation.

Press Enter to continue...
```

Congratulations! You have successfully configured a firewall module using the command line interface.

Installing a SmartCenter Server

If you chose to set up a SmartCenter server instead of a firewall enforcement module, select **SmartCenter** at the products installation page, not *VPN-1 Power*. If you select VPN-1 Power or UTM you will install a firewall enforcement module as well. Once you have SmartCenter highlighted press **n**.

```
The following products are available in this version
Please select product(s)
1 [ ] VPN-1 Power
2 [ ] UserAuthority
3 [*] SmartCenter
4 [ ] Eventia Suite
5 [ ] Integrity
6 [ ] Performance Pack
7 [ ] SmartPortal
```

Here you will be asked if you want to install a primary or secondary SmartCenter, or a log server. We will select **Primary SmartCenter**. Press **n** to continue.

```
Please specify the SmartCenter type you are about to install

1 (*) Primary SmartCenter
2 ( ) Secondary SmartCenter
3 ( ) Log Server
```

Now you will be prompted to install the Connectra Plug-in piece. If you run Connectra or plan to, it is a good idea to install this plug-in.

```
                    Check Point Software Technologies Ltd.

The Connectra Management NGX Plug-In enables you to centrally manage
Connectra NGX R62CM devices via SmartCenter.
This includes centralized policy configuration, global SmartDefense
updates, monitoring, logging and reporting.
The new Plug-Ins architecture introduces the ability to
dynamically add new features and support for new products,
without the need to upgrade to a new release.
For more information, please refer to "What's New" document

1 [*] Install Connectra NGX R62CM Plug-In
```

By pressing **n**, you will be taken to a summary page. If you are satisfied with the products you are about to install, press **n** to install.

The next screen presents the option to install licenses. You can also do this after you have set up your SmartCenter.

```
Welcome to Check Point Configuration Program
=================================================
This program will guide you through several steps where you
will define your VPN-1 configuration.
At any later time, you can reconfigure these parameters by
running cpconfig
Configuring Licenses...
========================
Host Expiration Signature Features

Note: The recommended way of managing licenses is using SmartUpdate.
cpconfig can be used to manage local licenses only on this machine.

Do you want to add licenses (y/n) [y] ?
```

In the next steps you will define Administrators and GUI clients. This is not the same account as the SecurePlatform system account. This account authenticates SMART Clients connecting to the SmartCenter.

```
Configuring Administrator...
============================
No VPN-1 Administrator is currently
defined for this SmartCenter Server.

Do you want to add an administrator (y/n) [y] ?
Administrator name: admin
Password:
Verify Password:
Administrator admin was added successfully and has
Read/Write Permission for all products with Permission to Manage Administrators
```

Now that you have successfully set up the administrator's account it is time to add GUI clients. These hosts access the SmartCenter using the SMART Clients. After you have defined all your GUI clients, remember to press **CTRL-D** to confirm and exit.

```
Configuring GUI Clients...
==========================
GUI Clients are trusted hosts from which
Administrators are allowed to log on to this SmartCenter Server
```

```
using Windows/X-Motif GUI.

No GUI Clients defined
Do you want to add a GUI Client (y/n) [y] ?
You can add GUI Clients using any of the following formats:
1. IP address.
2. Machine name.
3. "Any" - Any IP without restriction.
4. IP/Netmask - A range of addresses, for example 192.168.10.0/255.255.255.0
5. A range of addresses - for example 192.168.10.8-192.168.10.16
6. Wild cards (IP only) - for example 192.168.10.*

Please enter the list of hosts that will be GUI Clients.
Enter GUI Client one per line, terminating with CTRL-D or your EOF
character.
```

The next step is automatic. Once the Random Pool completes press **Enter** to proceed with the installation and initialization of the Internal Certificate Authority (ICA).

```
Configuring Random Pool...
===========================
Automatically collecting random data to be used in
various cryptographic operations.

          [...............]

Automatic collection of random data is done.

Configuring Certificate Authority...
====================================
The Internal CA will now be initialized
with the following name: cpmodule

Initializing the Internal CA...(may take several minutes)
   Internal Certificate Authority created successfully
   Certificate was created successfully
Certificate Authority initialization ended successfully
Trying to contact Certificate Authority. It might take a while...
cpmodule was successfully set to the Internal CA

Done
```

Upon successful completion, the SmartCenter will generate a fingerprint. Though it has been my experience that not many people keep this fingerprint, it is a good idea to save it to a file. The fingerprint is unique to your machine. Upon first logon you will see this fingerprint pop up. It is good to audit this fingerprint every now and again with the one you saved to a file.

Are You Owned?

My Fingerprint Changed!

There are several explanations for a changed fingerprint. Secureknowledge article sk31891 identifies things you should check:

- ICA regenerated (either through corruption or fwm sic_reset)
- Licensing changes
- IP address or object name of SmartCenter server was changed
- Internal Certificate passed 75% of its lifetime

Also, check and recheck with other administrators. Changes sometimes take place without your knowledge.

```
Configuring Certificate's Fingerprint...
==========================================
The following text is the fingerprint of this SmartCenter Server:
TUG BENT TUBA LACY SALK BURL SHD FIRM BLUM FREY KIN IF

Do you want to save it to a file? (y/n) [n] ?
Initializing the Internal CA...(may take several minutes)
   Internal Certificate Authority created successfully
   Certificate was created successfully
Certificate Authority initialization ended successfully
Trying to contact Certificate Authority. It might take a while...
cpmodule was successfully set to the Internal CA

Done

************* Installation completed successfully *************

Do you wish to start the installed product(s) now? (y/n) [y] ?
```

Press **y** to start the Check Point processes. Now only one more step remains. You must log out and log back in. Press **Enter** to drop to a command prompt. Type **exit** and press **Enter**. Doing this will drop you to a login prompt. Once you log in, you are ready to connect to your newly installed management station.

(Note: After this configuration is complete, I like to reboot the management station, just to verify all the services come up properly. To do this, instead of typing **exit**, type **reboot** and press **Enter**.)

Congratulations, you now have a fully functional management station, and if you follow the "Installing a Firewall Module" section you now have both a Smartcenter Server as well as a Checkpoint Firewall enforcement module. Well done!

Platform Shell

When first logging into SecurePlatform you are presented with an application-specific configuration interface. This interface does not operate like the bash shell of expert mode (which is covered in the next section). The simplest way to navigate this interface is by using **?**. The following commands are utilized with this interface in NGX R65.

```
[cpmanager]# ?
Commands are:
?                            - Print list of available commands
LSMcli                       - SmartLSM command line
LSMenabler                   - Enable SmartLSM
SDSUtil                      - Software Distribution Server utility
about                        - Print about info
addarp                       - Add permanent ARP table entries
adduser                      - Add new user
arp                          - Display/manipulate the arp table
audit                        - Display/edit commands entered in shell
backup                       - Backup configuration
checkuserlock                - Check if user is locked
cp_conf                      - Check Point system configuration utility
cpadmin                      - Control system administration portal
cpca                         - Run Check Point Internal CA
cpca_client                  - Manage/configure Check Point Internal CA
cpca_create                  - Create new Check Point Internal CA database
cpca_dbutil                  - Print/convert Check Point Internal CA database
cpconfig                     - Check Point software configuration utility
cphaprob                     - Defines critical process of High Availability
cphastart                    - Enables the High Availability feature on the machine
```

```
cphastop              - Disables the High Availability feature on the machine
date                  - Set/show date
delarp                - Remove permanent ARP table entries
deluser               - Remove existing user
diag                  - Send system diagnostics information
dns                   - Add/remove/show domain name resolving servers
domainname            - Set/show domain name
eth_set               - Control ethernet interface speed/duplex settings
etmstart              - Starts FloodGate-1
etmstop               - Stops FloodGate-1
exit                  - Switch to standard mode/Logout
expert                - Switch to expert mode
fgate                 - FloodGate-1 commands
fips                  - Turns on/off FIPS mode
fw                    - VPN-1/FireWall-1 commands
fwm                   - FW-1/VPN-1 management utility
help                  - Print list of available commands
hostname              - Set/show host name
hosts                 - Add/remove/show local hosts/IP mappings
idle                  - Set/show auto logout time in minutes
ifconfig              - Configure/store network interfaces
lockout               - Configure lockout parameters
log                   - Log rotation control
netstat               - Show network statistics
ntp                   - Configure ntp and start synchronization client
ntpstart              - Start NTP clock synchronization client
ntpstat               - Show NTP clock synchronization client state
ntpstop               - Stop NTP clock synchronization client
passwd                - Change password
patch                 - Install/Upgrade utility
ping                  - Ping a host
pro                   - Enable/Disable SecurePlatform Pro
reboot                - Reboot gateway
restore               - Restore configuration
revert                - Revert to saved Snapshot Image
rmdstart              - Start SmartView Reporter
rmdstop               - Stop SmartView Reporter
route                 - Configure/store routing tables
rtm                   - SmartView Monitor commands
rtmstart              - Start SmartView Monitor
rtmstop               - Stop SmartView Monitor
```

```
rtmtopsvc              - SmartView Monitor of Top Services
scroll                 - Allow scrolling the output of various commands
showusers              - List SecurePlatform administrators
shutdown               - Shut down gateway
snapshot               - Create Snapshot Image
snmp                   - Configure SNMP daemon
sysconfig              - Configure your SecurePlatform Gateway
syslog_servers         - Add/remove/show external syslog servers
time                   - Set/show time
timezone               - Set/show the time zone
top                    - Show the most active system processes
traceroute             - Trace the route to a host
unlockuser             - Unlock user
ups                    - Configure Smart UPS monitoring
vconfig                - Configure Virtual LANs
ver                    - Print SecurePlatform version
vpn                    - Control VPN
webui                  - Configure web UI
```

Expert Mode

Expert mode grants access to a traditional Linux bash shell, with the equivalent of root privileges, so be careful what you edit here. To enter expert mode type **expert** on the CPShell command line. You will be asked for a password; if this is the first time you are logging in the password will be the SecurePlatform administrative password, and you will be asked to change it once you have supplied your credentials. (Note: The CPShell password and the Expert password can be the same, but is not recommended.)

```
[cpmodule]# expert
Enter current password:

This is the first time you enter the expert mode.

Expert password must be changed.

Enter new expert password:
Enter new expert password (again):

You are in expert mode now.

[Expert@cpmodule]#
```

Now you are in Expert Mode. At the command prompt, Expert@ will precede the hostname. At this point you have unrestricted access to a bash shell, with root privileges. Most Check Point utilities are still available using this shell, such as sysconfig and cpconfig, however you now have the ability to navigate the file system of the security device.

Useful Commands

The previous list identifies the range of commands with SecurePlatform. But which ones should you note? After working with Check Point and SecurePlatform for many years there are some commands I use frequently. Ping and traceroute are available on most any system today, however, Backup/Restore and Patch will allow you to keep your system configured the way you want it—and protected in case something goes wrong.

Backup and Restore

Backup is a necessity for a firewall but is also important for a SmartCenter since this device stores the security configuration. There are several ways to back up and restore a system. First we will talk about the backup and restore options available using the CPShell.

Backup

Type **backup** on the CPShell and press **Enter**. To proceed, press **y** and then press **Enter** to continue. This will create a backup file with a timestamp. The file will store at */var/CPbackup/backups*. Usage of the backup command follows.

```
[Expert@cpmodule]# backup ?
usage:
backup [-h] [-d] [-l] [--purge DAYS] [--sched [on hh:mm <-m DayOfMonth> |
<-w DaysOfWeek>] | off] [--tftp <ServerIP> [-path <Path>] [<Filename>]]
[--scp <ServerIP> <Username> <Password> [-path <Path>] [<Filename>]]
[-file [-path <Path>] [<Filename>]]

where:
      -d                        Show debug messages
      -l, --logs                Back up log files
      -h, --help                Show this help information
      -t, --tftp                Transfer backup package to TFTP server
      -s, --scp                 Transfer backup package to SCP server
      -f, --file                Specify local backup package filename
      -e, --sched               Configure scheduled backup operation
      -p, --purge               Purge local backup packages older than DAYS
```

But what good, you ask, is a backup if the system fails and you cannot retrieve that file? Luckily, Check Point solves this problem with a clever option. Use the option to create a back up file and then secure copy (SCP) to an SCP server. To do this use the -s switch as illustrated:

```
[Expert@cpmodule]# backup -s 172.16.1.22 scpuser scppassword
Are you sure you want to proceed (y/n) [y]? y

Creating backup package...
Done
Transferring the backup package...
Done
```

Restore

Now that the file has been sent to your server, you can relax because you can restore your configuration with ease. The following explains the usage of the Restore command, and how to retrieve and restore your system from that same SCP server.

```
[Expert@cpmodule]# restore ?
usage:
restore             [-h] [-d] [[--tftp <ServerIP> <Filename>] |
                    [--scp <ServerIP> <Username> <Password> <Filename>] |
                    [--file <Filename>]]

where:
    -d                              Show debug messages
    -h, --help                      Show this help information
    -t, --tftp                      Transfer backup package from TFTP server
    -s, --scp                       Transfer backup package from SCP server
    -f, --file                      Specify local backup package filename
[Expert@cpmodule]#
```

In the following example we will utilize the −s switch to restore the configuration. If you do not want to utilize the restore feature using one command, type **restore** to access a menu screen that will enable you to choose how you want to restore. In this case we will use one command, taking advantage of SCP.

```
[Expert@cpmodule]# restore -s 172.16.1.22 scpuser scppassword backup_cpmodule_14_
1_2008_15_20.tgz

Examining the backup package, please wait...
Transferring the backup package…
Done
```

```
All information will be restored.
-----------------------------------------------
Choose one of the following:
-----------------------------------------------
[C]    Continue.
[M]    Modify which information to restore.
[Q]    Quit.
-----------------------------------------------
Your choice: c
Restoring backup package...
Done
[Expert@cpmodule]#
```

Other Ways to Back up and Restore Your System

Upgrade_export and Upgrade_import

This utility usually is reserved for upgrading, but it is a great way to save the configuration. There are two utilities: upgrade_export and upgrade_import. These tools are located in the $FWDIR/bin/upgrade_tools or /opt/CPsuite-R65/fw1/bin/upgrade_tools directory on the SmartCenter. Once you are in that directory type **./upgrade_export <filename>** and press **Enter**. This will create an export of your Checkpoint configuration. To restore the configuration type **./upgrade_import <filename>** and press **Enter**, and you're back in business.

```
[Expert@cpmodule]# ./upgrade_export SplatR65_export.tgz

You are required to close all Check Point clients before the Export
operation begins.
If the export fails, stop Check Point services and run the upgrade_export
command again.
Press ENTER when ready.

Checking the existence of necessary files...
Copying files to temp dir...
Building configuration file...
Compressing the files…

The export operation finished successfully.
[Expert@cpmodule]#
```

To restore the configuration, transfer the file back to that directory, type **./upgrade_import <the name of the file>**, and press **Enter**. This time you will notice numerous files scrolling across the screen. This is normal.

```
[Expert@cpmodule]# ./upgrade_import SplatR65_export.tgx.tgz

The 'Import' operation will stop all Check Point services (cpstop).
Do you want to continue? (y/n) [n] ? y
```

Finally, you can take a snapshot of your current configuration. This creates a complete image of your SecurePlatform system. The snapshot usage:

```
[Expert@cpmodule]# snapshot ?
usage:
snapshot        [-h] [-d] [[--tftp <ServerIP> <Filename>] |
                [--scp <ServerIP> <Username> <Password> <Filename>] |
                [--file <Filename>]]
where:
    -d                          Show debug messages
    -h, --help                  Show this help information
    -t, --tftp                  Transfer backup package to TFTP server
    -s, --scp                   Transfer backup package to SCP server
    -f, --file                  Specify local backup package filename
```

Here we will use the tftp option. (Note: As a personal preference when transferring configuration files, I *always* use a secure method. I am showing an alternative but I recommend using SCP.)

```
[Expert@cpmodule]# snapshot -t 172.16.1.159 Splat_R65_snapshot
Are you sure you want to proceed (y/n) [y]? y

Creating the Snapshot Image. This can take up to 20 minutes…
Note that all Check Point products will be stopped
and re-started after the snapshot completes.
```

Patch Command

As business needs change you may be called upon to add more products to your Check Point deployment. This can be done by utilizing the patch command.

```
[Expert@cpmodule]# patch ?
Usage: patch add tftp <ip> <patch_name>
       patch add scp <ip> <username> <remote_filename> [password]
       patch add cd [<patch_name>]
       patch add <full_patch_path>
```

In this example we will use the CD to upgrade then R65 installation.

```
[Expert@cpmodule]# patch add cd
```

```
Choose a patch to install:

1) SecurePlatform NGX R65 Upgrade Package (CPspupgrade_R65.tgz)
2) Exit

Your choice:
1
Calculating the MD5 checksum of the package.
The MD5 checksum is: 67d9c04796w7fd7sc71da7b93939becd1da0
Is that right (Y/N)? y
Extracting /mnt/cdrom/SecurePlatform/patch/CPspupgrade_R65.tgz package ..

Start Upgrading ..
Do you want to create a backup image for automatic revert (y/n)?: n
Verifying ..
```

Secure Shell

Secure Shell (ssh) is a useful firewall administration tool. SSH enables administrators to log in securely. It is the preferred way to connect to security devices because the channel is encrypted. Essentially ssh works by using public and private keys. During the initial connection, the server will send your ssh client a public key, and you will receive the following screen:

```
[Expert@cpmodule]# ssh -l admin 172.19.4.1
The authenticity of host '172.19.4.1 (172.19.4.1)' can't be established.
RSA key fingerprint is ca:2c:0b:f0:cc:51:84:d8:4e:17:ca:58:43:d5:5f:7a.
Are you sure you want to continue connecting (yes/no)? yes
Warning: Permanently added '172.19.4.1' (RSA) to the list of known hosts.
admin@172.19.4.1's password:
```

Type **yes** to continue. Once you do this, your client will generate both a public and private key. The server you are connecting to will take the public key. Now both the client and server have keys to encrypt and decrypt the connection. More detailed documentation is outlined in RFCs 4250–4554.

There are a number of ssh clients available, both free and commercial. Depending on your needs and the operating system you are running you can determine which client will best suit. If you are unsure of the right client there is a great comparison matrix located at http://en.wikipedia.org/wiki/Comparison_of_SSH_clients.

SecurePlatform Pro

SecurePlatform and SecurePlatform Pro differ in a few ways. SecurePlatform is a robust operating system facilitating many of the everyday functions of a security gateway or management station. However, more complex installations call for more robust components. Since firewalls are edge devices it stands to reason that routing needs to be as robust as possible. SecurePlatform Pro solves many of these problems with its advanced routing suite. SecurePlatform Pro has support for dynamic unicast routing protocols (BGP, OSPF, RIPv1, RIPv2) as well as multicast protocols (IGMP, PIM-DM, PIM-SM). The following link compares the features of SecurePlatform and SecurePlatform Pro: http://www.checkpoint.com/products/secureplatform/comparison.html.

The dynamic routing suite that is available with SecurePlatform Pro is enabled/disabled using *cpconfig*. To access the dynamic routing suite type **router** on the command line interface and press **Enter**. Most of the configuration can be done on this screen:

```
localhost.localdomain(config)#ip ?
  access-list            Configure an access list
  as-path                ASPATH configuration
  community-list         Configure a BGP community list
  community-set          Configure a BGP community set
  dvmrp                  Configure DVMRP
  igmp                   Configure IGMP
  pim                    Configure PIM
  prefix-list            Configure a prefix list
  prefix-tree            Configure a prefix tree
  route                  Static route configuration
  router-discovery       Configure Router Discovery server
  router-id              Configure a router-id
  routingtable-id        Configure routing table ID
```

Getting to this screen is quite easy if you remember to use the ?. Once you have accessed the router, type a command followed by ?. This will list any options available for that parameter. To get to this screen you will have to enter the following commands: **enable | configure terminal | ip**. Also remember you cannot configure static routes here, you will need to do this using the SecurePlatform utilities. If you try to add a static route here you will see the following:

```
localhost.localdomain(config)#ip route EU0 999 This command is not allowed.
Please use standard SecurePlatform tools to configure static routes.
```

Another difference between SecurePlatform and SecurePlatform Pro is that only SecurePlatform Pro supports RADIUS authentication for SecurePlatform Administrators. SecurePlatform support a number of authentication methods for administrators, SecurePlatform Pro builds on this by adding RADIUS. Furthermore there is no need for a special license to manage users via RADIUS. There are two ways to authenticate administrators via RADIUS—by individual or by group. Following is the usage of the **radius server add** command, this will aid in the configuration of RADIUS authentication.

```
[Expert@cpmodule]# radius server add
Usage:
Control   RADIUS servers:
      radius servers show
      radius servers add <server[:port]> <secret> <timeout> <label>
      radius servers del [<server[:port]>|<label>]
Control   RADIUS user groups:
      radius groups show
      radius groups add <groupname>
      radius groups del <groupname>

Control   local RADIUS users:
      radius users show
      radius users add <username>
      radius users del <username>
```

Hot Fix Accumulators

Installing Hot Fix Accumulators (HFAs) is an important part of keeping your security device up-to-date. HFAs are a collection of fixes to the Check Point software, operating system, security flaws, or enhancements for the device. Installing an HFA is not a complex process, but it is important. As a Check Point security administrator, you will need to be familiar with installing hot fix accumulators. This section will show you how to install HFAs using the command line.

Hot fix accumulators always come with release notes. Release notes outline the fixes included in the hot fix you are installing as well as fixes that were included in previous HFAs. It is *always* a good idea to review the release notes before installing the HFA. SecurePlatform hot fix accumulators are a bit different when compared to the HFAs for Nokia, Solaris, and Windows. SecurePlatform HFAs contain fixes for both the operating system as well as the Check Point software. If you have never installed an HFA I can assure you this process is quite straightforward.

HFA Installation

Before installing an HFA you must download it from Check Point. In this example we will install HFA 01. Remember hot fixes are additive: if you are going install HFA 05, you do not need to install HFAs 01-04 first, simply install HFA 05. Once you have the HFA that you want, FTP or SCP it to your management station and to your firewall enforcement modules.

> **NOTE**
>
> You will install the HFA on the management station *first*. This is very important. The management station has to be at or above the software level of the firewall module in order to preserve backward compatibility. Always install the HFA on the management station first, then the firewall modules.

As a personal preference I always make a directory in the /home/admin directory containing the HFA name.

```
[Expert@cpmodule]# pwd
/home/admin
[Expert@cpmodule]# mkdir R65_HFA_01
[Expert@cpmodule]# cd R65_HFA_01/
[Expert@cpmodule]# pwd
/home/admin/R65_HFA_01
```

Now it is time to FTP the file to your management station or firewall:

```
[Expert@cpmodule]# ftp 172.16.9.100
Connected to 172.16.9.100 (172.16.9.100).
220 3Com 3CDaemon FTP Server Version 2.0
Name (172.16.9.100:admin):xxxxxxxxx
331 User name ok, need password
Password:xxxxxxxxx
230 User logged in
Remote system type is UNIX.
Using binary mode to transfer files.
ftp> bin
200 Type set to I.
ftp> get VPN-1_R65_HFA_01_wrapper.SecurePlatform.tgz
```

```
local: VPN-1_R65_HFA_01_wrapper.SecurePlatform.tgz remote: VPN-1_R65_HFA_01_wrap
per.SecurePlatform.tgz
227 Entering passive mode (172,16,9,100,9,183)
125 Using existing data connection
226 Closing data connection; File transfer successful.
136060186 bytes received in 23.8 secs (5.6e+03 Kbytes/sec)
ftp> bye
221 Service closing control connection
[Expert@cpmodule]# ls
VPN-1_R65_HFA_01_wrapper.SecurePlatform.tgz
[Expert@cpmodule]#
```

The next part of the installation is to untar the file:

```
[Expert@cpmodule]# tar xzvf VPN-1_R65_HFA_01_wrapper.SecurePlatform.tgz
./
./PostInstall.sh
./PreInstall.sh
./packages.txt
./wrapper.conf
./UnixInstallScript
./CPvpn/
./CPvpn/fw1_R65_HFA.tgz
./SecurePlatform/
./SecurePlatform/SecurePlatform_R65_HFA.tgz
./CPppak/
./CPppak/sim_R65_HFA.tgz
./Eventia/
./Eventia/ReportingServer_R65_HFA.tgz
./CPEdgeCmp/
./CPEdgeCmp/edge_cmp_R65_HFA.tgz
[Expert@cpmodule]#
```

Now that the files are untarred, you are ready for installation. The UnixInstallScript will install both the SecurePlatform and Checkpoint HFAs. To install simply type **./UnixInstallScript** and press **Enter**. You will be asked if you want to continue with the installation. Press **Y** to continue. This process can take a while, so you will need to be patient.

```
[Expert@cpmodule]# ./UnixInstallScript
Welcome to HFA R65_01 installation.
Do you wish to continue [Y/n]?

y
```

```
Installing SecurePlatform ...
... SecurePlatform installation succeeded.
Installing VPN-1 ...
... VPN-1 installation succeeded.
Installing VPN-1 UTM Edge Compatibility Package …
... VPN-1 UTM Edge Compatibility Package installation succeeded.

************************************************************************
**************
The updated inspect files were installed successfully.
You must install the Security Policy after completing the HFA installation.
************************************************************************
*************

------------------------------------------------------------
The installation of HFA R65_01 has completed successfully.
You must reboot your computer for the changes to take effect.
------------------------------------------------------------
[Expert@cpmodule]#
```

Now it is time to reboot. Once this is done you can verify the installation is complete by typing **fw ver** on the command line interface:

```
[cpmodule]# fw ver
This is Check Point VPN-1(TM) & FireWall-1(R) NGX (R65) HFA_01, Hotfix
601 - Build 019
[cpmodule]#
```

That's it—you have now successfully installed a hot fix on your SecurePlatform system.

Summary

In this chapter you have learned how to install, configure, and maintain a SecurePlatform or SecurePlatform Pro installation. SecurePlatform is quite easy to install and configure. I have shown you several ways to do so. The WUI is a browser-based method of configuring SecurePlatform. The CLI will also allow you to configure SecurePlatform, and is preferred since there are many more options than the WUI. The CLI offers you a CPShell to configure system and Check Point products. Expert mode offers a bash shell for configuring and editing the file system. Remember that expert mode holds the same privileges as root.

Some of the utilities that SecurePlatform has to offer are backup/restore, upgrade_export/upgrade_import, and patch add. These utilities will enable you to keep your SecurePlatform installation up to date and safe. We also looked at applying HFAs to SecurePlatform. Doing this helps to keep the operating system as well as the Check Point products running smoothly and securely.

Finally we explored some of the differences between SecurePlatform and SecurePlatform Pro. These differences included management of administrators via RADIUS, and the dynamic routing suite. SecurePlatform Pro needs special licenses to run.

Solutions Fast Track

Installation

☑ The installation of SecurePlatform or SecurePlatform Pro is designed to be easy.

☑ Installation can be done with either a bootable CD or a combination of a floppy disk and a network share.

☑ While installing you will be prompted to choose between SecurePlatform or SecurePlatform Pro.

Configuration

☑ Browser-based configuration is available using the WUI.

☑ Both initial and post configuration parameters can be set/changed with the WUI.

☑ All configuration can be done from the command line.

☑ The "?" is your best friend if you are not sure of a command parameter.

☑ *sysconfig* is the utility used to configure both Check Point and SecurePlatform.

☑ Expert mode is available only from the CLI.

☑ Expert mode gives you access to a bash shell with "root" privileges to the entire system.

SecurePlatform Shell

☑ When first logging in to SecurePlatform, you are presented with an application-specific configuration interface.

☑ Expert mode grants access to a traditional Linux bash shell, with the equivalent of root privileges.

☑ Backup/Restore and Patch will allow you to keep your system configured the way you want it.

Secure Shell

☑ Secure Shell is the preferred way to connect to security devices because the channel is encrypted.

☑ Essentially Secure Shell works by using public and private keys.

☑ A number of free and commercial versions of Secure Shell clients are available.

SecurePlatform Pro

☑ Dynamic routing is available only if you are using SecurePlatform Pro.

☑ Unicast protocols supported: BGP, OSPF, RIPv1, RIPv2.

☑ Multicast protocols supported: IGMP, PIM-DM, PIM-SM.

Hot Fix Accumulators

☑ HFAs help keep both the operating system and product suite up to date.

☑ Installation to both OS and Check Point product suite can be done using the UnixInstallScrtipt via the command line.

☑ Always read the release notes before applying an HFA.

Frequently Asked Questions

Q: I have SecurePlatform installed. Do I have to reinstall in order to use the features or SecurePlatform Pro?

A: No. The easiest way to switch from SecurePlatform to SecurePlatform Pro is to type **pro enable** on the command line. However, make sure you have the proper licenses installed on the management station managing the enforcement modules.

Q: I have a configuration file, and I did not import it when I built the SmartCenter. Do I have to rebuild and import it?

A: No. You can import the configuration post installation. To accomplish this, change the directory to *$FWDIR/bin/upgrade_tools*. Then FTP/SCP the configuration file to this directory and type **./upgrade_import <your filename>** and press **Enter**.

Q: I do not have a CD-ROM or floppy drive installed on the server I plan to use to install SecurePlatform. Can I still use this server?

A: Yes, you can perform the installation. There are detailed instructions on how to accomplish this. They are located in Appendix A of the CheckPoint_R65_ SecurePlatform_SecurePlatformPro_AdminGuide, entitled "Installation on Computers without Floppy or CD-ROM Drives."

Chapter 10

Advanced Troubleshooting

Solutions in this chapter:

- **NGX Debugging**
- **Packet Analysis**
- **Log Troubleshooting**
- **VPN Analysis**
- **VPN Client Analysis**
- **ClusterXL Troubleshooting**

☑ **Summary**

☑ **Solutions Fast Track**

☑ **Frequently Asked Questions**

Introduction

Any advanced network security product needs a set of troubleshooting tools. This chapter covers the debugging and troubleshooting features available on the Check Point NGX R65 suite. Many of the troubleshooting methods detailed in this chapter will work on any NG- or NGX-based Check Point firewall.

NGX Debugging

To understand troubleshooting methodology, a deep understanding of the Check Point internal workings and directory structure is in order. As mentioned earlier in this book, Check Point VPN-1 is a software-based firewall product. Check Point can run on Check Point Secure Platform, Red Hat Linux, Sun Solaris, HP-UX, IBM AIX, Nokia IPSO (BSD), and Windows Server. The only major differences between the different operating system installs are the install scripts and the kernel bindings. The Check Point directory structure is the same across the different operation systems, with the exception of Windows, which adds an extra line feed to the various text files.

The firewall creates two directory trees. The SVN Foundation tree (a.k.a. the cpshared tree) is installed in the $CPDIR directory. This Windows install installs in %CPDIR%, following the Microsoft environment variable format. The firewall package installs in the $FWDIR directory. Note that the $CPDIR/bin and $FWDIR/bin directories are in the root/admin user's *path* environment variable.

Here are some of the directories created that are important to mention:

- **$CPDIR/bin** Contains the cpconfig and cplic utilities
- **$FWDIR/bin** Contains the firewall and management daemons
- **$FWDIR/conf** Contains the firewall configuration
- **$FWDIR/lib** Contains the custom Check Point Inspect code for protocols
- **$FWDIR/log** Contains the log files
- **$FWDIR/spool** Contains the e-mail in the Simple Mail Transfer Protocol (SMTP) queue used by the SMTP resource
- **$FWDIR/tmp** Contains temporary files, used for utilities such as fw monitor

When a SmartDashboard client connects to a Management Server, the following files are downloaded to the client:

- $FWDIR/conf/objects_5_0.C

- $FWDIR/conf/rulebases_5_0.fws

- $FWDIR/conf/fwauth.NDB

The objects_5_0.C file contains all firewall properties, objects, automatic network address translator (NAT) settings, global properties, user groups, and implicit rules. The rulebases_5_0.fws file contains all the explicit rules and manual NAT rules of every rulebase, concatenated. All rulebases use the same objects file, which is a primary reason for using Database Revision Control instead of creating new rulebases for internal policy backups. The fwauth. NBD file contains all of the users, and is also known as the User Database.

When a policy is pushed to a firewall, the firewall will take the particular rulebase being pushed and save it to a W file. If the policy name is Standard, the Standard rulebase from the rulebases_5_0.fws file is saved to $FWDIR/conf/Standard.W. The compile process takes this file along with the objects, the user database, and the contents of the $FWDIR/lib directory to create the policy, $FWDIR/conf/ Standard.pf.

Notes from the Underground…

Resolving Policy Install Issues

Sometimes a policy does not push for some reason. You can take several steps to troubleshoot this issue. Check to see whether the firewall is indeed up and online. If this is a new firewall, the default policy blocks all but Check Point traffic, which is desirable unless a route needs to be added to allow the Management Server to reach the firewall. You can modify the $FWDIR/ conf/initial_module.pf policy if required, but most administrators just unload the policy with *fw unloadlocal* to access the firewall appliance with Secure Shell (SSH).

Check to see that the firewall daemon, fwd, is actually running. You can do this using the *ps* command in UNIX, or by checking the Windows Task Manager. If the daemon is not running, you can run the daemon in debug mode using the command *fwd –d* to find out why it is unloading. On the firewall,

Continued

> you can pull the last pushed policy from the manager using the *fw fetch <management server ip>* command. If you cannot gain access to any network, or if you do not want to for some reason, you can load the policy locally. For example, for the Standard rulebase, copy the Standard.pf file to the $FWDIR/ conf directory of the firewall and issue the *fw load Standard.pf* command.

You can place each firewall daemon into debug mode for troubleshooting the operation of the binary itself. The output of these debug files has a very high level of detail. To put the firewall daemon into debug mode issue the following command:

```
fw debug fwd on TDERROR_ALL_ALL=5
```

The firewall daemon logging will output to $FWDIR/log/fwd.elg. This file will be in clear text and can be read into a text editor or parsed with grep. To stop logging issue the following command:

```
fw debug fwd off TDERROR_ALL_ALL=0
```

You also can place the Management Server into debug mode by substituting "fwm" for "fwd" in the preceding commands. The management daemon logging will output to $FWDIR/log/fwm.elg. The Check Point resources, also known as security servers and proxies, can also be placed into debug mode. To be able to debug a resource, the resource must have a process id (PID). The PID references are in the $FWDIR/tmp directory and end with .pid. Resources are named in the following manner: in.a<PROTOCOL>d. For example, to start debugging the Hypertext Transfer Protocol (HTTP) security server issue the following command:

```
fw debug in.ahttpd on FWAHTTPD_LEVEL=3
```

To stop debugging the HTTP security server use this command:

```
fw debug in.ahttpd off FWAHTTPD_LEVEL=3
```

The output of the debugging is stored in $FWDIR/log/ahttpd.elg in this instance. You can achieve more advanced troubleshooting using the *fw ctl debug* command, which will dump the actual kernel memory to a file.

SIC Troubleshooting

Check Point communicates internally using secure internal communication (SIC). You can encrypt this communication using certificates, cut from the certificate authority (CA) running on the primary management station, and it is based on OpenSSL.

There is no built-in interface to manage the CA; however, there is a Knowledge Base article on Check Point's support site that explains how to install one. You can use these certificates for authentication and encryption. This system replaced Check Point's older "putkey" system, which is still there for backward compatibility.

You can resolve most SIC issues by resetting the communication on the remote end. Using the *cpconfig* command on a firewall offers an option to Reset Secure Internal Communication. This will ask for a one-time password, which is used in the SmartDashboard GUI to establish a new certificate for the firewall.

There is a chance the CA can become corrupt. This can happen in certain scenarios when the name or Internet Protocol (IP) address of the Management Server is changed without taking the proper steps to ensure a smooth transition. Once Check Point is configured on a Management Server, the name or IP address should not be changed in the firewall object, or on the operating system. Follow the R65 Upgrade Guide for procedures on changing these settings properly.

You can reinitialize the CA using the *fwm sic_reset* command. You need to run this command in expert mode if you are running it on Secure Platform. This will reset all certificate operations and require new one-time passwords to be generated for every firewall, along with a reimport of the licensing. After running the command on the management station, you need to run cpconfig again and choose the Certificate Authority option to tell Check Point to initialize a new CA.

SIC uses Transmission Control Protocol (TCP) ports 18209 through 18211. You can verify access to SIC services by accessing port 18211 or by using *netstat −na* and searching for the open TCP port. The fwd and fwm debug logs, as well as the cpd daemon logs, can help you to troubleshoot SIC issues. You can put the SVN Foundation process into debug mode by issuing the following commands:

```
cpd_admin debug on TDERROR_ALL_ALL=5
cpd_admin debug on OPSEC_DEBUG_LEVEL=9
```

The following commands will turn off cpd debugging:

```
cpd_admin debug off TDERROR_ALL_ALL=0
cpd_admin debug off OPSEC_DEBUG_LEVEL=0
```

If all else fails, try to delete the firewall object and create a new one. It is possible for independent objects to contain problematic configuration options.

Packet Analysis

Sometimes you need more information than what is available in Check Point's logging mechanisms. Several utilities are available to troubleshoot packet issues, including snoop, tcpdump, and fw monitor.

snoop

snoop is the packet sniffer built into the Sun Solaris operating system. A long time ago, Check Point was a Solaris-only product and the Check Point documentation contained many references to snoop. Some of those references still exist. snoop is similar to tcpdump, as it grabs raw packets and either displays them in a readable format or dumps them to a file. snoop has the ability to parse packet dump files and format them for text-based display as well.

tcpdump

tcpdump is the packet sniffer utility that is available for most flavors of UNIX and Linux. This utility is installed by default on Check Point's Secure Platform. Like snoop, tcpdump can read raw packets from any or all interfaces and display them in a text-based terminal or dump them into a file. It is recommended that you use filters to limit what tcpdump writes to a file.

fw monitor

Check Point has a built-in packet sniffer that you can access by running the command *fw monitor*. This is the sniffer of choice on a Check Point appliance. The *fw monitor* command is available on every operating system on which Check Point will run. The output is displayed on the console by default. If redirected to a file, the fw monitor utility stores its packet dumps in libpcap format, which is the same format that tcpdump uses. You can use a graphical utility such as Wireshark, CPethereal, or Sniffer Pro to analyze these capture files later.

Several command-line switches are available for fw monitor. Some of the more important ones are:

- *fw monitor −o <filename>* This outputs to a file instead of the console.
- *fw monitor −m* The capture mask tells the monitor where to sniff out of four places.

- *fw monitor –p* The position allows for a more granular inspection.

- *fw monitor –e* Expressions allow for filtering of what to capture.

- *fw monitor –f* Multiple expressions can be placed into a filter file.

- *fw monitor –x* The offset allows for capture of the data portion of the packets.

- *fw monitor –c* The count option limits how many packets are captured.

The *fw monitor –m* switch allows you to pick where the firewall captures packets. The firewall kernel is loaded in two places: on the inbound direction and on the outbound direction, with routing in between. By default, fw monitor sniffs in four places. Here is the process:

1. The packet arrives at the inbound interface. This is signified by *–m i.*

2. The packet flows through the inbound firewall kernel. This is signified by *–m I.*

3. The operating system routes the packet.

4. The packet arrives at the outbound interface. This is signified by *–m o.*

5. The packet flows through the outbound interface. This is signified by *–m O.*

So, the default capture contains all four places: *fw monitor –m iIoO.* You can pick and choose which ones you want to capture. This is sufficient for most needs, but what if you wanted to capture in between firewall processes? The *fw monitor –p* command allows for more granular capturing.

Before looking into the *–p* parameter, let's reference the output of the *fw ctl chain* command, as shown in Figure 10.1.

Figure 10.1 Referencing the Output of the *fw ctl chain* Command

```
[cpModule]#
[cpModule]#
[cpModule]#
[cpModule]#
[cpModule]#
[cpModule]#
[cpModule]# fw ctl chain
in chain (8):
        0: -   1fffff6 (9098fbf0) (00000001) Stateless verifications (asm)
        1: -   1000000 (909c8520) (00000003) SecureXL conn sync (secxl_sync)
        2:           0 (90937010) (00000001) fw VM inbound  (fw)
        3:           1 (90998200) (00000002) wire VM inbound  (wire_vm)
        4:          10 (9094c230) (00000001) fw accounting inbound (acct)
        5:    10000000 (909c8cb0) (00000003) SecureXL inbound (secxl)
        6:     7f600000 (90988bb0) (00000001) fw SCV inbound (scv)
        7:     7f750000 (90aaa970) (00000001) TCP streaming (in) (cpas)
out chain (7):
        0: -   1ffff0 (90aaaaf0) (00000001) TCP streaming (out) (cpas)
        1: -   1f00000 (9098fbf0) (00000001) Stateless verifications (asm)
        2:           0 (90937010) (00000001) fw VM outbound  (fw)
        3:           1 (90998200) (00000002) wire VM outbound  (wire_vm)
        4:    10000000 (909c8cb0) (00000003) SecureXL outbound (secxl)
        5:     7f800000 (9094c230) (00000001) fw accounting outbound (acct)
        6:     7f700000 (90aaacf0) (00000001) TCP streaming post VM (cpas)
[cpModule]# _
```

This command displays most of the positions that a packet traverses through a Check Point firewall. More processes handle packets, but the *fw ctl chain* output displays everything that is possible to capture using the *–p* parameter. The first number is a position ID, and the other numbers are memory offsets and absolute memory locations, which vary depending on the operating system and firewall version. The text in parentheses at the end represents aliases. You can use the ID or the alias using the *–p* parameter. The *fw monitor –m* command captures at the firewall VM inbound listed in the chain output. Here is an example of using the *–p* parameter to capture at the inbound virtual private network (VPN) decryption:

```
fw monitor -pi 2
```

Here is the same command using an alias:

```
fw monitor -pi -fw
```

You can also sniff in every possible place using the *–p all* parameter. This will log 15 packets for every one packet. Running this on a busy firewall without a filter would be a recipe for disaster, so let's get into filtering our capture to get just what we need. The *–e* parameter allows for custom expressions to be written. This expression is written in Check Point's proprietary Inspect language. Here is an example:

```
fw monitor -e 'accept [9:1]=6;'
```

The preceding command captures packets whose ninth byte, the length of 1 byte, is equal to 6. In an IP header, the ninth byte is the protocol ID. The protocol ID for TCP is 6. This expression captures all TCP packets that the firewall rulebase accepted.

When an fw monitor is compiled, it includes the $FWDIR/lib/fwmonitor.def file, which also includes the $FWDIR/lib/tcpip.def file. These files contain aliases that you can use in expressions. For example, one of the lines in the tcpip.def file contains the text *#define ip_p [9 : 1]*. This allows us to issue the following command instead:

```
fw monitor -e 'accept ip_p=6;'
```

See the tcpip.def file for more references. When you execute fw monitor the following text appears:

```
   monitor: getting filter (from command line)
   monitor: compiling
monitorfilter:
Compiled OK.
   monitor: loading
   monitor: monitoring (control-C to stop)
```

When the monitor is invoked a miniature inspect code base is generated and stored in the $FWDIR/tmp/monitorfilter.pf file. If you used an elaborate expression, you can copy this monitorfilter.pf file to another location so that you can use it in the future using the *–f* parameter. Your custom filter file can contain your own custom *#define* aliases as well.

The expressions also understand logical operations and order of operations. Let's say we want to capture all traffic between 192.168.1.1 and 10.1.1.1, using the Internet Control Message Protocol (ICMP):

```
fw monitor -e 'accept ip_p=1, ((src=192.168.1.1, dst=10.1.1.1) or (src=10.1.1.1,
dst=192.168.1.1));'
```

The *–x* parameter allows for data capture. For example, let's say we want to capture the first 100 bytes of the data portion of the packets. An offset is required, and with TCP packets the data portion starts at offset 52:

```
fw monitor -x 52,100
```

The last option that can be useful is the *–c* parameter, which stops monitoring after a specified number of packets. You can specify inbound and outbound directions using this command. Keep in mind that it will still log as many positions as you specify. For example, if you use defaults, four entries are created for each packet, so if you count five packets, you will capture 20 packets (5 × 4). For example:

```
fw monitor -ci 5 -co 5
```

More command-line options are available for fw monitor, but the preceding command-line options are the ones that are most frequently used. Good references for capture scripts are available on the Check Point User Group (CPUG) forums, Check Point's own Knowledge Base, Nokia's Knowledge Base, and the Check Point "How to use fw monitor" document.

Tools & Traps…

Which Sniffer Do I Choose?

As you can see, you essentially can choose between two utilities when collecting packets. The major difference between the two is the data link layer contents of the packet dump. When you use snoop or tcpdump, raw packets are sniffed before Check Point gets the packets. These packets contain Media Access Control (MAC) addresses and are useful for troubleshooting Layer 1 and Layer 2 issues.

When you use fw monitor, Check Point overwrites the MAC addresses of the packets with firewall information. These packets contain information that is useful for troubleshooting Layers 3 through 7, and for handling routing issues.

CPethereal and Wireshark

Check Point has a client application available for analysis of tcpdump and fw monitor capture files. CPethereal is available from Check Point's Support Download Web site under NG Utilities. The advantage of this application is that it has an additional field for the FW Chain position of the packet. The downside of this application is that it is based on a rather dated version of Ethereal.

You also can load the fw monitor output into the latest version of Wireshark, which used to be Ethereal. Finding the FW Chain location is still possible by looking at the first several bytes in the hex output at the bottom of the interface, where the hex dump is displayed. The first byte is the basic location: i, I, o, or O. The second byte contains a number 0 through 9 signifying the absolute FW Chain location. The next several bytes spell out the inbound or outbound interface name.

Log Troubleshooting

All Check Point firewalls can generate logs locally. The *fw log* command will allow an administrator to view log entries on the command shell. Most issues with logging are the result of connectivity issues with the Management Server and/or Logging Server. Logging issues can also occur when there is an issue with the SIC certificates, as Check Point uses these certificates to secure the logging traffic.

Check Point will populate an empty $FWDIR/log directory on startup of various services. If you have a corrupt log file and *fw repairlog* does not seem to resolve your issues, you can issue a *cpstop* and move or delete the contents of the $FWDIR/log directory, and then issue a *cpstart* to bring the services back up. Do not remove the actual log directory or symlink in $FWDIR. The directory has to exist for Check Point to initialize.

VPN Analysis

When troubleshooting VPN traffic, you can resolve most issues by studying the Info field of the SmartView Tracker logs. Usually a break in an existing VPN is caused by a recent configuration change in the policy. If a Database Revision Control backup has been made recently, open it in a new window and compare the current policy with the backup. Also, double-check that the encryption domains have not been modified, as the encryption domain group may be used in other rules in the policy and is sometimes modified for other purposes by accident. It may also be a good idea to check CPU usage and memory usage of the VPN gateway. If a runaway process uses up all available resources, all VPN traffic can be affected.

If there are certificate issues, switching to a preshared secret is a valid step to fix the VPN issue while the certificate issues are being worked on. Another common issue, which directly affects VPNs that are using certificates, is time and date settings on the gateways. Make sure the time and date settings are within the certificate valid date fields.

TIP

Make sure routing has not been affected. It may seem obvious that two gateways need to be able to route to each other for a VPN tunnel to establish, but many VPN tunnels have failed as a result of improper routing.

Now we'll discuss some examples of errors that show up in the Info view of the SmartView Tracker.

Encryption failure, decrypted methods did not match rule

If you receive the error *Encryption failure, decrypted methods did not match rule*, this typically means there are overlapping encryption domains. VPN-1 supports proper subsets, which is an encryption domain fully contained within another encryption domain, and fully overlapping encryption domains when clusters are involved. Otherwise, any encryption domain overlap will cause the VPN to fail.

Received notification from peer: no proposal chosen

The error message *Received notification from peer: no proposal chosen* is rather common. This usually means the VPN settings do not match on both ends. This error could also mean there is a subnet negotiation mismatch. Make sure the **Support key exchanges for subnets** setting is enabled on older versions of Check Point, or that VPN tunnel sharing settings are configured properly in the advanced section of the VPN community on the R65. Both ends must agree on these settings for a proper VPN tunnel to be established.

Tools & Traps…

VPN Checklist

Here is a quick checklist we have found to be helpful when setting up a VPN tunnel. Both ends of a VPN tunnel need to match, and providing this checklist to other VPN administrators may help the process go a little bit easier.

Phase 1: Internet Key Exchange (IKE)

- Which key exchange algorithm? (IKE)

- Which encryption algorithm? (Data Encryption Standard [DES], 3DES, AES-128, AES-256)

- Which hash algorithm? (Message Digest 5 [MD5], Secure Hash Algorithm [SHA-1])

- Key size? (Group 2 – 1024)
- Main mode or aggressive mode? (Main mode)
- IKE renegotiation timeout? (24 hours)
- Authentication? (Preshared key or certificate)

Phase 2: IPSec Quick Mode

- Which encryption algorithm? (DES, 3DES, AES-128, AES-256, Null)
- Which hash algorithm? (MD5, SHA-1)
- Key size? (Group 2 – 1024)
- IPSec renegotiation timeout? (3,600 seconds/one hour)
- Enable perfect forward secrecy? (Yes, if the other end supports it)
- Enable compression? (Yes, if mostly clear text packets are being transferred in the VPN)
- Disable NAT? (Yes)
- Tunnel mode or transport mode? (Tunnel mode)

Cannot identify peer for encrypted connection

You will receive the error message *Cannot identify peer for encrypted connection* when NAT is not being applied properly. Make sure that if NAT is applied to a packet the NAT IP address is part of the encryption domain.

Encryption failure: packet is dropped as there is no valid SA

The SA is the Security Association in a VPN tunnel. The error *Encryption failure: packet is dropped as there is no valid SA* can occur when packets are corrupted before they reach the other VPN gateway. Look into data link errors or links that are over capacity. This error can also occur when the *fwha_sync_outbound_sa* setting in the firewall object is set to *false*. To resolve this issue use *guidbedit* or *dbedit* to set this variable to *true* in the firewall properties.

Encryption failure: Clear text packet should be encrypted or clear text packet received within an encrypted packet

If you receive the error message that reads *Encryption failure: Clear text packet should be encrypted or clear text packet received within an encrypted packet*, it means that the IP and subnet mask are incorrect in the firewall Topology tab, or the VPN is terminating to the wrong interface. Make sure the external IP address of the gateway is the IP address in the General tab of the firewall object. In a cluster object, the external routable Virtual Internet Protocol (VIP) address of the cluster should be the IP on the main gateway properties page.

Encryption Failure: Packet was decrypted, but policy says connection should not be decrypted

An improper VPN domain can cause the error message *Encryption Failure: Packet was decrypted, but policy says connection should not be decrypted*. Double-check that the VPN domains on the Topology tab of the VPN objects are set properly.

If all else fails, you can run a VPN debug on a VPN gateway. To start VPN debugging issue the following commands:

```
vpn debug on
vpn debug ikeon
```

The output of these commands dumps logging information in the $FWDIR/log/vpnd.elg file. You can open this log file in the IKEView.exe utility, which is available from the NG Utilities section of Check Point's support Web site. To stop VPN debugging issue the following commands:

```
vpn debug ikeoff
vpn debug off
```

VPN Client Analysis

Troubleshooting issues with SecuRemote and Secure Client is typically very similar to standard IKE VPN troubleshooting. Check the VPN domains, as well as connectivity to the external side of the VPN gateways from the client network.

The most common issue is connectivity to the encryption gateway on the proper ports. Check Point uses several ports with client-side VPN. If these ports are not open, you may need to connect via Visitor Mode, which emulates a Secure Sockets Layer (SSL) VPN on TCP port 443. Check Point has a limited SSL VPN built into VPN-1, called SSL Network Extender (SNX). For a full-blown SSL VPN, Check Point offers Connectra, which requires an additional host. As of R65, Connectra management is built into the SmartCenter Server.

A packet capture utility is available on all SecuRemote clients. The *srfw monitor* command allows for client-side analysis and is similar to the fw monitor utility.

ClusterXL Troubleshooting

You can cluster Check Point firewalls in several ways. In this section, we will discuss how to diagnose issues with Check Point's built-in clustering functionality, ClusterXL.

ClusterXL has four modes: Legacy High Availability, New Mode High Availability, Load-Sharing Multicast, and Load-Sharing Unicast. Communication among these nodes is facilitated using the Cluster Control Protocol (CCP) using User Datagram Protocol (UDP) port 8116.

State synchronization is optional with the High Availability modes and mandatory with the Load-Sharing modes. To check the status of state sync, use the *fw ctl pstat* command. The status of the sync will be at the end of the output. Another way to check the status of state sharing is to view the number of state table entries on both nodes by running the following command:

```
fw tab -s -t connections
```

The output under the *VALS* parameter is the number of state table entries in memory. Check the physical statistics on the Ethernet port that state sync is using and make sure there are no data link errors. Also make sure you can ping the other nodes as well, but keep in mind that a rule may by required to allow ICMP between the nodes.

Verify that there are no IP conflicts on the firewall networks. New Mode High Availability and the Load-Sharing modes require a physical IP address per network as well as a VIP. IP conflicts will show up in the Info view of the SmartView Tracker as well as the various devices that have the IP address causing the conflict.

The Load-Sharing Multicast method has the most issues on many networks, as it requires that all locally connected devices support Multicast traffic. Static Address Resolution Protocol (ARP) and/or static Content Addressable Memory (CAM) entries may be necessary on switches and routers. Also make sure the spanning tree is configured on switches. If the local switches do not understand Multicast, they may treat the traffic as broadcast traffic. Without the spanning tree, this traffic may cause routing loops and essentially cause an internal denial of service (DoS). In case of this emergency, immediately change the load-sharing method to Unicast until the internal network is reconfigured to handle the Multicast traffic.

For advanced troubleshooting techniques, refer to the Check Point Advanced Technical Reference Guide for NGX. This guide contains the specifications and detailed analysis of the Check Point High Availability (CPHA) and state sync packets.

Summary

In this chapter, we covered several different methods of troubleshooting various issues on Check Point gateways. When troubleshooting, check the obvious first. Make sure basic connectivity is established and the link layer is operating properly.

You can resolve most issues by studying the logs in the SmartView Tracker. If further analysis is required, Check Point's built-in packet capturing utilities can gather packets for additional study. The capture format is libpcap, which is compatible with all of the popular packet analysis client software.

All of the Check Point daemons can run in debug mode for troubleshooting issues with internal functionality. Debug output is placed into text files with an .elg extension in the $FWDIR/log directory.

Solutions Fast Track

NGX Debugging

☑ The *fw debug* command is used to put various firewall daemons into debug mode.

☑ The *cpd_admin debug* command is used for SIC troubleshooting.

Packet Analysis

☑ For Layer 2 troubleshooting use snoop or tcpdump to capture packets.

☑ The fw monitor utility built into the Check Point firewall can capture packets in multiple places.

☑ The *fw ctl chain* command displays the path a packet takes through VPN-1.

☑ Use the CPethereal or Wireshark utility to analyze packet data on a client PC.

Log Troubleshooting

☑ Check Point logs are stored in the $FWDIR/log directory.

☑ The *fw log* command allows for viewing of logs in a local command shell.

☑ The $FWDIR/log directory can be empty when Check Point services start.

VPN Analysis

☑ Study the Info field of the Check Point logs for Phase 1 and Phase 2 initiation details.

☑ Use the *vpn debug* command for detailed IPSec analysis.

☑ Verify that both sides of a VPN connection have the same settings.

VPN Client Analysis

☑ Verify that the correct ports are open from the client to the firewall.

☑ Use the *srfw monitor* command for client-side packet analysis.

☑ If all else fails, look into SNX or the full-blown SSL VPN, Connectra.

ClusterXL Troubleshooting

☑ The *fw ctl pstat* command will show state synchronization status.

☑ Verify that there are no IP conflicts on the firewall subnets.

☑ Ensure that Multicast traffic is handled properly. Use Unicast mode if there are issues.

Frequently Asked Questions

Q: Can Check Point enforce security on Internetwork Packet Exchange (IPX) or AppleTalk traffic?

A: No, Check Point is a strictly Transmission Control Protocol/Internet Protocol (TCP/IP)-based network security product. In fact, those protocols may bypass the firewall, so it is important to make sure those protocols are not installed on the host operating system.

Q: How would I debug Security Servers?

A: The Security Servers are separate processes on the firewall's host operating system and each one has its own debug command. For example, the e-mail proxy uses the $FWDIR/spool directory to store e-mail and the *fw mdq* command can restart the process. To debug this process use *fw debug in.asmtpd*.

Q: Can I view a Check Point log file on a client system?

A: You must place a Check Point log file on a VPN-1 Management Server or firewall to view its contents. Once the log file is on one of these systems, you can export it to a comma-separated value (CSV) file for import into another analysis tool.

Q: In which firewall chain does Check Point route packets?

A: This is a trick question, as Check Point does not route packets, the host operating system does. Routing occurs between the inbound kernel, I, and the outbound kernel, o.

Q: Why can anyone on the Internet access my Secure Platform Web UI login page?

A: In the firewall object, there is a setting for Visitor Mode. This allows VPN clients to connect over HTTPS, TCP port 443. If the Secure Platform Web UI is listening on port 443, which is the default, Visitor Mode cannot bind to that port. Change the port that Secure Platform is using and restart Check Point services.

Index

Syngress: *The Definition of a Serious Security Library*

Syn·gress (sin-gres): *noun, sing.* Freedom from risk or danger; safety. See *security.*

Syngress: *The Definition of a Serious Security Library*

Syn·gress (sin-gres): *noun, sing.* Freedom from risk or danger; safety. See *security.*

Cyber Spying: Tracking Your Family's (Sometimes) Secret Online Lives

Dr. Eric Cole, Michael Nordfelt,
Sandra Ring, and Ted Fair

Have you ever wondered about that friend your spouse e-mails, or who they spend hours chatting online with? Are you curious about what your children are doing online, whom they meet, and what they talk about? Do you worry about them finding drugs and other illegal items online, and wonder what they look at? This book shows you how to monitor and analyze your family's online behavior.

ISBN: 1-93183-641-8

Price: $39.95 US $57.95 CAN

Stealing the Network: How to Own an Identity

Timothy Mullen, Ryan Russell, Riley (Caezar) Eller,
Jeff Moss, Jay Beale, Johnny Long, Chris Hurley, Tom Parker, Brian Hatch

The first two books in this series "Stealing the Network: How to Own the Box" and "Stealing the Network: How to Own a Continent" have become classics in the Hacker and Infosec communities because of their chillingly realistic depictions of criminal hacking techniques. In this third installment, the all-star cast of authors tackle one of the fastest-growing crimes in the world: Identity Theft. Now, the criminal hackers readers have grown to both love and hate try to cover their tracks and vanish into thin air...

ISBN: 1-59749-006-7

Price: $39.95 US $55.95 CAN

Software Piracy Exposed

Paul Craig, Ron Honick

For every $2 worth of software purchased legally, $1 worth of software is pirated illegally. For the first time ever, the dark underground of how software is stolen and traded over the Internet is revealed. The technical detail provided will open the eyes of software users and manufacturers worldwide! This book is a tell-it-like-it-is exposé of how tens of billions of dollars worth of software is stolen every year.

ISBN: 1-93226-698-4

Price: $39.95 U.S. $55.95 CAN

SYNGRESS®

Syngress: *The Definition of a Serious Security Library*

Syn·gress (sin–gres): *noun, sing.* Freedom from risk or danger; safety. See *security*.

Syngress: *The Definition of a Serious Security Library*

Syn·gress (sin-gres): *noun, sing.* Freedom from risk or danger; safety. See *security*.

Syngress: *The Definition of a Serious Security Library*

Syn·gress (sin-gres): *noun, sing.* Freedom from risk or danger; safety. See *security*.

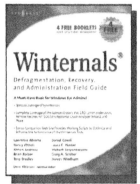
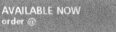

Syngress: *The Definition of a Serious Security Library*

Syn·gress (sin-gres): *noun, sing.* Freedom from risk or danger; safety. See *security*.

How to Cheat at Designing Security for a Windows Server 2003 Network

Neil Ruston, Chris Peiris

While considering the security needs of your organiztion, you need to balance the human and the technical in order to create the best security design for your organization. Securing a Windows Server 2003 enterprise network is hardly a small undertaking, but it becomes quite manageable if you approach it in an organized and systematic way. This includes configuring software, services, and protocols to meet an organization's security needs.

ISBN: 1-59749-243-4

Price: $39.95 US $55.95 CAN

How to Cheat at Designing a Windows Server 2003 Active Directory Infrastructure

Melissa Craft, Michael Cross, Hal Kurz, Brian Barber

The book will start off by teaching readers to create the conceptual design of their Active Directory infrastructure by gathering and analyzing business and technical requirements. Next, readers will create the logical design for an Active Directory infrastructure. Here the book starts to drill deeper and focus on aspects such as group policy design. Finally, readers will learn to create the physical design for an active directory and network Infrastructure including DNS server placement; DC and GC placements and Flexible Single Master Operations (FSMO) role placement.

ISBN: 1-59749-058-X

Price: $39.95 US $55.95 CAN

How to Cheat at Configuring ISA Server 2004

Dr. Thomas W. Shinder, Debra Littlejohn Shinder

If deploying and managing ISA Server 2004 is just one of a hundred responsibilities you have as a System Administrator, "How to Cheat at Configuring ISA Server 2004" is the perfect book for you. Written by Microsoft MVP Dr. Tom Shinder, this is a concise, accurate, enterprise tested method for the successful deployment of ISA Server.

ISBN: 1-59749-057-1

Price: $34.95 U.S. $55.95 CAN

SYNGRESS®

Syngress: *The Definition of a Serious Security Library*

Syn·gress (sin-gres): *noun, sing.* Freedom from risk or danger; safety. See *security*.

Configuring SonicWALL Firewalls

Chris Lathem, Ben Fortenberry, Lars Hansen

Configuring SonicWALL Firewalls is the first book to deliver an in-depth look at the SonicWALL firewall product line. It covers all of the aspects of the SonicWALL product line from the SOHO devices to the Enterprise SonicWALL firewalls. Advanced troubleshooting techniques and the SonicWALL Security Manager are also covered.

ISBN: 1-59749-250-7

Price: $49.95 US $69.95 CAN

Perfect Passwords:
Selection, Protection, Authentication

Mark Burnett

User passwords are the keys to the network kingdom, yet most users choose overly simplistic passwords (like password) that anyone could guess, while system administrators demand impossible to remember passwords littered with obscure characters and random numerals. Author Mark Burnett has accumulated and analyzed over 1,000,000 user passwords, and this highly entertaining and informative book filled with dozens of illustrations reveals his findings and balances the rigid needs of security professionals against the ease of use desired by users.

ISBN: 1-59749-041-5

Price: $24.95 US $34.95 CAN

SYNGRESS®

Syngress: *The Definition of a Serious Security Library*

Syn·gress (sin-gres): *noun, sing.* Freedom from risk or danger; safety. See *security*.

Skype Me! From Single User to Small Enterprise and Beyond
Michael Gough

This first-ever book on Skype takes you from the basics of getting Skype up and running on all platforms, through advanced features included in SkypeIn, SkypeOut, and Skype for Business. The book teaches you everything from installing a headset to configuring a firewall to setting up Skype as telephone Base to developing your own customized applications using the Skype Application Programming Interface.

ISBN: 1-59749-032-6

Price: $34.95 US $48.95 CAN

Securing IM and P2P Applications for the Enterprise
Brian Baskin, Marcus H. Sachs, Paul Piccard

As an IT Professional, you know that the majority of the workstations on your network now contain IM and P2P applications that you did not select, test, install, or configure. As a result, malicious hackers, as well as virus and worm writers, are targeting these inadequately secured applications for attack. This book will teach you how to take back control of your workstations and reap the benefits provided by these applications while protecting your network from the inherent dangers.

ISBN: 1-59749-017-2

Price: $49.95 US $69.95 CAN

SYNGRESS®

Syngress: *The Definition of a Serious Security Library*

Syn·gress (sin-gres): *noun, sing.* Freedom from risk or danger; safety. See *security.*

How to Cheat at Managing Windows Server Update Services

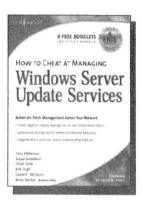

Brian Barber

If you manage a Microsoft Windows network, you probably find yourself overwhelmed at times by the sheer volume of updates and patches released by Microsoft for its products. You know these updates are critical to keep your network running efficiently and securely, but staying current amidst all of your other responsibilities can be almost impossible. Microsoft's recently released Windows Server Update Services (WSUS) is designed to streamline this process. Learn how to take full advantage of WSUS using Syngress' proven "How to Cheat" methodology, which gives you everything you need and nothing you don't.

ISBN: 1-59749-027-X

Price: $39.95 US $55.95 CAN

How to Cheat at IT Project Management

Susan Snedaker

Most IT projects fail to deliver – on average, all IT projects run over schedule by 82%, run over cost by 43% and deliver only 52% of the desired functionality. Pretty dismal statistics. Using the proven methods in this book, you'll find that IT project you work on from here on out will have a much higher likelihood of being on time, on budget and higher quality. This book provides clear, concise, information and hands-on training to give you immediate results. And, the companion Web site provides dozens of templates for managing IT projects.

ISBN: 1-59749-037-7

Price: $44.95 U.S. $64.95 CAN

Printed and bound by CPI Group (UK) Ltd, Croydon, CR0 4YY

03/10/2024

01040340-0012